THE
MAMMALS
OF BRITAIN AND EUROPE

Text by
Gordon Corbet

Illustrated by
Denys Ovenden

Collins · St James's Place, London

William Collins Sons & Co Ltd
London · Glasgow · Sydney · Auckland
Toronto · Johannesburg

First published 1980
© 1980 Gordon Corbet and Denys Ovenden
ISBN Hardback edition 219772 3
ISBN Paperback edition 219774 X
Colour reproduction by Adroit Photo Litho Ltd, Birmingham
Filmsetting by Jolly & Barber Ltd, Rugby
Printed and bound by
Wm Collins Sons & Co Ltd, Glasgow

Contents

How to use this book

This book deals with all species of mammals that now occur in a wild state in Europe west of the USSR, including the islands of Spitzbergen and Iceland, and in the northeastern Atlantic north of 35°N. In addition to resident, indigenous species, the following categories are included:

- vagrant bats, whales and dolphins that only occasionally and irregularly reach the region

- species that have been introduced accidentally or deliberately and that now maintain themselves as wild populations

- 'feral' populations, i.e. domesticated forms that have established self-perpetuating wild populations

- some domesticated forms that, although not truly feral, are represented by semi-wild local populations of primitive breeds.

Species that are extinct in the region are not included. Additional species that are not included may occur spasmodically as escapes from captivity.

There are 185 species illustrated in colour and a further five species shown in monochrome drawings with the text. Any additional species that are not illustrated as whole animals are virtually indistinguishable by external features from their illustrated relatives but their diagnostic characters are given in the text. Most good sightings, as well as animals found dead, should be identifiable from the colour plates. Note that mouse-sized mammals are represented by the shrews (plates 2 and 3) as well as by the true mice and related rodents (plates 13 to 20). Pattern, colour and size often vary considerably amongst the individuals of one species. Some of these variations are shown, especially where there are clear differences between males and females (as in some seals), between winter and summer coat (as in deer) or between young and adults (as in some shrews), but there are many others that cannot be shown. In many groups of mammals, such as bats and rodents, young animals are considerably darker and greyer than the adults.

Footprints and droppings can be identified (usually only approximately) from the illustrations on pages 102–111. Skulls can be placed in their main group by reference to pages 112–118 and in some cases a more precise identification can be achieved by using the drawings in the colour plates or in the main text. Further general hints on identification are given on pages 20–21.

Maps of the present European range are given opposite the colour illustration while more detailed maps of Britain and Ireland are given on pages 231–244. In the European maps space has sometimes made it necessary to show more than one species on the same map. They have been distinguished by using different colours which are explained by an accompanying key for each map. On the distribution maps for the seals breeding and other regularly used areas are shown solid and dispersal areas by hatching. No maps are included for the whales, dolphins or porpoises, many of which have world-wide ranges. Nor are they given for domesticated species or such localized populations as, for example, that of the Barbary ape and the Wallaby. Adjoining non-European territories have been omitted from the maps since they are outside the range of this book. All maps must be interpreted in conjunction with the information on habitat given in the text since on this scale it is not possible to distinguish between species with scattered and continuous distributions. In particular it is as well to keep in mind that most species will be much scarcer and more scattered on the edge of their range than at the centre. Migrant bats are sometimes blown off course and turn up in unexpected localities.

Measurements are usually given only on the page facing the colour plates. One measure of overall size is given, usually the combined length of the extended head and body, along with any others that are of particular diagnostic value. The aim has been to indicate the normal range of adult animals, ignoring extremes. This is practicable for example with shrews, which have almost reached adult size when they leave the nest, and with bats in which subadult animals can be recognized by the knobbly and translucent joints between the wing-bones. For most groups it is impracticable to draw a sharp line between young and adult and only the normal upper size limit is given.

When using the main text, note that in some cases a considerable amount of information that is common to a number of species is given under the preceding heading of the genus, family or order.

The figure on page 12 was adapted from one in the Journal of Zoology by kind permission of the Zoological Society of London and Dr Hans Kruuk; that on page 173 is taken from *Din viata rozatoarelor* (Bucharest, 1967) by kind permission of the author Dr M. Hamar and of Dr T. Baicu.

Introduction

The diversity of mammals

A typical mammal such as a weasel has the following characteristics (amongst many others):

- a jointed, internal bony skeleton
- milk glands by which the young are fed
- a coat of hair almost completely covering the body
- young that are not enclosed in an eggshell at birth
- four legs with five-toed feet adapted for walking and running
- a projecting tail containing an extension of the back-bone
- projecting lobes or 'pinnae' around the ear-holes
- the ability to control the temperature of the body at a constant, high, level (that is, high in relation to the average environmental temperature)
- a large brain, with a considerable capacity for learning and for varying behaviour as a result of experience

All mammals have a bony skeleton and suckle their young on milk, and all but the Australasian monotremes (platypus and spiny anteaters) give birth to young devoid of any kind of eggshell. The other features listed above vary greatly in their expression, giving rise, amongst the groups of mammals represented in Europe, to an enormous diversity of appearance and way of life.

Most carnivores, including the weasels, cats, foxes and bears, have all the above attributes, except that in some the toes are reduced to four. The same applies to the rodents (mice, squirrels etc.), the lagomorphs (rabbits and hares) and the insectivores (shrews, hedgehogs, moles), but in these the learning ability is usually less well developed. Some rodents and insectivores, for example the dormice and hedgehogs, reduce their bodily temperature and become inactive in winter, that is they hibernate. The ungulates – deer, goats, horses etc. – take reduction of the toes further, to a single one in the horse, associated with fast running.

Much more extreme deviations from the typical mammal are shown by the bats, in which the front legs have been transformed into wings and a high temperature is maintained only during periods of activity, the temperature falling during the daily roosting period as well as during hibernation. Seals show deviations of a different kind, in adaptation to their aquatic environment. The limbs have been reduced to paddle-like flippers, still retaining the skeletal elements of five digits, ear pinnae have disappeared and the tail is little more than a rudiment. The whales and dolphins have gone even further – the hind limbs and the hair have disappeared as well as the ears (the external ears, that is), while the tail has become large and muscular, with a horizontally flattened 'fluke' to provide the main propulsive organ. In spite of these apparently unmammalian features, whales show their mammalian nature by the possession of warm blood, and the production of active young that are suckled, as well, of course, as by their need to breath air.

The European mammal fauna

The composition of the European mammal fauna, ignoring domesticated forms, is as follows:

Terrestrial	Indigenous	Introduced	Irregular vagrants
Rodents	52	8	
Bats	31		2
Insectivores	21	1	
Carnivores	19	6	
Ungulates	11	7	
Lagomorphs	3		
Primates		1	
	137	23	2
Marine			
Cetaceans	22		7
Pinnipedes	8		
	30		7

The above figures for rodents and insectivores are slightly inflated by the occurrence of groups of very closely related species that are superficially extremely similar and that replace each other geographically, for example amongst the Common shrew and its allies and the pine voles. The treatment of these as groups of separate species is based mainly upon differences in chromosomes that suggest that they would be incapable of interbreeding – in other words the differences, although trivial in our eyes, are such that the animals themselves would distinguish between 'us' and 'them' if they should ever meet. The distinctiveness and distribution of some of these 'sibling species' is still somewhat uncertain and it is probable that other examples will come to light.

Introduced species

Exotic mammals have been introduced into Europe in a variety of circumstances. There are those, like the House mouse and Common rat, that arrived uninvited and unwelcome, as parasites and pests, many centuries ago, and are now widespread. There are other long established species that are treated as introductions on more circumstantial evidence, for example the Egyptian mongoose and the Genet. In these cases the overall distribution of the species (mainly Africa), the absence of fossil records or related species in Europe, and the fact that there is a plausible motive for introduction, namely the control of rodent pests, all increase the probability that they owe their presence in Europe to man. The Algerian hedgehog and the Barbary ape are two other species whose arrival is undocumented but probably assisted.

In the case of more recent introductions the origin is clearer. There are several rodents (Coypu, Canadian beaver, Muskrat) and carnivores (American mink, Raccoon, Raccoon-dog) that were brought to Europe as fur-bearers and either escaped from fur-farms (for example the Muskrat and Mink) or were deliberately released (for example the Canadian beaver in Finland). Exotic deer have been introduced either as ornaments, initially in enclosed parks, or for hunting. These have come mainly from eastern Asia (for example Sika deer and Muntjac) but also from America (for example the White-tailed deer). In addition several indigenous European ungulates (for example the Fallow deer) have had their ranges within Europe enlarged for the same purposes.

Feral and domestic mammals

Feral animals are ones that have escaped, or been released, from captivity and have established self-perpetuating populations living uncontrolled by man. The term is best reserved for cases where the captive ancestors were domesticated to the extent of being clearly distinguishable from the ancestral wild species, as in the case of most populations of feral goats and cats. The American mink is a borderline case since many of the escapees were of distinctive, domestic breeds, but most of the wild-born descendants resemble the ancestral wild American mink sufficiently closely to be virtually indistinguishable.

Several forms of domestic mammals that are commonly but erroneously described as feral, such as the Camargue horses and the Chillingham cattle, are nevertheless given entries in the book (under 'Domestic horse', 'Domestic cattle' etc.) since they are of considerable interest to students of truly wild mammals. They are called 'domestic' rather than 'feral' because their breeding is often controlled by the addition, removal or confinement of animals and they are often given supplementary food. Their zoological interest lies in the fact that in both appearance and behaviour they represent relatively primitive, unimproved and localized breeds that are closer to the ancestral wild species (which in the case of cattle is extinct) than are most modern breeds. In addition they are often sufficiently 'free-ranging' to establish social organizations, breeding cycles and feeding ecologies that relate more to those of the ancestral wild species than to modern farm stock.

Domesticated forms are sometimes considered, as far as naming is concerned, to be part of the ancestral wild species. However, where they are sufficiently different from the ancestral species to be easily distinguishable, for example the dog and wolf, sheep and mouflon, there is a very strong case for treating them as separate entities, for most of which well established and well known Latin names exist, and to avoid using these names to include also the wild species.

Habitat and distribution

Europe provides a great variety of habitats for mammals, lacking only desert and dry steppe amongst the principal temperate-zone vegetation types. Mammals, being warm-blooded, are not greatly restricted in their distribution by the direct effects of temperature, but rather by the availability of suitable food and by the physical nature of the plant cover which provides protection from predators or, in the case of predators, concealment in stalking their prey.

Many of the terrestrial mammals have ranges that correspond rather closely with one or more of the main vegetation zones shown on the map. The Norway lemming for example is confined to the tundra and Scandinavian montane zones, characterized by short vegetation of dwarf shrubs, sedges etc. with a short growing season and long cold winters. Wolverine and Elk are confined to the northern coniferous forests, the Alpine marmot to the treeless alpine zone of the central European mountains and the Steppe polecat to the drier grassland zone of the southeast. The largest zone in Europe as far as natural vegetation is concerned is the deciduous forest zone. Many of Europe's mammals are adapted especially to this habitat which, more than any other, has been destroyed

The natural vegetation zones of Europe

Tundra and alpine

Coniferous forest

Deciduous forest

Grassland

Mediterranean woodland and scrub

The deciduous forest and Mediterranean zones have been most severely affected by deforestation and cultivation.

and fragmented by the spread of agriculture. Man's activity has not only transformed forest to fields but most of the remaining fragments of forest have themselves been greatly altered by felling and replanting, by coppicing or by the effects of domestic animals. Many of the smaller mammals of the original forests have not only survived in the remnants but have also adapted to such substitute habitats as hedgerows, orchards and gardens, for example the Bank vole and, to a lesser extent, the Hazel dormouse. Roe deer need larger areas of woodland but have been versatile enough to accept plantations of exotic trees in lieu of the native forests. The largest of the forest mammals, the Bison and the Brown bear, have fared less well and have disappeared from most of western Europe.

The Mediterranean zone of Europe has been subjected to severe human disturbance for even longer than has the rest of Europe. Little undisturbed forest has survived but a variety of dry woodland, scrub and grassland habitats still provide suitable conditions for mammals. Most of these are the same as those of central Europe, such as the Eastern and Western hedgehogs and the Wood mouse, but others are found only in the south, for example the Rock mouse in the Balkans and the Pygmy white-toothed shrew throughout the Mediterranean lowlands, the latter species being so small – indeed the smallest of all mammals – that virtually any habitat provides suitable cover and insect food.

There are a few species of mammal that are so versatile that they not only occupy all the natural vegetation zones of Europe but have adapted to many of the man-made ones as well. Such for example is the Red fox, found from the Arctic tundra to the Mediterranean scrub, from the eastern steppes to Scottish mountains and from agricultural land to city parks. The Weasel is almost as ubiquitous.

Some patterns of distribution cannot be interpreted simply in terms of vegetation zones with or without human interference. Several woodland species of central Europe, for example the Garden dormouse and the Common pine vole, are absent from Britain, reflecting the fact that the severance of Britain from the Continent took place (about 8000–9000 years ago) when the climate had not yet ameliorated sufficiently following the last glaciation for suitable forest to have extended so far north.

Bats are less affected by water barriers but are more susceptible to temperature and are scarce in the far north. Most bats are basically forest animals but many make extensive use of buildings, bridges and other human artifacts for roosting. Many species of bats make limited southward migrations in the autumn but very little is known of the extent or the regularity of these. They are more pronounced where the winters are severe – great numbers of bats for example migrate from central European Russia to winter in the Balkans.

Amongst the marine mammals there is a clear distinction between the seals and walrus on the one hand, which are tied to land or ice during the breeding season, and the cetaceans which remain permanently at sea. But that is not to say that the cetaceans are entirely nomadic – most species have distinct ranges, some in coastal waters, some in deeper waters, most making regular annual migrations between north and south. Several species of dolphins occur in the Mediterranean and Black Seas and the Baltic, but none are confined to them and many cetaceans have distributions that extend far beyond the North Atlantic.

Ecology and behaviour

From the point of view of any one species of animal, its ecology can be considered as the sum total of its relationships with its environment, not only the physical environment of earth, water and weather, but also the living environment of plants and other animals. And since an animal's behaviour is adapted to its environment both in a general way and in response to the needs of the moment, the two subjects of ecology and behaviour are intimately connected. Food is probably the most fundamental aspect of an animal's ecology. With most mammals it is possible to recognize a feeding strategy peculiar to the species that enables it to exploit a particular source of food with the minimum of competition from other species. Some species are highly specialized in their feeding habits – most European bats for example eat nothing but insects – while others are more versatile. In order to determine the strategy used by any particular species it is often necessary to consider especially its feeding behaviour at the time of year when food is in shortest supply. Most vegetarians for example feed on a wide variety of plants in summer – animals as diverse as beavers, roe deer, elk, hares, bank voles and water voles will feed on succulent herbaceous plants such as are found on a river bank. But in severe winter conditions they specialize in very different ways: beavers feed on the twigs of trees they have felled and stored under water, roe on leaves of brambles and evergreen shrubs, elk on conifer foliage, hares on the bark of small trees, bank voles on acorns and water voles on the rhizomes of grasses and sedges.

Many rodents are primarily seed-eaters. Some, like the Wood mouse and the Red squirrel, remain active all winter, feeding especially on acorns or beech-mast and conifer seed respectively, although they are versatile enough to turn to other foods if the main seed crop fails. Others avoid the winter shortage by hibernating, for example the various species of dormice, the souslik and the hamsters. These last two make large stores of seeds in their burrows. It is a common misconception to believe that it is amongst the animals of the far north that hibernation is most common. In fact winters in the Arctic are too long for hibernation to be a practicable strategy and it is in the temperate zone, and especially in areas with a continental climate, with short but severe winters, where most of the hibernators are found. Red and grey squirrels do not hibernate but they store food by burying items such as acorns at random rather than in one hoard. Another species that makes good use of a heavy crop of acorns is the Wild boar which stores them internally in the form of fat, and most deer will also feed on acorns to recover condition after the autumnal rutting season and thereby enhance their chances of surviving the winter.

An important factor in defining the ecological role of a species is its social organization. Some mammals, such as red deer, grey seals, rabbits and many bats, are conspicuously colonial, but even species that are generally described as 'solitary' have a characteristic social organization. Solitary animals, such as red foxes and shrews, are generally territorial, each animal defending a particular piece of ground, patrolling the boundaries and being very aware of its neighbours on all sides, partly through direct meetings but more often through the deposition of scent. In shrews it is the young animals that are territorial, irrespective of sex, and they tend to oust the older generation at the end of the breeding season and maintain their territories until the beginning of their own

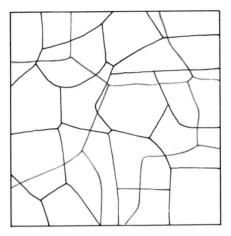

Winter territories of pygmy shrews (blue) and common shrews (black) in a 100 metre square of rough grassland. Males and females of each species have separate territories but the two species overlap at random. There is however some vertical separation, with the pygmy shrews spending less time underground than the larger common shrews.

breeding season the following spring. Territories are related to food supply and where two closely related species occur together they tend to exploit the food resources in different ways rather than to have mutually exclusive territories (see illustration). In most 'solitary' mammals it is the adult males that are most strictly territorial. Very often, as in red foxes, a breeding male's territory may include several smaller territories of females, and roving young males may be tolerated if they show proper deference and are no threat to the reproductive supremacy of the territory-holding male. Badgers are also territorial but it is a group or 'clan' rather than an individual that holds the territory (see illustration overleaf). All individuals of the group will mark the boundary with scent and can distinguish between the scent of their own and neighbouring clans.

In many small rodents such as the mice and voles a hierarchical structure develops especially when numbers are high, with a considerable number of young subordinate animals being tolerated, but not breeding, within the territory of the breeding adults.

In most of the large deer and other ungulates such as ibex and chamois the adult females and young animals are permanently gregarious, while adult males are either solitary or form separate bachelor herds. During the short mating season or 'rutting' period the dominant males join the matriarchal herds and fight off rival males, more by display than by force. Bats show some similarities to deer in that the sexes are usually in separate colonies in summer when the young are born but come together in autumn when mating takes place. Seals are also gregarious but in this case the mating and birth seasons coincide. In the case of the Grey seal, for example, the adult males or bulls hold territories on the breeding beaches and usually mate with several cows after they have given birth but before they desert their pups.

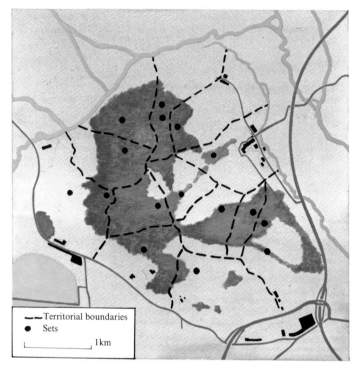

Territories occupied by groups of badgers in an area of 10 square kilometres of woodland (green) and farmland. Each territory contains one or two principal systems of burrows ('sets') and is occupied by a group of up to twelve badgers. The sets are mostly in woodland but their location is also influenced by the distribution of suitable substrate for burrowing, in this case soft sandstone. The peripheral area was not included in the survey.

Mammals and man

A great many different kinds of mammals have played important roles in human affairs ever since man was a primitive hunter, and likewise few species of mammals have escaped being influenced to a substantial extent by man's activities. Predators that might have preyed directly upon people, such as the Sabre-toothed cat and the Lion, have long since been eliminated from Europe. Man in his turn has preyed upon all the large herbivores for food and later for sport, upon the large whales for food and a variety of other products, and upon most of the carnivores for fur. Of the ungulates the very largest – Bison, Aurochs, Horse – were almost or completely exterminated. Most of the deer on the other hand have been preserved for sport and although much of their habitat has been lost they remain widespread, frequently assisted by reintroduction and translocation, and supplemented by several exotic species. In most European countries the hunting of all deer, along with Wild boar and other ungulates, is carefully controlled and close seasons are enforced, although controlled shooting is also carried out to avoid over-population, with damage to trees and to farm crops. Amongst small game the hares and rabbits are the principal species. They also have been important food and sporting animals but their small size, high breeding potential and ability to adapt to farmland have ensured their survival and in the case of rabbits their spread and increase to become a major agricultural pest.

The large carnivores, particularly the Wolf and the Brown bear, have suffered severely through persecution, mainly on the grounds of the protection of domestic stock and game animals. All of the carnivores have been subjected to considerable persecution. Some, such as the Red fox, the Badger, the Stoat and the Weasel have survived in good numbers, through their adaptability or their elusiveness. Others have suffered severe reduction through loss of forest or from excessive persecution, especially in the interests of game preservation, but have survived well enough to recover when these pressures are released – examples are the Pine marten and Wild cat in Britain. Otters survived the pressures of fur-trapping and persecution by fishing interests surprisingly well, but have recently declined very seriously in many lowland areas, such as in Germany and in central England, probably as a result of pollution of rivers by industrial and agricultural chemicals as well as by increasing disturbance.

A great deal of research has recently been undertaken both on the social organization and ecology of carnivores and on the factors controlling the numbers of game animals (including birds). It is becoming increasingly clear that carnivores have very little effect upon the annual 'crop' of game species and that they are mostly very versatile, adapting their behaviour to particular habitats and generally opting for whichever prey is most abundant and easily obtained at the moment.

Amongst the great whales, the large, slow-moving, inshore species – the Bowhead, the Black right whale and the Humpback – were almost exterminated from European waters during the era of sailing ships and hand harpoons and one species, the Grey whale, was completely exterminated from the Atlantic. The faster rorquals of the deeper waters – the Blue, Sei and Fin whales – have been drastically reduced during the past century by commercial whaling activity although the last two still survive in sufficient numbers for annual catches to be agreed by the International Whaling Commission. There is however considerable concern that the quotas might not be low enough to arrest the decline of these species.

One group of mammals with a unique relationship with man are the bats. As with the similarly aerial and insectivorous swallows and swifts, bats have adopted human constructions – houses, bridges, mines etc. – as roosting sites in a big way. These to some extent substitute for the greater number of old, hollow trees that must once have been much more numerous than now. In many areas bats are very heavily dependant upon human artifacts and are consequently very vulnerable because of rapid technological change – new building methods, chemical treatment against wood-boring insects etc. Because of the vast quantities of insects they consume bats are wholly beneficial to human interests, although they suffer from a 'bad press' through superstition and ignorance of their ways. Bats have legal protection in some degree in several European countries. Some species are declining at an alarming rate and since they migrate across state boundaries international measures are required to ensure their survival.

Finding mammals

The different groups of mammals need very different techniques for their detection. Amongst the large, terrestrial mammals it is important to distinguish between the vegetarian species – the ungulates – and the predatory carnivores. Ungulates are easier to watch. Those that live on open country, such as the reindeer of Lapland, the ibex of the Alps or the red deer in some areas such as the Highlands of Scotland, generally form herds of considerable size. Although they may be very wary they can be stalked by day. The careful use of binoculars – any size from 8×30 to 10×50 is suitable – enables herds to be detected on distant hillsides before they are excessively disturbed. Any attempt at a closer approach should if possible be made up-wind, but remember that observation from a distance, using binoculars or a telescope, is more likely to reveal animals behaving naturally, whereas with too close an approach all other activity will be suspended while the animals watch the observer.

Woodland ungulates are less gregarious. Many of them, such as roe deer, sika deer, mouflon and wild boar, do much of their feeding in clearings or on open ground adjacent to woodland, generally emerging at dusk to feed, and retiring to the shelter of the woods during the day. Dawn is often the best time for observation since there is less human disturbance than at dusk. A search for droppings (see pages 110–111) and for frayed trees will suggest suitable places to watch since deer are often very regular in their habits. For all woodland species, lying concealed at a suitable vantage point is essential since any movement of the observer will be detected by the quarry long before it is visible.

Some groups of smaller mammals are sufficiently active and visible by day to be watched directly, although in every case the early morning is by far the best time for observation. Rabbits and hares come into this category, as do squirrels, ground squirrels, marmots and the aquatic rodents – water voles, musk rat, coypu and beaver. Remember that common rats are also frequently seen swimming, often by day.

Carnivores of all sizes, from weasels to bears, are particularly difficult to see. Most are strictly nocturnal, especially where there is human disturbance, and they are generally solitary and much more thinly dispersed than the herbivores. Long and patient watching is usually necessary and in many cases the best that can be expected is a brief glimpse in poor light or in the beam of a torch. However the determined watcher can use a variety of techniques to improve the chances of making contact. The burrows or den may be found and watched at dusk for the animal emerging. Badger sets in lowland country are particularly easy to recognize by the numerous holes and very large accumulation of soil, but where dens are amongst rocks they are much more difficult to detect. Otter dens can be recognized by the accumulation of droppings containing fish bones and sometimes crab shells if they are near the coast.

A search for footprints may show which paths are in regular use and if the ground is not suitable for imprinting it may be practicable to prepare a section of path by spreading sand or mud. Thorny twigs or sticky tape placed at strategic points, for example where a path goes under a fence, may pick up telltale hairs that are identifiable – the black and white guard hairs of badgers are particularly distinctive. Another technique is to place bait at a site that is convenient to watch – the regular placing of bait, for example a rabbit carcase, combined with a study of the footprints around it, may give quite a detailed picture of the local carnivores without ever seeing one.

The small rodents and shrews are about as difficult to watch directly as the carnivores but there are many indirect ways of finding them. One way of watching small rodents is to place bait, such as grain or other seeds, at a regular feeding place which can then be watched, especially at night using a red light. Shrews, voles and mice can sometimes be found under logs or under planks of wood or sheets of corrugated iron. Driftwood lying above high water mark on boulder beaches is always worth lifting to look for shrews which thrive on the sandhoppers and maggots of seaweed flies that are abundant in such places. Traps of many different designs can be used to catch small mammals, ranging from ordinary household snap-traps to complicated live traps designed for ecological research. All such traps should normally be placed well hidden amongst vegetation, in or immediately adjacent to runways if these can be found. A commonly used and effective bait is a mixture of peanut butter and cereal but many traps can be used without bait, either set across a runway or, in the case of live traps, depending upon the animal's exploratory behaviour to entice it inside. A simple but effective live trap that is particularly suitable for the periodic monitoring of small mammals at one site is the pitfall. A smooth-sided container (glass jar, polythene drum etc.) is sunk into the ground and covered by a piece of wood. To 'set' the trap the lid is propped up on stones two or three centimetres above the rim and bait is placed at the bottom of the container. A depth of 30cm is adequate for shrews and voles but something deeper is required for mice. All live traps must be provided with ample food and bedding (dry hay, for instance). They should be examined at least twice a day and made ineffective when not in use.

Two other useful ways of recording small mammals are searching for remains in discarded bottles and in the pellets cast up by owls or other raptors. Unstoppered bottles that are lying at an angle, for example amongst grass or bushes on a roadside bank, frequently trap small mammals whose remains can usually be identified by the skull and teeth. Likewise bird pellets contain the fur and bones of the latest prey and if teased apart the skulls can in most cases be isolated and precisely identified. Pellets of barn owls are particularly useful. They not only feed upon a wide variety of shrews and rodents but the skulls tend to be less damaged than those from other raptors.

A pellet regurgitated by a tawny owl, partly opened to expose the lower jaw of a shrew (left) and of a vole (right).

Flying bats are fairly easy to locate at dusk but extremely difficult to identify. Precise identification generally requires finding the roosting site. Potential sites, for example a cave entrance, a hollow tree or an isolated rural building, can be watched at dusk for bats emerging. Within caves, cellars or attics some species of bats hang conspicuously from the roof, for example most horseshoe bats and the mouse-eared bats. Others however cling closely against the walls or squeeze into small crevices and careful searching is necessary to locate them. The most difficult bats to find are those like Bechstein's bat and the Barbastelle that live dispersed in woodland, without forming colonies.

Identifying mammals

With mammals varying so enormously in both appearance and visibility, the problems involved in making precise identifications are equally diverse and a large part of the main text of this book, dealing with individual species or groups, is devoted to identification features. There are however a few general points to remember that will help to avoid some of the problems encountered, especially when trying to make a precise identification of an animal 'in the hand', whether alive or dead.

Measurements can often be helpful and are sometimes critical for an accurate identification. The measure of overall size most often used is 'head and body', measured from the tip of the nose to the base of the tail with the body fully relaxed and extended. The length of the tail is measured to the tip excluding the terminal hairs. In many rodents the length of the tail relative to the head-and-body is a useful diagnostic character but it is important to note that the body may look very much shorter in a living animal.

In order to use measurements as identification characters it is necessary to be able to recognize young animals as such. In many species, including most rodents, bats and carnivores, young animals have the coat much greyer than the adults and often of a different, softer texture. Without experience the appearance of the genitalia is not always a clear-cut guide to age since most wild mammals are seasonal breeders and the genitalia may revert to a state resembling those of the immature animals during the non-breeding season. The feet, and especially the hind feet, generally reach their full size before the body is fully grown so that the young animals have disproportionately large feet. Because they vary less with age than other parts of the body the length of the hind feet is particularly useful in distinguishing some species, for example of shrews and mice. They are measured from the back of the heel to the tip of the longest toe, excluding the claw.

When dealing with skulls, young animals can be recognized by the general fragility and lack of fusion of the separate bones, by the presence of teeth in the process of erupting or replacement, and by the unworn appearance of the teeth.

The coat or 'pelage' may vary with age, season and sex. Only some of the more clear-cut differences are shown in the illustrations. The winter coat is longer than the summer and, in carnivores especially, may contain a large proportion of fine woolly fibres concealed beneath the long straight 'guard hairs' that form the visible surface of the pelage. In some deer, for example the Roe, the winter coat is strikingly different from the summer, being greyish rather than reddish brown, while in northern Europe several species change to a

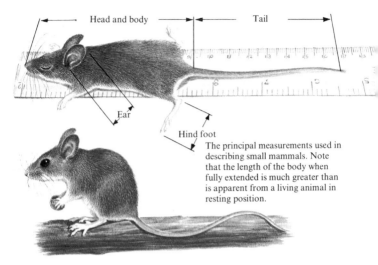

The principal measurements used in describing small mammals. Note that the length of the body when fully extended is much greater than is apparent from a living animal in resting position.

more or less completely white coat in winter. These seasonal colour changes are brought about by a moult, extending over a period of a few weeks to several months and during the process many intermediate conditions may be seen. Most small mammals moult back into their summer pelage in spring but many carnivores do not have a distinct spring moult although the coat may become gradually thinner by abrasion and loss of hair.

In most species of mammals there is little difference in general appearance between male and female. The main exceptions are amongst the ungulates, some seals and a few cetaceans. In these the adult males carry specialized structures – antlers in deer, an inflated muzzle in the Hooded seal, a long tusk in the Narwhal – or are more boldly patterned, for example in the Mouflon and Harp seal. In only a few cases are males conspicuously larger than the females, for example in the Stoat, Weasel and Sperm whale, although it is common for males to be slightly larger.

Within any one sex/age group there is usually little variation in appearance, but there are some conspicuous exceptions. In many areas red squirrels occur in two strikingly different colour forms, usually reddish brown and black, and ship rats also occur in several colour varieties. Conspicuous geographical variation in colour is likewise the exception rather than the rule. Water voles are mostly black in the north of Scotland, brown elsewhere; lynx are more heavily spotted in southern than in northern Europe; in Ireland the Mountain hare is much browner than elsewhere.

PLATE 1

Western hedgehog *Erinaceus europaeus*   Page 120
Underside uniformly coloured but ranging from dark brown to almost white. Spine-free 'parting' on crown very narrow. Head and body 225–275mm.

Eastern hedgehog *Erinaceus concolor*   Page 121
Breast white, contrasting with darker belly. Otherwise as Western hedgehog. Head and body 225–275mm.

● Western hedgehog
● Eastern hedgehog

Algerian hedgehog *Erinaceus algirus*   Page 121
Very pale below, face pattern obscure, spine-free 'parting' on crown wide enough to insert a pencil. Note that Western hedgehog is also very pale in S. Spain. Distribution sporadic, probably introduced. Head and body 200–250mm.

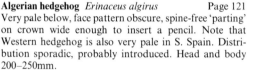

Northern mole *Talpa europaea*   Page 121
Large. Eyes can be opened. Head and body 120–150mm, hind feet (without claws) 17–19.5mm.

See also Roman mole (p. 122).

● Northern mole
● Roman mole

Blind mole *Talpa caeca*   Page 122
Small. Eyes permanently covered by membrane. Head and body 100–130mm, hind feet (without claws) 15.5–17.5mm.

Pyrenean desman *Galemys pyrenaicus*   Page 123
Muzzle very long, flattened and spatulate. Front feet not enlarged, tail long. In rivers and canals. Cf. smaller water shrews, plate 3. Head and body 110–135mm.

Mole hills are round, have no entrance and soon become flattened.

Hills of yellow ants remain steep-sided and develop vegetation

defensive position

Western hedgehog

Eastern hedgehog

Algerian hedgehog

Northern mole

Blind mole

23

Pyrenean desman

PLATE 2

All species on this page have red-tipped teeth and five single-pointed (uni-cuspid) teeth on each side of the upper jaw. Measurements of feet are without claws.

Common shrew *Sorex araneus*　　　　　Page 124
Three-coloured, with flanks distinct from upper and undersides. Juvenile paler, with tufted tail. Second uni-cuspid tooth about equal to 1st, 3rd smaller. Head and body 60–85mm, hind feet 12–13mm.

See also very similar Millet's shrew (p. 124), Spanish shrew (p. 124) and Appennine shrew (p. 125).

● Common shrew　　● Millet's shrew　　● Spanish shrew

Pygmy shrew *Sorex minutus*　　　　　Page 125
Small, two-coloured, tail relatively long and thick com-pared with Common shrew. Third unicuspid tooth larger than 2nd. Head and body 45–60mm, hind feet 11–12mm.

Laxmann's shrew *Sorex caecutiens*　　　　Page 125
Medium size. Tail very prominently tufted in juvenile. Unicuspid teeth small and well-spaced. Head and body 50–70mm, hind feet 11–12mm.

Least shrew *Sorex minutissimus*　　　　Page 125
Extremely small; short hind feet particularly distinctive. Head and body 35–45mm, hind feet 8–9mm.

Dusky shrew *Sorex sinalis*　　　　　Page 126
Large, underside dark, tail shorter than head and body. Unicuspid teeth decrease in size uniformly. Head and body 60–80mm, hind feet 13–15mm.

Alpine shrew *Sorex alpinus*　　　　　Page 126
Grey, dark below. Tail as long as head and body. Fifth unicuspid tooth as large as 4th. Head and body 60–75mm, hind feet 13–16mm.

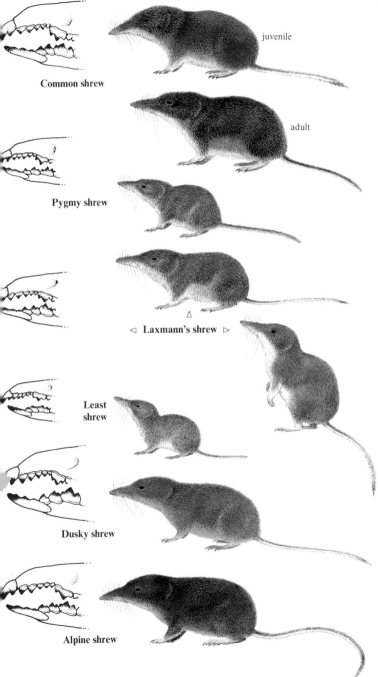

RED-TOOTHED SHREWS

juvenile

adult

Common shrew

Pygmy shrew

◁ **Laxmann's shrew** ▷

Least shrew

Dusky shrew

Alpine shrew

PLATE 3

Water shrew *Neomys fodiens* Page 126
Black above, variable below. Fringe of long hair on whole length of underside of tail and on sides of hind feet. Teeth red-tipped, 4 unicuspids. Head and body 70–90mm, hind feet 16–20mm.

Miller's water shrew *Neomys anomalus* Page 126
As Water shrew but tail fringe absent, or slight and confined to terminal third. Feet also less well fringed. Head and body 65–85mm, hind feet 14–18mm.

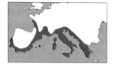

Pygmy white-toothed shrew *Suncus etruscus* Page 127
Exceedingly small. Tail with whiskers. Teeth white, 4 unicuspids. Head and body 35–45mm, hind feet 7–8mm.

Greater white-toothed shrew *Crocidura russula* Page 127
Greyish brown, tail with whiskers, gradual transition from dark to light on flanks. Teeth white, 3 unicuspids. Head and body 65–85mm, tail 35–50mm, hind feet 12–13mm.

Lesser white-toothed shrew
Crocidura suaveolens Page 128
As Greater white-toothed shrew but smaller. Head and body 55–70mm, tail 30–40mm, hind feet 11–12mm.

Bicoloured white-toothed shrew
Crocidura leucodon Page 128
Clear line of demarcation between dark back and pale belly. Otherwise as Greater white-toothed shrew. Head and body 65–85mm, hind feet 12–13mm.

Rotting seaweed on a boulder beach provides a rich habitat for shrews.

WATER SHREWS AND WHITE-TOOTHED SHREWS

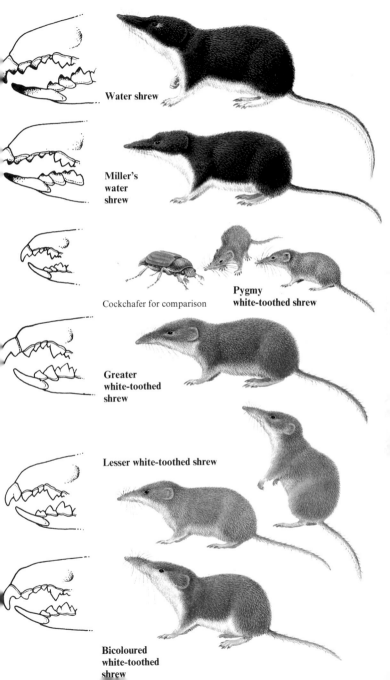

Water shrew

Miller's water shrew

Cockchafer for comparison

Pygmy white-toothed shrew

Greater white-toothed shrew

Lesser white-toothed shrew

Bicoloured white-toothed shrew

PLATE 4

Horseshoe bats are the only European bats with complex lobes of skin on the nose.

Lesser horseshoe bat *Rhinolophus hipposideros*   Page 130
Smallest horseshoe bat. Sella in front view tapering above, in profile with a blunt upper angle. Forearm 35–42mm.

Greater horseshoe bat
Rhinolophus ferrumequinum   Page 131
Largest horseshoe bat. Sella in front view saddle-shaped, in profile upper angle prominent but blunt. Forearm 50–61mm.

Mediterranean horseshoe bat
Rhinolophus euryale   Page 131
Intermediate in size. Sella in front view parallel-sided, in profile with slender, pointed upper angle. Forearm 43–49mm.

Blasius's horseshoe bat *Rhinolophus blasii*   Page 131
Intermediate in size. Noseleaf broad; sella in front view constricted above. Forearm 44–50mm.

Mehely's horseshoe bat *Rhinolophus mehelyi*   Page 131
Large, pale. Lancet abruptly contracted to slender point. Forearm 48–55mm.

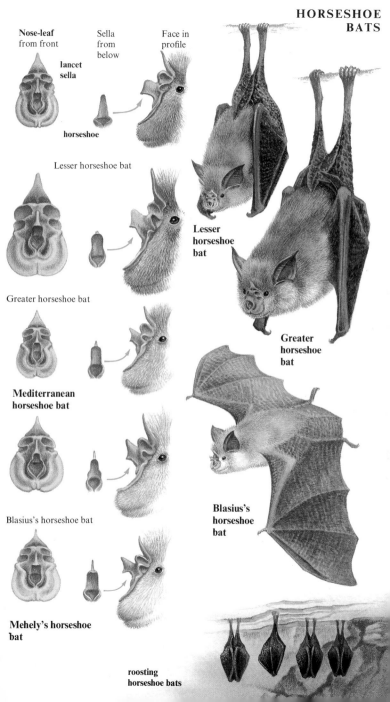

Nose-leaf from front

lancet
sella

Sella from below

Face in profile

horseshoe

Lesser horseshoe bat

Lesser horseshoe bat

Greater horseshoe bat

Greater horseshoe bat

Mediterranean horseshoe bat

Blasius's horseshoe bat

Blasius's horseshoe bat

Mehely's horseshoe bat

roosting horseshoe bats

PLATE 5

All the bats on this page and the next have a long, erect, pointed 'tragus' in the ear.

Daubenton's bat *Myotis daubentoni*   Page 132
Muzzle pinkish brown, feet large, upper surface rather reddish brown, tail membrane scantily haired. Forearm 33–40mm.

See also very similar Nathalina bat (p. 132).

Long-fingered bat *Myotis capaccinii*   Page 132
As Daubenton's bat but slightly larger. Coat more yellowish brown, tail membrane hairy, especially around shin. Forearm 40–44mm.

Pond bat *Myotis dasycneme*   Page 133
As Daubenton's bat but considerably larger. Coat greyer, tail membrane almost naked. Forearm 43–48mm.

Brandt's bat

Brandt's bat *Myotis brandti*   Page 133
Small, face and membranes dark, feet very small. Coat reddish brown above, buff below (but grey in first year). Forearm 32–37mm.

◁ **Whiskered bat** *Myotis mystacinus*   Page 134
Small, skin very dark, coat greyish brown above, dirty grey below. Feet small. Forearm 31–36mm.

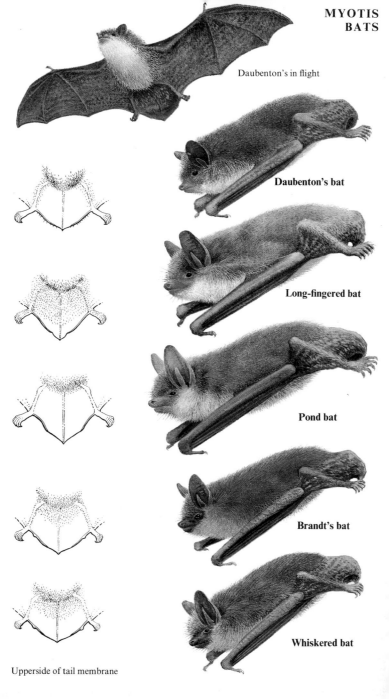

MYOTIS BATS

Daubenton's in flight

Daubenton's bat

Long-fingered bat

Pond bat

Brandt's bat

Whiskered bat

Upperside of tail membrane

PLATE 6

In all the species on this page the wing membrane meets the foot at the base of the outer toe.

Geoffroy's bat *Myotis emarginatus*   Page 134
Small, reddish brown; sharply angled step in hind margin of ear. Edge of tail membrane sparsely hairy. Forearm 36–42mm.

Natterer's bat *Myotis nattereri*   Page 134
Small, greyish brown; hind margin of ear with a slight step. Edge of tail membrane densely haired on either side of tail-tip. Tragus very long and narrow. Forearm 37–42mm.

Bechstein's bat *Myotis bechsteini*   Page 135
Small, reddish, ears very long but widely separated, extending far beyond nose when folded forwards. Forearm 39–44mm.

Greater mouse-eared bat *Myotis myotis*   Page 135
Very large. Pointed tragus distinguishes from other large bats. Tragus wider and muzzle shorter and deeper than in Lesser mouse-eared bat. Forearm 57–67mm.

Lesser mouse-eared bat *Myotis blythi*   Page 135
Only slightly smaller than Greater mouse-eared bat. Muzzle and tragus narrower. Cranial and dental measurements necessary for critical identification. Forearm 54–60mm.

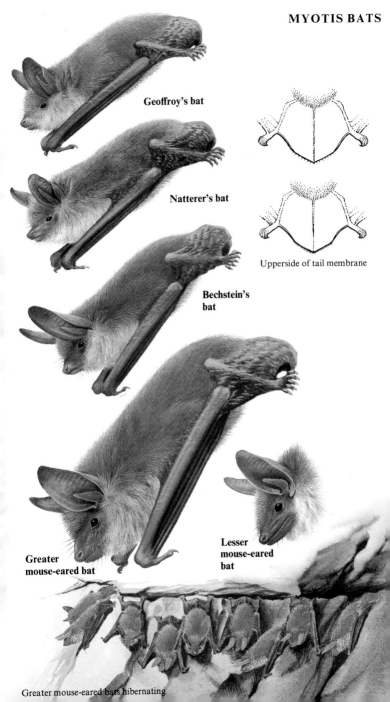

MYOTIS BATS

Geoffroy's bat

Natterer's bat

Upperside of tail membrane

Bechstein's bat

Greater mouse-eared bat

Lesser mouse-eared bat

Greater mouse-eared bats hibernating

PLATE 7

All these species have short, rounded ears containing short, blunt traguses.

Noctule *Nyctalus noctula* Page 136
Coat golden brown all over, colour of hairs extending to roots. Wings narrow. Forearm 46–55mm.

Leisler's bat *Nyctalus leisleri* Page 136
Coat with a slight golden brown tinge, but hair dark towards the roots. Otherwise like small Noctule. Forearm 39–46mm.

Greater noctule *Nyctalus lasiopterus* Page 136
Like Noctule but distinctly larger. Forearm 62–69mm.

Serotine *Eptesicus serotinus* Page 137
Ear rounded, tragus short and rounded but narrow. Tail extends beyond membrane by about 1½ vertebrae. Naked skin very dark. Forearm 48–55mm.

Northern bat *Eptesicus nilssoni* Page 137
Smaller and paler than Serotine, ears and tail similar. Yellow hair-tips give a light, glossy sheen above. Forearm 38–46mm.

Parti-coloured bat *Vespertilio murinus* Page 137
Ear and tragus very broad and rounded. Upper surface with white hair-tips giving frosted appearance, underside almost white with sharp demarcation. Forearm 40–48mm.

34

Noctule in flight

Noctule

Leisler's bat

Serotine

Northern bat

Greater noctule

Parti-coloured bat

PLATE 8

Pipistrelles are small (forearm under 39mm) with small rounded ears containing short blunt traguses, and an extension of the tail membrane on the outside of the spur from the ankle. Examination of the teeth may be necessary for critical identification (see p. 139).

Common pipistrelle *Pipistrellus pipistrellus*   Page 138
Wings narrow (5th finger *c*. 40mm), thumb short (equal to width of wrist). Colour uniform. Forearm 28–34mm.

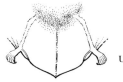

Upperside of tail membrane
Pipistrellus spp.

Nathusius's pipistrelle *Pipistrellus nathusii*   Page 139
Colour less uniform than in Common pipistrelle. Wings broader (5th finger *c*. 45mm), thumb larger than width of wrist. Forearm 32–35mm.

Kuhl's pipistrelle *Pipistrellus kuhli*   Page 139
Lighter than other pipistrelles, wing membrane with narrow white margin (occasionally present in other species). Thumb short. Forearm 32–35mm.

Savi's pipistrelle *Pipistrellus savii*   Page 139
Light hair tips contrasting with dark bases, underside distinctly paler than upper. Thumb short. Forearm 32–38mm.

Hoary bat *Lasiurus cinereus*   Page 140
Tail membrane densely hairy above. Mottled and frosted coat unique. A vagrant from North America. Forearm 51–54mm.

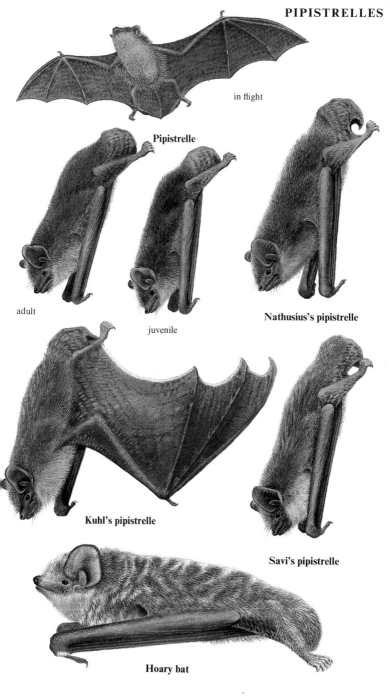

PIPISTRELLES

in flight

Pipistrelle

adult

juvenile

Nathusius's pipistrelle

Kuhl's pipistrelle

Savi's pipistrelle

Hoary bat

PLATE 9

Common long-eared bat *Plecotus auritus*   Page 140
Extremely long ears. Coat greyish brown, appearing brown when hair is parted. Young animals greyer and more like next species. Tragus translucent and narrow (5mm at widest). Forearm 34–41mm.

Grey long-eared bat *Plecotus austriacus*   Page 140
As Common long-eared bat but slightly larger and always greyish. Coat appears dark and slaty when parted. Tragus opaque and grey, *c.* 6mm at widest. Forearm 38–43mm.

Barbastelle *Barbastella barbastellus*   Page 141
Small, very dark all over. Ears short but joined on top of head. Forearm 37–42mm.

Schreiber's bat *Miniopterus schreibersi*   Page 141
Small, muzzle very short, hair on head short and erect. Wings very long, terminal segment bent sharply back at rest. Forearm 42–48mm.

Free-tailed bat *Tadarida teniotis*   Page 141
Very large. Tail long and extending far beyond short membrane. Ears large, joined, projecting forwards. Forearm 58–64mm.

BATS

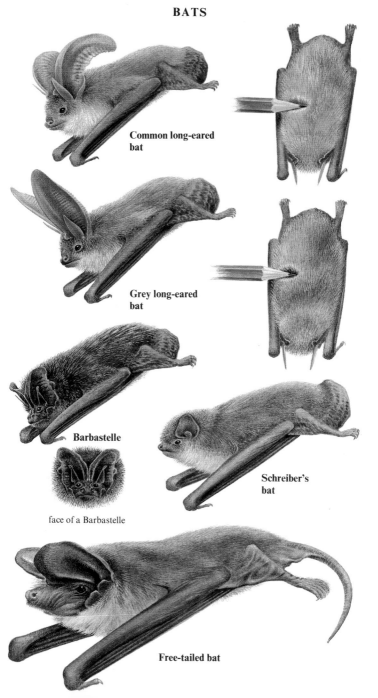

Common long-eared bat

Grey long-eared bat

Barbastelle

face of a Barbastelle

Schreiber's bat

Free-tailed bat

PLATE 10

Red-necked
wallaby

Rabbit

Rabbit *Oryctolagus cuniculus*   Page 143
Ears without black tips, ears and legs shorter than in
hares. Colonial, usually close to cover. Head and body
35–45cm, hind feet 7.5–9.5cm, ear from notch 6–7cm.

Brown hare *Lepus capensis*   Page 144
Yellowish brown throughout the year, long legs, long
black-tipped ears. Tail sharply black and white. Head and
body 50–65cm, hind feet 11.5–15cm, ear from notch
8.5–10.5cm.

◁ **Mountain hare** *Lepus timidus*   Page 144
Greyish brown in summer, white in winter (except in
Ireland where more yellowish brown throughout the
year). Ears short, tail wholly white. Head and body
45–60cm, hind feet 12–15.5cm, ear from notch 6–8cm.

Red-necked wallaby *Macropus rufogriseus*   Page 119
Long thick tail, very long hind legs and feet, bounding
gait on hind legs only, young carried in pouch. Head and
body 60–70cm, tail about same.

WALLABY, RABBIT AND HARES

Rabbit

Brown hare

Mountain hare
(Irish race)

Mountain hare
(Scottish race)

summer

winter

moulting

PLATE 11

All these species but the Flying squirrel are diurnal and easily observed by day.

Red squirrel *Sciurus vulgaris*   Page 146
Very variable. In summer red and dark greyish brown forms coexist on continent, red only in Britain and Ireland. In winter more greyish but ear-tufts prominent. Always in or near trees. Head and body 18–25cm, tail 14–20cm.

Grey squirrel *Sciurus carolinensis*   Page 147
Predominantly grey at all seasons but with a variable amount of reddish or yellowish on back and flanks (lowest illustration shows about the maximum). Ears never tufted, tail with white fringes. Always in or near trees. Head and body 23–30cm, tail 20–24cm.

Flying squirrel *Pteromys volans*   Page 147
Nocturnal, rarely seen by day. Gliding membrane unique but not prominent when not in use. Cf. Fat dormouse, plate 13. Head and body 14–20cm, tail 9–14cm.

European souslik *Spermophilus citellus*   Page 148
Tail short but hairy, eyes large, ears very short, back faintly mottled but not clearly spotted. Always on ground, living in burrows in colonies. Head and body 19–22cm, tail 6–7cm.

Spotted souslik *Spermophilus suslicus*   Page 148
As European souslik but distinctly spotted and tail shorter. Head and body 18–25cm, tail 3–4cm.

See also Siberian chipmunk (p. 149).

Food remnants of squirrels

pine   spruce   larch   hazel

SQUIRRELS AND SOUSLIKS

summer, red phase

spring
British race

winter, red phase

Red squirrel

winter,
dark phase

winter

Grey squirrel

**Flying
squirrel**

summer, extreme reddish form

Spotted souslik

European souslik

PLATE 12

Alpine marmot *Marmota marmota* Page 148
A large terrestrial rodent living in burrows in alpine pastures. Tail short but well haired. Head and body 50–58cm, tail 14–19cm.

European beaver *Castor fiber* Page 149
The largest European rodent, always in or close to water. Tail very broad, flat and scaly. Fells small trees leaving characteristically shaped stumps with prominent tooth marks. Head and body 75–100cm, tail 30–40cm.

See also Canadian beaver (p. 151).

● European beaver   ● Canadian beaver

Porcupine *Hystrix cristata* Page 151
Armour of spines unique. Easily detected by cast spines outside wide burrows. Cf. hedgehogs, plate 1. Head and body *c*. 70cm.

Detached quills of Porcupine

head

upper back

lower back

tail

Coypu *Myocastor coypus* Page 151
Usually seen in water, marshes and on riverbanks. Much larger than Water vole (plate 17) and Common rat (plate 18). Tail not flattened. Head and body 40–60cm, tail 30–45cm.

Alpine marmot

European beaver

Stump of tree felled by Beaver

Porcupine

Coypu

Water vole

Musk rat

Coypu

PLATE 13

Garden dormouse *Eliomys quercinus*   Page 152
Black mask, large ears, tail with tufted, black-and-white tip. Head and body 100–170mm, tail 90–120mm.

Forest dormouse *Dryomys nitedula*   Page 152
Black mask, short ears, uniform tail. Head and body 80–130mm, tail 80–95mm.

Fat dormouse *Glis glis*   Page 153
Large, grey; no mask but dark rings make eyes appear very large and dark. Cf. Grey squirrel and Flying squirrel (plate 11). Head and body 130–190mm, tail 110–150mm.

Hazel dormouse *Muscardinus avellanarius*   Page 153
Small, short ears, orange-brown. Nest amongst shrubs, untidy, not entirely of grass, no obvious entrance. Cf. Harvest mouse (plate 20). Head and body 60–90mm, tail 55–75mm.

Mouse-tailed dormouse *Myomimus roachi*   Page 154
Small, grey, tail short-haired, slightly shorter than head and body. Head and body 70–110mm, tail 60–80mm.

DORMICE

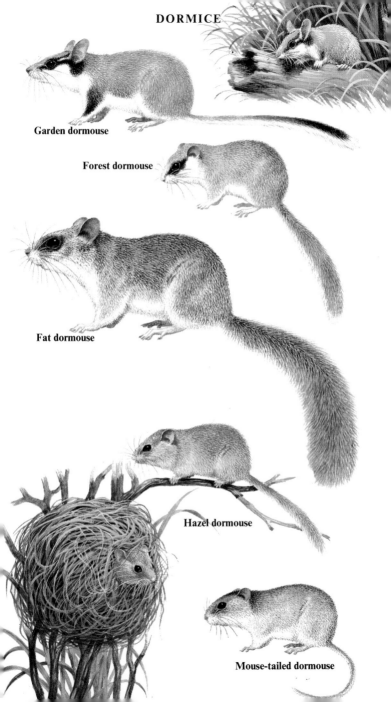

Garden dormouse

Forest dormouse

Fat dormouse

Hazel dormouse

Mouse-tailed dormouse

PLATE 14

Common hamster *Cricetus cricetus*　　Page 154
Size of Guinea pig. Extensive black below, short tail.
Head and body 220–300mm, tail 30–60mm.

◁ **Rumanian hamster** *Mesocricetus newtoni*　　Page 155
As Common hamster but much smaller, less black below.
Head and body 150–180mm, tail 10–20mm.

Golden hamster *Mesocricetus auratus*　　Page 154
Domesticated hamsters are very variable in colour but
usually have the pattern of dark marks on the shoulder
and neck less pronounced than in the wild species.

Grey hamster *Cricetulus migratorius*　　Page 155
No dark markings. Similar to grass voles and pine voles
(plates 16, 17) but eyes and ears larger, tail shorter. Head
and body 90–110mm, tail 22–28mm.

Mongolian gerbil

Mongolian gerbil *Meriones unguiculatus*　　Page 156
May occur as an escape. Tail long, well haired. Underside
and feet white, upper incisor teeth grooved. Cf. true mice
(plate 19).

◁ **Norway lemming** *Lemmus lemmus*　　Page 156
Bold pattern unique. Ears and tail very short. Head and
body 130–150mm, tail 15–20mm.

◁ **Wood lemming** *Myopus schisticolor*　　Page 157
Slaty grey above and below. Rusty streak on back. Coniferous forest. Head and body 85–95mm, tail 15–20mm.

Hamster skulls have rooted cheek-teeth with rather simple, rounded patterns
on the wearing surface. Lemming skulls have un-rooted cheek-teeth with
angular patterns.

Lemming runs revealed by melting snow

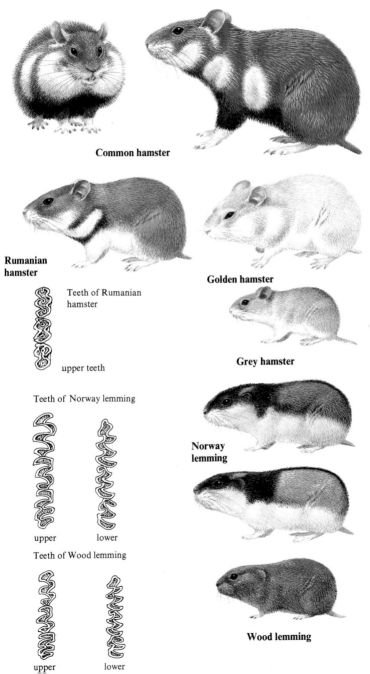

Common hamster

Rumanian hamster

Teeth of Rumanian hamster

upper teeth

Teeth of Norway lemming

upper   lower

Teeth of Wood lemming

upper   lower

Golden hamster

Grey hamster

Norway lemming

Wood lemming

PLATE 15

Juveniles of all voles are darker and greyer than adults, and therefore less distinctive, for the first month or so after leaving the nest. In all the species on this page the cheek-teeth become rooted, sometimes late in life.

Bank vole *Clethrionomys glareolus*   Page 157
Russet back, tail moderately long, ears more prominent than in grass and pine voles. Head and body 80–110mm, tail 35–65mm.

Northern red-backed vole
Clethrionomys rutilus   Page 158
Lighter and brighter than other species, tail short, well-haired with prominent terminal tuft. Head and body 80–100mm, tail 25–35mm.

Grey-sided vole *Clethrionomys rufocanus*   Page 158
Flanks grey, russet confined to narrow zone on back. Head and body 100–120mm, tail 30–40mm.

Balkan snow vole *Dinaromys bogdanovi*   Page 158
Pale grey and white, coat long and soft. Tail about three-quarters length of head and body. Cf. Snow vole (plate 16). Head and body 100–140mm, tail 75–110mm.

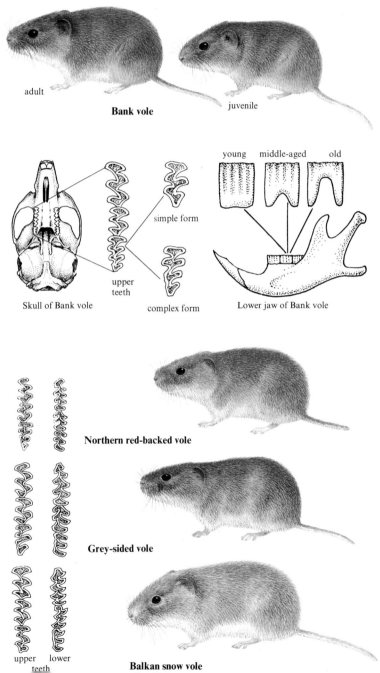

adult

juvenile

Bank vole

young   middle-aged   old

simple form

upper teeth

complex form

Skull of Bank vole

Lower jaw of Bank vole

Northern red-backed vole

Grey-sided vole

upper   lower
teeth

Balkan snow vole

PLATE 16

Field vole *Microtus agrestis* Page 159
Coat usually dark, long and shaggy. Tail sharply two-coloured. Second upper cheek-tooth distinctive. Head and body 90–130mm, tail 30–45mm, usually *c.* 30% of head and body.

Common vole *Microtus arvalis* Page 159
Coat usually paler, shorter and neater than in Field vole. Tail obscurely two-coloured. Head and body 90–120mm, tail 30–45mm, *c.* 30% of head and body.

See also Sibling vole (p. 160)

Root vole *Microtus oeconomus* Page 160
As Field vole but usually slightly larger and tail slightly longer, two-coloured. First lower cheek-tooth distinctive. Head and body 110–150mm, tail 40–65mm, *c.* 40% of head and body.

Snow vole *Microtus nivalis* Page 160
Pale greyish brown, tail long and very pale. First lower cheek-tooth distinctive. Head and body 110–140mm, tail 50–75mm, *c.* 50% of head and body. Cf. Balkan snow vole, plate 15.

Günther's vole *Microtus guentheri* Page 161
Feet white, tail very short and pale. Cheek-teeth as in Common vole but deeply indented. Head and body 100–120mm, tail 20–30mm, *c.*25% of head and body.

See also Cabrera's vole (p. 161).

● Günther's vole ● Cabrera's vole

In all grass voles the cheek-teeth remain unrooted. The distinctive features of the teeth are mainly at the posterior ends of the 2nd and 3rd upper teeth and the anterior end of the 1st lower tooth.

Droppings of Field vole in run, covered with chopped grass

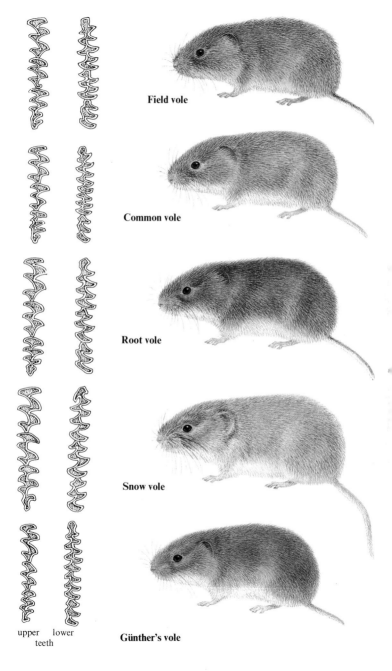

Field vole

Common vole

Root vole

Snow vole

upper | lower
teeth

Günther's vole

PLATE 17

Pine voles are like grass voles, but eyes, ears and feet are smaller. First lower cheek-tooth is distinctive, and hind feet have only 5 pads.

Common pine vole *Pitymys subterraneus*   Page 162
Dark. Last upper tooth complex. Head and body 80–100mm, tail 28–40mm, hind feet 13–15mm.

See also Alpine, Bavarian, Tatra and Liechtenstein's pine voles (pp. 162–3).

● Common pine vole   ● Alpine pine vole

Mediterranean pine vole
Pitymys duodecimcostatus   Page 163
More yellowish above and paler silvery grey below than other pine voles. Fur very soft and dense. Tail very short. Last upper tooth simpler, outer ridges uneven. Head and body 85–105mm, tail 20–30mm, hind feet 15–18mm.

See also Lusitanian and Thomas's pine voles (p. 163).

● Mediterranean pine vole   ● Lusitanian pine vole   ● Thomas's pine vole

Savi's pine vole *Pitymys savii*   Page 163
As Common pine vole but last tooth simple, outer ridges evenly developed. Head and body 85–105mm, tail 25–35mm, hind feet 14–16mm.

Water voles are like very large grass voles, with long tails, usually by water.

Northern water vole *Arvicola terrestris*   Page 164
Large size, long tail. All-black individuals common in some areas. May be terrestrial in south. Head and body 16–19cm in north, 14–16cm in south; tail 8–10cm in north, 4–8cm in south.

Southwestern water vole *Arvicola sapidus*   Page 165
Larger, darker and longer-tailed than neighbouring form of Northern water vole. Always by water. Head and body 17–20cm, tail 11–13cm.

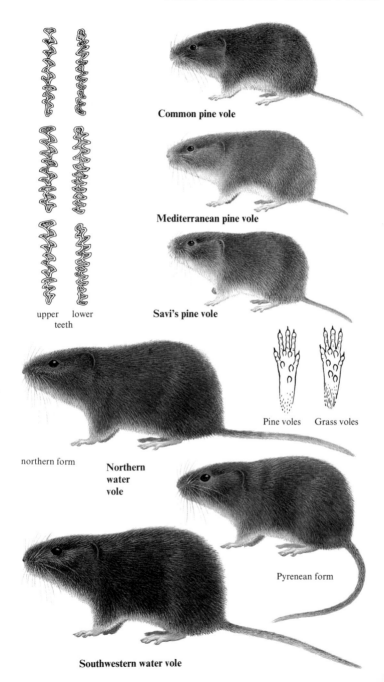

Common pine vole

Mediterranean pine vole

Savi's pine vole

upper lower
teeth

northern form

**Northern
water
vole**

Pine voles   Grass voles

Pyrenean form

Southwestern water vole

PLATE 18

Muskrat *Ondatra zibethicus*   Page 165
Always aquatic, larger than water voles (plate 17), smaller than Coypu and Beaver (plate 12). Tail flattened in vertical plane, ears short. Head and body 30–40cm, tail 20–27cm.

Greater mole-rat *Spalax microphthalmus*   Page 166
Subterranean. No visible eyes, ears nor tail. Larger than Lesser mole-rat. Head and body up to 31cm, hind feet 24–30mm.

Lesser mole-rat *Spalax leucodon*   Page 166
As Greater mole-rat but slightly smaller. Head and body up to 26cm, hind feet 20–25mm.

Hills of Mole-rats

Common rat *Rattus norvegicus*   Page 167
Usually brown, occasionally black. Tail a little shorter than head and body, almost naked, rather thick. Head and body 20–26cm, tail 17–23cm, hind feet 40–45mm, ears 19–22mm.

Ship rat *Rattus rattus*   Page 167
Smaller than Common rat. Colour variable – black, brown and grey, or brown and white. Tail slender, longer than head and body. Ears large and scantily haired. Head and body 16–23cm, tail 18–25cm, hind feet 30–40mm, ears 24–27mm.

RAT-SIZED RODENTS

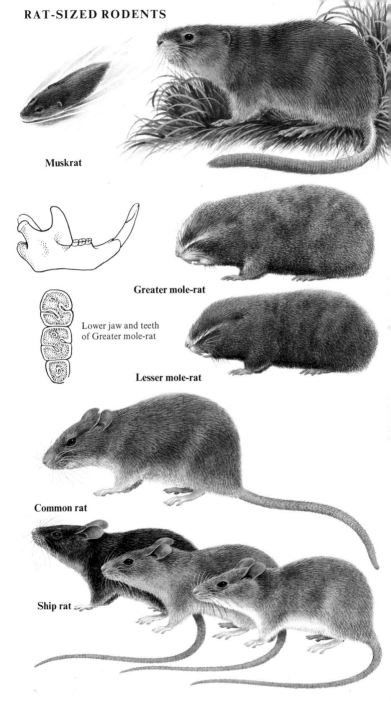

Muskrat

Greater mole-rat

Lower jaw and teeth
of Greater mole-rat

Lesser mole-rat

Common rat

Ship rat

PLATE 19   **WOOD MICE AND ALLIES**

Wood mouse *Apodemus sylvaticus*   Page 168
Tail about equal to head and body. Feet, eyes and ears
larger than in House mouse (plate 20). Underside pale
grey, usually with yellow streak on chest. Head and body
80–110mm, tail 70–115mm, hind feet 20–24mm, ear
15–17mm.

Yellow-necked mouse *Apodemus flavicollis*   Page 169
Slightly larger and brighter than Wood mouse, paler
below; chest-spot usually large, sometimes forming collar. Head and body 90–120mm, tail 90–135mm, hind feet
23–26mm, ear 16–20mm.

Pygmy field mouse *Apodemus microps*   Page 169
Smaller than Wood mouse – see especially hind feet and
ears. Chest-spot small or absent. See also House mouse
and Steppe mouse (plate 20). Head and body 70–95mm,
tail 65–95mm, hind feet 17–20mm, ear 13–15mm.

Rock mouse *Apodemus mystacinus*   Page 170
Large and greyish but much smaller than Ship rat (plate
18) and feet more slender. No chest-spot. Head and body
100–130mm, tail 105–140mm, hind feet 24–28mm, ear
17–21mm.

Striped field mouse *Apodemus agrarius*   Page 170
Dark stripe along back unique in *Apodemus* but see also
birch mice (plate 20). Tail shorter than head and body. No
chest-spot. Head and body 90–115mm, tail 70–85mm,
hind feet 17–21mm.

All species of *Apodemus* have complex, rooted cheek-teeth with rounded cusps,
becoming flatter and more featureless with wear.

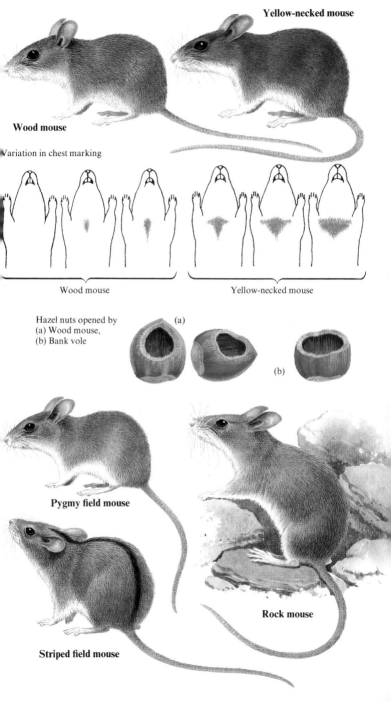

Yellow-necked mouse

Wood mouse

Variation in chest marking

Wood mouse

Yellow-necked mouse

Hazel nuts opened by
(a) Wood mouse,
(b) Bank vole

(a)

(b)

Pygmy field mouse

Striped field mouse

Rock mouse

PLATE 20

Harvest mouse *Micromys minutus*   Page 170
Smallest European mouse, ears very short, tail long, thin, prehensile. Nest distinctive, of shredded grass, 8–10cm diameter, above ground in grass or shrubs. Head and body 60–75mm, tail 50–70mm, hind feet 13–16mm, ear 8–10mm.

House mouse *Mus musculus*   Page 171
Very variable. Eyes, ears and hind feet smaller than in Wood mouse (plate 19). Tail thicker and more prominently ringed, about equal to head and body. No chest-spot. Upper incisors with characteristic notch on wearing surface (in profile), last tooth very small. Darkest in north-west, paler in south and east. Head and body 75–95mm, tail 70–95mm, hind feet 17–19mm, ear 12–16mm.

Algerian mouse *Mus spretus*   Page 172
Smaller than House mouse, paler grey below, feet white, tail shorter than head and body. Incisors without notch. Head and body 70–85mm, tail 55–70mm, hind feet 15–17mm, ear 11–14mm.

See also Steppe mouse (p. 172).

● Algerian mouse
● Steppe mouse

Cretan spiny mouse *Acomys cahirinus*   Page 173
Only on Crete. Back spiny. Ears very large. Colour varies from yellowish brown to grey. Tail easily broken, often damaged in life. Head and body 90–120mm, tail 90–120mm.

Birch mice have a dark stripe, tail much longer than head and body, ears small. Rare.

Northern birch mouse *Sicista betulina*   Page 174
Back uniform in colour apart from median dark stripe. Head and body 50–70mm, tail 80–105mm.

Southern birch mouse *Sicista subtilis*   Page 174
Central dark stripe bordered by pale stripes. Head and body 55–70mm, tail 70–85mm.

MISCELLANEOUS MICE

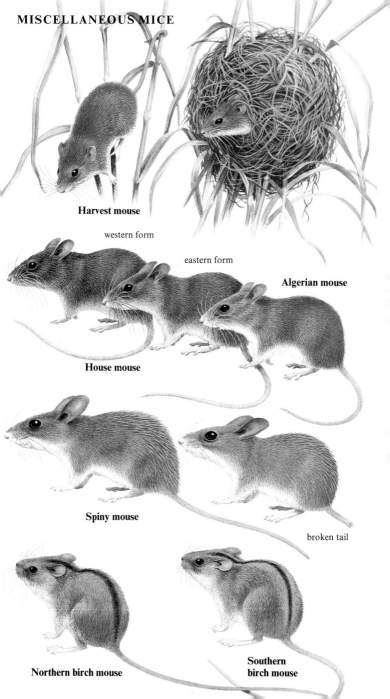

Harvest mouse

western form

eastern form

Algerian mouse

House mouse

Spiny mouse

broken tail

Northern birch mouse

Southern birch mouse

PLATE 21

Barbary ape *Macaca sylvanus*   Page 175
The only monkey in Europe, confined to Gibraltar, and
almost the only monkey (as distinct from the great apes)
without a tail. Head and body 60–70cm.

Polar bear *Thalarctos maritimus*   Page 176
Confined to the coasts and sea-ice of the high Arctic.
Always white. Ears shorter than in Brown bear, no angle
between muzzle and forehead. Head and body 1.5–2.5m.

Brown bear *Ursus arctos*   Page 176
Colour very variable, pale fawn to dark brown. Ears
prominent, muzzle forming angle with forehead. Footprints about the size of a man's but broader and claw
marks prominent. Head and body 1.5–2.5m.

Barbary ape

Polar bear

Brown bear

PLATE 22

Wolf   Alsatian   Jackal

Wild species of canines always have the ears erect even if short, never drooping as in many domestic dogs, and the tail drooping, never erect or curled.

Wolf *Canis lupus*   Page 177
Like a large Alsatian but ears shorter and less pointed, head broad. Colour rather uniform over body but varies from pale grey to medium greyish brown. Head and body up to 130cm, tail up to 50cm.

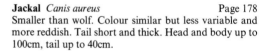

Jackal *Canis aureus*   Page 178
Smaller than wolf. Colour similar but less variable and more reddish. Tail short and thick. Head and body up to 100cm, tail up to 40cm.

Raccoon-dog *Nyctereutes procyonoides*   Page 179
Black mask (but see also Raccoon, plate 26). Legs short, ears short and rounded. Head and body up to 65cm, tail up to 20cm.

Arctic fox *Alopex lagopus*   Page 179
Colour variable, never reddish. Brown or grey in summer, white or grey in winter. Ears and muzzle shorter than in Red fox. Head and body up to 65cm, tail up to 35cm.

● Raccoon dog
● Arctic fox

Red fox *Vulpes vulpes*   Page 179
Usually reddish brown, sometimes with black markings on underside and nape. Muzzle narrow, ears large and pointed, tail very bushy, usually with white tip. Silver variety does not occur naturally in Europe but may escape from captivity. Head and body up to 75cm, tail up to 45cm.

Wolf

Jackal

Raccoon-dog

summer

winter

Arctic fox

'blue' form

Red fox

'cross' variety

Silver fox (ranch variety of Red fox)

PLATE 23

Stoat *Mustela erminea*   Page 180
Size variable, sometimes as small as large weasel, but tail always with black tip. Pure white, except for tail-tip, in winter in north, may be partly white farther south. Head and body 20–30cm, tail 6–12cm.

Weasel *Mustela nivalis*   Page 181
Size very variable (males much larger than females), tail relatively short and never with black tip. Dividing line on flank variable – straight or irregular. Head and body 13–23cm, tail 3–6cm.

European mink *Mustela lutreola*   Page 181
Dark brown all over except for white on chin *and* on upper lip. No white behind eye (compare Polecat, plate 24). Head and body 35–40cm, tail 13–14cm.

American mink *Mustela vison*   Page 181
As European mink but white confined to lower jaw. Many colour varieties bred for fur and these may be found as escapes. Head and body 35–40cm, tail 13–14cm.

Ranch varieties of American mink

Marbled polecat *Vormela peregusna*   Page 183
Facial pattern as in Polecat (plate 24) but boldly mottled pattern on back and tail is unique. Head and body 30–38cm, tail 15–20cm.

STOAT, WEASEL, MINK AND MARBLED POLECAT

winter

summer

winter (north)

Stoat

Weasel

♂

♀

European mink

American mink

Marbled polecat

PLATE 24

Western polecat *Mustela putorius*   Page 182
Dark all over except for pattern of white on head; light
underfur sometimes shows through dark surface of coat
(compare mink, plate 23). Head and body 32–44cm, tail
13–18cm.

Steppe polecat *Mustela eversmanni*   Page 182
As Western polecat but much paler on body; feet and
underside dark. Head and body 32–44cm, tail 13–18cm.

Ferret *Mustela furo*   Page 183
Domestic form of polecat used especially for catching
rabbits. Coat varies from creamy white to a form almost
as dark as Western polecat. Feral animals usually like
Western polecat but paler and with more white on head.
Size as for Western polecat.

Pine marten *Martes martes*   Page 183
Larger than polecats and mink, with more prominent
ears, longer bushier tail and longer legs. Throat patch
varies from pale yellow to dull orange, never white.
Frequently seen in trees. Head and body 40–55cm, tail
22–27cm.

Beech marten *Martes foina*   Page 184
As Pine marten but throat patch pure white and very
variable in size, often divided, in places, e.g. on Crete, very
reduced. Head and body 40–48cm, tail 22–26cm.

Polecat

Steppe polecat

typical

Domestic ferret

dark form

Pine marten

Cretan form

Beech marten

Badger set

Badger *Meles meles* Page 185
Combination of face pattern, black underparts, grey back and short, unpatterned tail is unique. Compare with Raccoon (plate 26) and Raccoon-dog (plate 22). Burrows – 'sets' – are distinctive, especially in woodland, with large mounds of excavated earth. Head and body 67–80cm, tail 12–19cm.

Wolverine *Gulo gulo* Page 184
Like a large heavy marten or small slim bear, but pale stripe on flank is unique. Usually on ground. Head and body 70–80cm, tail 16–25cm.

Otter *Lutra lutra* Page 184
Usually seen in or near water. Long, thick, tapering tail. Bounding gait on land, extremely agile swimmer. Compare with Beaver, Coypu (plate 12) and Muskrat (plate 18). Head and body 60–80cm, tail 35–45cm.

Egyptian mongoose *Herpestes ichneumon* Page 186
Like mink and polecats (plates 23, 24) but larger, and grizzled coat and long tapering tail distinctive. Head and body 50–55cm, tail 35–45cm.

See also Indian grey mongoose (p. 186).

Genet *Genetta genetta* Page 187
Prominent ears, spotted coat, very long, ringed tail. Much slimmer and shorter-legged than cat. Head and body 50–60cm, tail 40–48cm.

PLATE 25   MISCELLANEOUS CARNIVORES

Badger

Wolverine

Otter

Egyptian mongoose

Genet

PLATE 26

Raccoon *Procyon lotor*   Page 187
Combination of black mask and banded tail is unique, but cf. Raccoon-dog (plate 22) and Genet (plate 25). Head and body 50–60cm.

Lynx *Felis lynx*   Page 187
Large, long legs, tufted ears and cheeks, short tail. Amount of spotting variable. Head and body 80–130cm.

Wild cat *Felis silvestris*   Page 188
As domestic cat but always striped, never blotched. Tail short, thick and blunt, paws pale. Head and body 50–65cm.

Feral domestic cats are widespread in Europe and are interfertile with wild cats. Tabbies – those most resembling wild cats – usually have longer, slender, tapering tails and often show rounded blotches rather than vertical stripes.

Domestic cats in variety

RACCOON
AND CATS

Raccoon

Scandinavia

Lynx

Carpathians

Iberia

Wild cat

PLATE 27

Common seals on sandbanks

The species on this page are the only ones likely to be seen south and west of the Baltic.

Common seal *Phoca vitulina*   Page 189
Small, sexes similar. Muzzle short, profile concave between forehead and muzzle, nostrils forming V. Pups brown, swim from birth. Head and body up to 1.9m.

■ Breeding   /// Non-breeding

Grey seal *Halichoerus grypus*   Page 190
Large, males larger than females. Muzzle long, profile of forehead straight or convex, nostrils widely separated. Pups white, remain ashore. Head and body up to 3.2m (males) or 2.5m (females).

■ Breeding   /// Non-breeding

Monk seal *Monachus monachus*   Page 190
Only seal in Mediterranean. Large, sexes similar, white markings variable. Pups on land for 6 weeks.

Common seal

Grey seal

♀

♂

Monk seal

PLATE 28

All the species on this page are confined to Arctic waters (except for Ringed seal also in the Baltic) and only rarely wander further south. All these seals produce their pups on ice where they remain for several weeks.

Ringed seal *Phoca hispida*   Page 189
Small, pattern of rings, dark markings coalesce on back. Variable, sometimes difficult to distinguish from Common seal (plate 27). Head and body *c*.1.5m, sexes equal.

 Breeding   /// Non-breeding

Harp seal *Pagophilus groenlandicus*   Page 191
Adult females only gradually acquire pattern resembling faded version of males. Subadults similar to Common and Ringed seals but head dark and spots usually sparse. Head and body to 2m.

Breeding   /// Non-breeding

Bearded seal *Erignathus barbatus*   Page 191
Prominent whiskers, adults unspotted, subadults faintly spotted. Head and body 2–2.5m.

Breeding

/// Non-breeding

Male Hooded seal

hood deflated   hood inflated

Hooded seal *Cystophora cristata*   Page 191
Only adult male has prominent, inflatable hood. Otherwise similar to Grey seal but more white. Bluish grey pups unique. Head and body to 3m in male, slightly less in female.

Breeding   /// Non-breeding

Walrus *Odobenus rosmarus*   Page 191
Unmistakable. Note hind feet turned forward on land as in Sea-lion. Females with smaller, more slender tusks. Head and body up to 4m in males, 3m in females.

Breeding   /// Non-breeding

ARCTIC SEALS AND WALRUS

Ringed seal

Harp seal

♂

♀

subadult

Bearded seal

Hooded seal

♀

Walrus

♂

PLATE 29

Wild boar *Sus scrofa*   Page 195
Like a domestic pig but with a dense bristly coat and a long snout. Male with protruding tusks. Young striped. Head and body up to 180cm, shoulder height up to 100cm.

Bison *Bison bonasus*   Page 196
Like domestic cattle but with mane on neck and shoulders, especially in bull. Head and body *c.* 250cm, shoulder height *c.*190cm.

Musk ox *Ovibos moschatus*   Page 196
Smaller than domestic cattle. Long shaggy coat, horns meeting on top of head. Head and body *c.* 240cm, shoulder height *c.* 150cm in males, females smaller.

Domestic cattle *Bos taurus*   Page 196
Several primitive breeds, e.g. the Chillingham herd of white park cattle, in Northumberland, have survived with little change from Medieval times, but no truly wild nor feral animals exist in Europe.

See also Domestic water buffalo (p. 196).

Chillingham bull   **Hereford bull**   **Friesian cow**

WILD BOAR AND WILD CATTLE

Wild boar

Bison

Musk ox

PLATE 30

Mouflon *Ovis musimon*   Page 197
As domestic sheep but wool short and concealed by normal hair. Horns small or absent in female. Only mature males have reddish colour with pale patch on flank; younger males as females. Head and body 110–120cm, shoulder height 65–75cm.

See also Domestic sheep (p. 198).

Alpine ibex *Capra ibex*   Page 199
Goat-like, horns of male curved backwards in one plane, with prominent closely spaced ribs on front. Only at high altitude. Head and body 140–150cm, shoulder height 70–80cm.

◁ **Spanish ibex** *Capra pyrenaicus*   Page 199
As Alpine ibex but horns curved outwards and upwards. Head and body 120–140cm, shoulder height 65–75cm.

Wild goat *Capra aegagrus*   Page 199
As domestic goat but horns curving backwards in one plane, with sharp keel on front margin and widely spaced, low ribs. Only on some Greek islands.

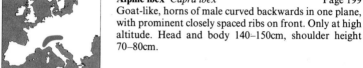

Feral goats

Domestic goat *Capra hircus*   Page 200
Primitive breeds like Wild goat but often long-haired, often piebald and horns usually divergent or with corkscrew spiral. Feral in some areas, e.g. Scotland, Mediterranean islands. Size very variable.

◁ **Chamois** *Rupicapra rupicapra*   Page 200
Goat-like. Smaller than ibex. Bold facial pattern, short hooked horns in both sexes. Dark in winter, pale in summer. Head and body 100–130cm, shoulder height 70–80cm.

Mouflon

♂

♀

Alpine ibex

♂

♀

♂

Spanish ibex

Chamois

summer

Wild
goat

winter

PLATE 31

Red deer *Cervus elaphus*   Page 201

Large. Pale patch on rump buff in both sexes at all ages, never white. Antlers of fully mature stags with *two* forward branches close to base, but young males have only one as in Sika deer (plate 32) and in rare individuals (hummels) antlers fail to develop. Antlers growing and covered with 'velvet', from spring to early autumn, clear of velvet by about September, shed in following spring. Coat reddish brown in summer, greyish brown in winter, young calves spotted. Head and body up to 260cm, shoulder height up to 150cm.

Except in Reindeer, only male deer carry antlers and only for part of the year. Although those of fully mature males are distinctive, those of young animals can be confusing. The pattern of the tail and rump is almost constant within a species and is especially useful for identification.

Red deer

Sika

Fallow deer

Roe deer

RED DEER

Red deer

♂ autumn

young ♂ winter

♀ winter

hummel ♂ winter

♀ summer

calf

♂ early summer, in velvet

PLATE 32

Sika deer *Cervus nippon*   Page 202

Spotted in summer, dark and almost unspotted in winter. Tail mostly white, rump patch white, bordered black. Antlers with never more than one forward branch at base. Head and body up to 120cm, shoulder height up to 85cm.

Spotted deer *Cervus axis*   Page 203

Heavily spotted at all seasons. Tail long, dark, rump patch small, not bordered with black. Antlers simple, not flattened. Head and body up to 130cm, shoulder height up to 90cm.

Fallow deer *Cervus dama*   Page 202

Very variable. Usually spotted in summer, unspotted and greyer in winter. Permanently dark and permanently light varieties common. Tail long with dark stripe, rump bordered with black. Antlers flattened at tips in mature bucks, but not in young animals. Head and body up to 150cm, shoulder height up to 110cm.

normal spotted form   albino   melanistic

Variation in fallow deer

84

DEER

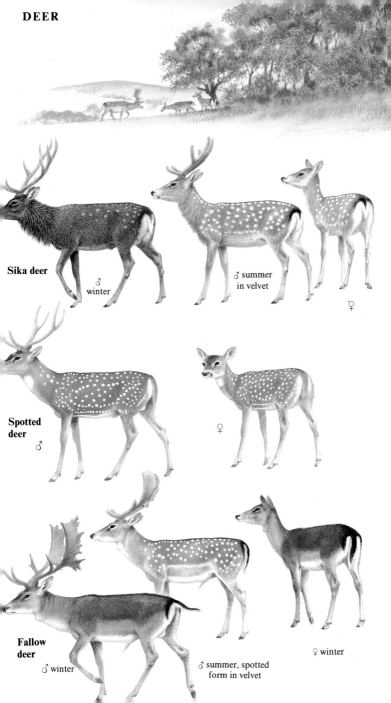

Sika deer

♂ winter

♂ summer
in velvet

♀

Spotted deer

♂

♀

Fallow deer

♂ winter

♂ summer, spotted
form in velvet

♀ winter

PLATE 33   NORTHERN DEER

Elk *Alces alces*   Page 203
Very large, with long legs. Dark at all seasons. Antlers in males only, usually flattened but sometimes remaining simply branched. Muzzle inflated, overlapping mouth. Head and body up to 280cm, shoulder height up to 220cm.

Reindeer *Rangifer tarandus*   Page 203
Very variable in colour and pattern, especially amongst domesticated animals. Antlers in both sexes, smaller in females. First forward branch itself branched. Feet large. Head and body up to 210cm, shoulder height up to 120cm, often much less.

White-tailed deer *Odocoileus virginianus*   Page 204
Reddish brown in summer, greyish in winter. Tail long and thick, raised in flight showing prominent white underside and rump. Antlers arching forwards. Head and body up to 180cm, shoulder height up to 105cm.

Variation in domestic Reindeer

1 year old ♂

autumn
(mate antlers)

Elk

♂ with simple
antlers

♂ summer
(velvet)

calf summer

♂ winter

Reindeer

♀ summer

calf

♂ winter

♀ summer

**White-tailed
deer**

calf

PLATE 34

Tree frayed
by antlers of
Roe deer

Roe deer *Capreolus capreolus*   Page 204
Smallest widespread deer. Reddish brown in summer,
greyish brown in winter. White rump patch prominent in
winter, obscure in summer. Antlers short, rough, up to 3
points. Frayed bark on young trees is characteristic sign.
Head and body up to 120cm, shoulder height up to 75cm.

Muntjac *Muntiacus reevesi*   Page 205
Very small, dark throughout year, rump patch only conspicuous when tail raised. Antlers very small on permanent projections. Head and body up to 90cm, shoulder
height up to 50cm.

Chinese water deer *Hydropotes inermis*   Page 205
No antlers, but males have protruding tusks. Rump patch
obscure, ears large. Head and body up to 100cm, shoulder
height up to 60cm.

Chinese water deer buck showing large canine
teeth

SMALL DEER

♂ winter

♀ winter

♂ summer

♀ summer

Roe deer

Roe deer calf

♂ summer

♀ winter

Muntjac

Chinese water deer

♂ summer

♀ winter

PLATE 35

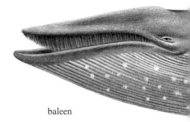

baleen

All these whales have plates of horny baleen in the mouth and no teeth. The colour of the baleen is useful in identifying stranded animals. All the species on this page, the rorquals, are long and slender, with the throat deeply furrowed, the flippers narrow and pointed, a small fin on the back and relatively straight jaws. At sea, the 'blow' is erect and appears single (see plate 36).

Fin whale *Balaenoptera physalis*   Page 207
Black above, white below, pigment on head and baleen asymmetrical. Back fin smaller than in Sei whale. Length up to 20m.

Blue whale *Balaenoptera musculus*   Page 208
Lighter above than other baleen whales, underside same as back. Back fin very small. Baleen black, up to 80cm. Length up to 30m.

Sei whale *Balaenoptera borealis*   Page 208
As Fin whale but not so slim and back fin larger and more pointed. Colour symmetrical. Baleen black with pale fringes. Length up to 18m.

Minke whale *Balaenoptera acutorostrata*   Page 208
Smallest rorqual. White spot on flipper diagnostic. Baleen white or yellowish, not over 30cm long. Length up to 10m.

BALEEN WHALES

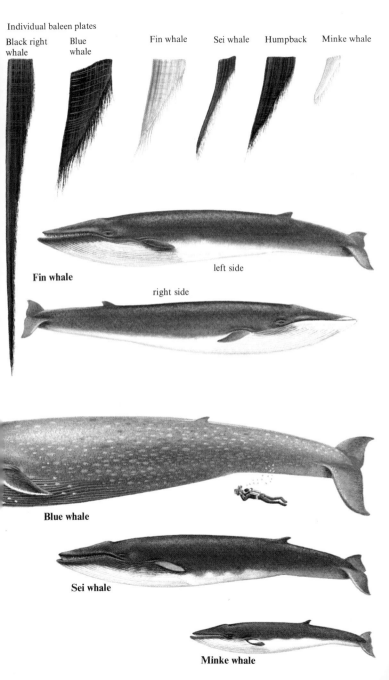

Individual baleen plates

Black right whale

Blue whale

Fin whale

Sei whale

Humpback

Minke whale

Fin whale

left side

right side

Blue whale

Sei whale

Minke whale

PLATE 36

HUMPBACK, RIGHT WHALES
AND SPERM WHALES

Humpback whale *Megaptera novaeangliae*   Page 209
Small fin on back. Tail emerges from water on diving.
Flippers very long, mainly white. Throat grooved. Baleen
black, up to 80cm long. Length up to 15m.

Black right whale *Balaena glacialis*   Page 209
No fin on back. All black. Jaw arched, flippers broad
and rounded, head large. Blow erect and double. Baleen
black, up to 2.5m long. Length up to 17m.

Bowhead whale *Balaena mysticetus*   Page 209
As Black right whale, but usually some white below and
head even larger. Baleen up to 3m. Length up to 18m.

Sperm whale *Physeter catodon*   Page 210
Obscure fin on back. Head bulbous, lower jaw slender,
with numerous teeth. Females much smaller than males.
Blow single, directed forwards. Length of males up to
18m, of females up to 10m.

See also Pygmy sperm whale, plate 39.

Whales blowing

Blue   Fin whale   Humpback   Right

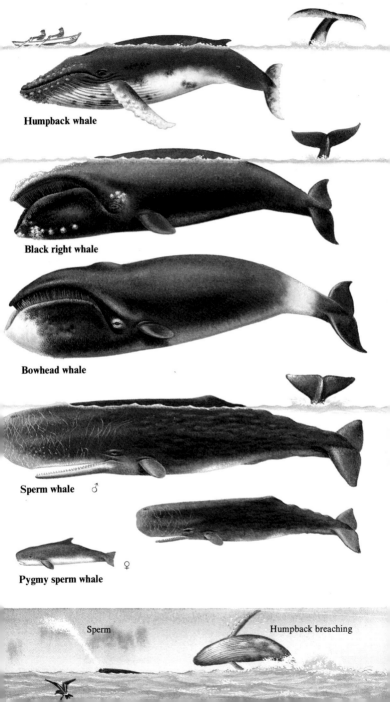

Humpback whale

Black right whale

Bowhead whale

Sperm whale ♂

Pygmy sperm whale ♀

Sperm

Humpback breaching

PLATE 37

Apart from the Bottle-nosed whale these species are rarely seen in coastal waters and rarely become stranded. They have no baleen but only a single pair of tusk-like teeth in the lower jaw, in males only. The tail fluke has no central notch and the back fin is well behind the centre of the body. Pale scratch marks on the skin are common.

Bottle-nosed whale *Hyperoodon ampullatus* Page 211
Forehead bulbous, especially in large males. Compare Pilot whale (plate 38). Prominent beak, flippers small and rounded. Tusks at tip of lower jaw. Length up to 9m, more often 7–8m.

Cuvier's whale *Ziphius cavirostris* Page 211
Colour and pattern variable; form with white head and back distinctive but other patterns occur including uniform grey. Tusks at front of lower jaw. Length up to 7 or 8m.

Sowerby's whale *Mesoplodon bidens* Page 211
Body strongly compressed from side to side, all black or lighter below. Beak slender. Tusks near centre of lower jaw. Length up to 5m.

True's beaked whale *Mesoplodon mirus* Page 212
Pale below, often spotted. Tusks at front of lower jaw, very flattened (as in all *Mesoplodon*). Length up to 5m.

Gray's whale *Mesoplodon grayi* Page 212
Similar to Sowerby's whale but smaller and lighter. Tusks further forward. Length up to 4.5m.

Gervais' whale *Mesoplodon europaeus* Page 212
Larger than Sowerby's whale, otherwise similar. Tusks small, just behind tip of lower jaw. Length up to 6m.

Stranded beaked whales are best identified by the position and shape of the tusks in the lower jaw. These normally erupt fully only in males; in females they usually remain embedded in the jaws.

Bottle-nosed   Sowerby's   Cuvier's

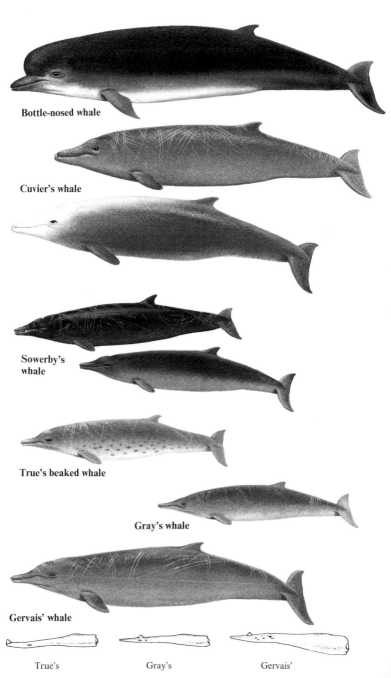

BEAKED WHALES

Bottle-nosed whale

Cuvier's whale

Sowerby's
whale

True's beaked whale

Gray's whale

Gervais' whale

True's   Gray's   Gervais'

PLATE 38

White whale *Delphinapterus leucas*   Page 213
Adults completely white, juveniles grey. Bulbous fore-
head, no back fin. Flippers rather short and rounded.
Length up to 5m.

Narwhal *Monodon monoceros*   Page 213
As White whale but mottled pattern. Male only has unique, spirally grooved tusk. Length (without tusk) up to
5.5m, tusk up to 3m, usually less.

Narwhal tusk

Long-finned pilot whale *Globicephala melaena* Page 213
Large recurved fin centrally on back, bulbous forehead,
very short beak. Flippers long and pointed. Sociable.
Length up to 8m.

Killer whale *Orcinus orca*   Page 214
Back fin erect and triangular, especially large in adult
male. Flippers broad and rounded. Pattern fairly constant. Length up to 9m in males, females rather smaller.

Basking sharks (fish, not mammals) also have a triangular
fin on the back but this is followed by the vertical tail fin.

Basking sharks

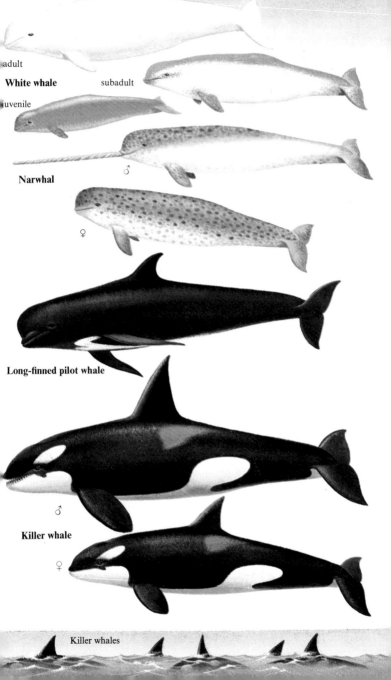

adult

White whale   subadult

juvenile

Narwhal   ♂

♀

Long-finned pilot whale

♂

Killer whale

♀

Killer whales

PLATE 39

Bottle-nosed dolphin *Tursiops truncatus*   Page 214
Grey, obscurely patterned, back fin large, central; short beak. The species most used in dolphinaria. Length up to 4m.

Risso's dolphin *Grampus griseus*   Page 215
Grey, no beak, bulbous forehead. Skin often scarred. Length up to 3.5m.

Rough-toothed dolphin *Steno bredanensis*   Page 215
Small, spotted, beak white. Teeth distinctively furrowed. Length up to 2.5m.

False killer whale *Pseudorca crassidens*   Page 215
All black, rounded head, no beak, short slender flippers. Rare but sometimes becoming stranded in large groups. Length up to 5.5m.

Pygmy sperm whale *Kogia breviceps*   Page 210
Head shark-like, overhanging mouth, prominent fin on back. Teeth in lower jaw only. Length up to 3.5m.

School of False killer whales stranded on beach

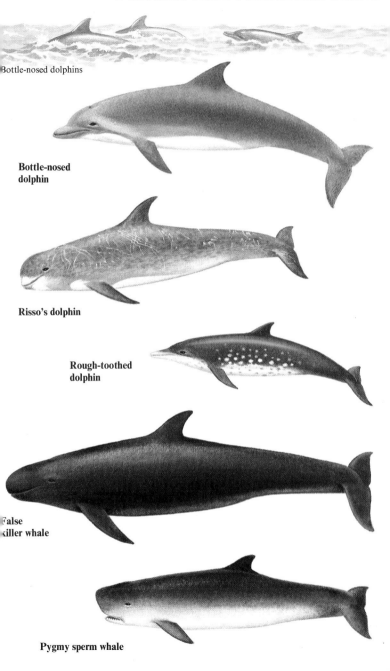

Bottle-nosed dolphins

**Bottle-nosed
dolphin**

Risso's dolphin

**Rough-toothed
dolphin**

**False
killer whale**

Pygmy sperm whale

PLATE 40

Common dolphin *Delphinus delphis*   Page 216
Bold pattern with lines crossing below back fin. Colour varies in intensity. Beak slender, fin large, recurved. Follow ships. Length up to 2.5m, more often about 2m.

Striped dolphin *Stenella coeruleoalba*   Page 216
Complex marks, without crossover pattern of Common dolphin. Length up to 2m.

White-sided dolphin *Lagenorhynchus acutus*   Page 217
Large, with large back fin and short, dark beak. Pale line on flank. Tail deep and narrow in front of flukes. Length up to 2.7m.

White-beaked dolphin
Lagenorhynchus albirostris   Page 217
Beak white, back fin very large and erect, pattern complex. Length up to 3m.

Porpoise *Phocoena phocoena*   Page 217
Smallest cetacean. Back fin low and blunt, no beak. Plump body. Length up to 1.8m.

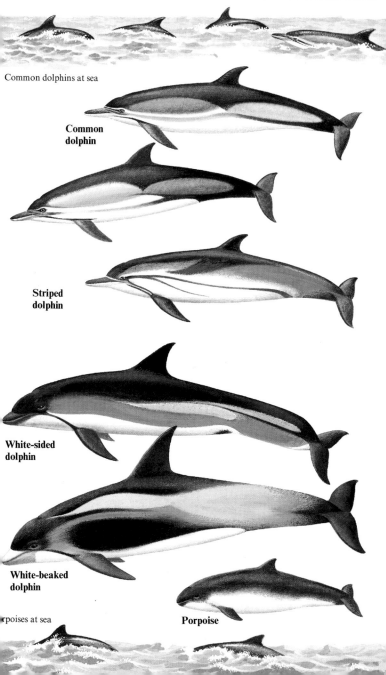

Common dolphins at sea

Common dolphin

Striped dolphin

White-sided dolphin

White-beaked dolphin

Porpoises at sea

Porpoise

Tracks

The footprints or 'spoor' of mammals, if clearly imprinted, for example on firm mud, can sometimes enable the particular species to be identified. More often only an approximate identification can be made. As well as the number and relative length of the toes and the arrangement of pads and claws, attention should be paid to the relative position of the prints of fore and hind feet and the overall pattern of the trail, keeping in mind that these can vary greatly according to the speed of the animal. Tracks in snow often become misleadingly enlarged as the snow melts and refreezes.

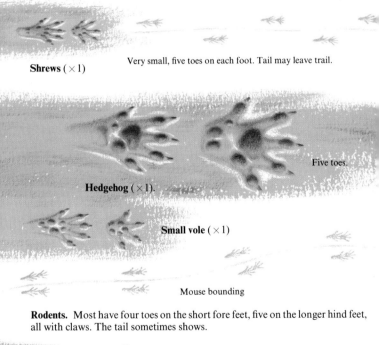

Shrews ($\times 1$)

Very small, five toes on each foot. Tail may leave trail.

Hedgehog ($\times 1$).

Five toes.

Small vole ($\times 1$)

Mouse bounding

Rodents. Most have four toes on the short fore feet, five on the longer hind feet, all with claws. The tail sometimes shows.

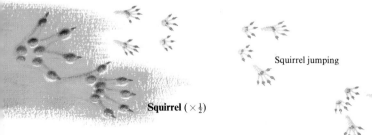

Squirrel jumping

Squirrel ($\times \frac{1}{2}$)

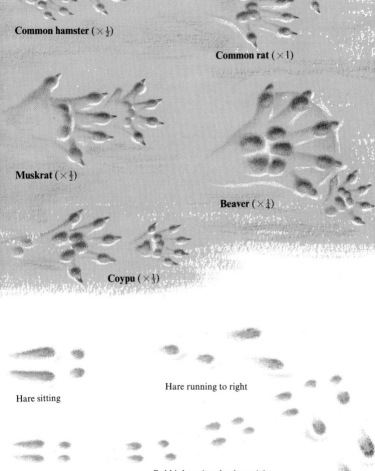

Common hamster ($\times \frac{1}{2}$)

Common rat ($\times 1$)

Muskrat ($\times \frac{1}{2}$)

Beaver ($\times \frac{1}{4}$)

Coypu ($\times \frac{1}{3}$)

Hare sitting

Hare running to right

Rabbit hopping slowly to right

Rabbits and hares. The individual prints show little detail since the soles are hairy, but the pattern of the trail is very characteristic, with combination of short fore and long hind feet. When running fast the prints of the hind feet come *in front* of those of the front feet and the prints are no longer side by side.

Ungulates The footprints of cloven-hoofed ungulates are easy to recognize as such, but the individual species can rarely be identified with certainty. Most leave prints of the main, central pair of hooves only, but on soft ground the short lateral toes of wild boars, the 'dewclaws', usually show and sometimes those of deer leave a pair of faint marks behind the main print.

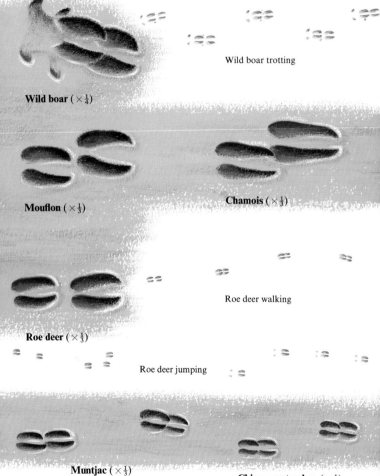

Wild boar trotting

Wild boar ($\times \frac{1}{4}$)

Mouflon ($\times \frac{1}{3}$)

Chamois ($\times \frac{1}{3}$)

Roe deer walking

Roe deer ($\times \frac{1}{3}$)

Roe deer jumping

Muntjac ($\times \frac{1}{3}$)

Chinese water deer ($\times \frac{1}{3}$)

In muntjac the two hooves of each pair tend to be slightly asymmetrical. When deer are walking the prints of fore and hind feet often overlap or coincide.

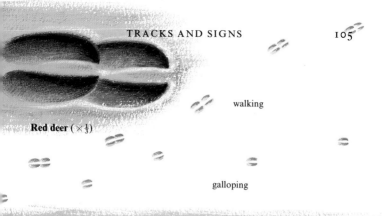

walking

Red deer ($\times \frac{1}{3}$)

galloping

Fallow deer ($\times \frac{1}{3}$)

Sika deer ($\times \frac{1}{3}$)

In prints of white-tailed deer the dewclaw marks of the hind feet are more widely separated from the main print than those of the fore feet.

White-tailed deer ($\times \frac{1}{3}$)

Elk ($\times \frac{1}{4}$)

The dewclaws of white-tailed deer, elk and reindeer are more prominent than those of other deer. The curved prints of reindeer are quite distinctive.

Reindeer ($\times \frac{1}{4}$)

Carnivores Fore and hind feet similar, toes four or five, usually short with thick pads and prominent claws (except in cats) but often obscured by hair, especially in winter.

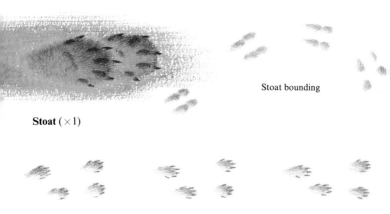

Stoat bounding

Stoat ($\times 1$)

Polecat bounding

Small members of the weasel family (above) usually move with a bounding gait. The larger carnivores may walk or bound. When walking the prints of the hind feet may almost or precisely coincide or 'register' with those of the fore feet.

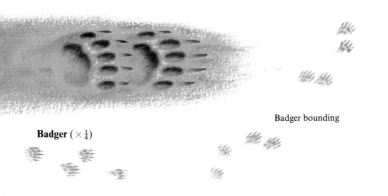

Badger bounding

Badger ($\times \frac{1}{4}$)

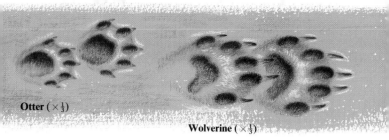

Otter ($\times \frac{1}{3}$)

Wolverine ($\times \frac{1}{3}$)

The webbed feet of otters show in prints on riverside mud. Otters usually progress on land by bounding. Wolverine prints are as large as or larger than foxes' but show five toes on each foot.

Fox ($\times \frac{1}{3}$)

Dog ($\times \frac{1}{3}$)

Fox trotting

Foxes and dogs show only four toes, the outer pair much shorter than the central ones, all with prominent claws. Dog prints of course vary greatly in size but are usually relatively wider than those of foxes. Those of wolves and jackals are not distinguishable from dogs of similar size.

Common seal on sand

Cat ($\times \frac{1}{3}$)

Cat prints show four toe pads but no claws since these are retracted when the cat is walking. Prints of lynx are similar but twice the size, about 6cm broad. Seals travel on land by a wriggling movement of the body helped by the front flippers.

Feeding signs

Signs left by feeding activity are useful in locating animals and in studying their activity. It is rarely possible to identify the species exactly from the sign alone although one can usually be fairly certain what species is responsible if the local mammal species are known.

Bark is eaten mainly in winter and especially during hard weather when rabbits, hares, voles, deer and other ungulates will all remove bark within reach of the ground, especially from young hardwood trees.

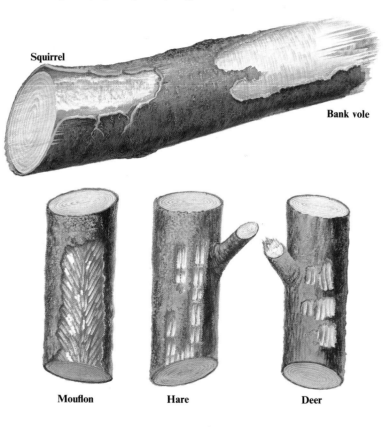

Squirrel

Bank vole

Mouflon   **Hare**   **Deer**

Squirrels will also strip sappy bark from high branches in summer, filling the seasonal gap between the spring buds and the autumn seeds, nuts and fruit.

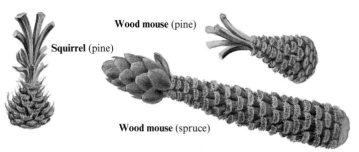

Squirrel (pine)

Wood mouse (pine)

Wood mouse (spruce)

Squirrels and mice remove the scales of cones to get at the nutritious seeds which lie between them, mice generally making a neater job than squirrels. (Crossbills and woodpeckers also feed on cones but usually leave the scales attached although sometimes split or disarranged.)

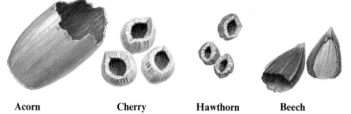

Acorn   **Cherry**   **Hawthorn**   **Beech**

Nuts and fruit-stones are gnawed by rodents to reach the kernel, often after storing them in hoards, e.g. under a log by mice, or buried singly amongst grass in the case of squirrels.

Rosehip debris is often found under hedges or in old bird nests where mice have been feeding by extracting the kernels from the pips. Fallen apples are eaten by all kinds of rodents and ungulates and even by carnivores such as foxes, especially in hard weather.

Droppings (natural size)

Droppings of herbivores (this page) usually occur in groups and are fairly constant in shape in any one species. They tend to be darker, and to stick together (especially in deer) in summer, and to be lighter, drier and more fibrous in winter. They also become paler as they dry out and weather.

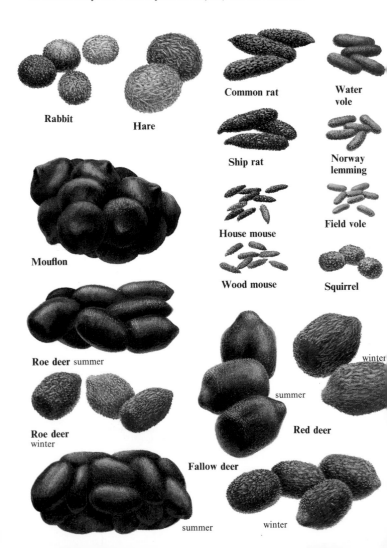

Rabbit

Hare

Common rat

Water vole

Ship rat

Norway lemming

House mouse

Field vole

Wood mouse

Squirrel

Mouflon

Roe deer summer

Roe deer winter

Fallow deer summer

Red deer summer

winter

winter

Elk

winter   summer

Droppings of predators are elongate, irregular, usually with hair, feathers, bone or insect cuticle showing. They often become white and chalky on weathering. Content and size are better clues to the species than is shape.

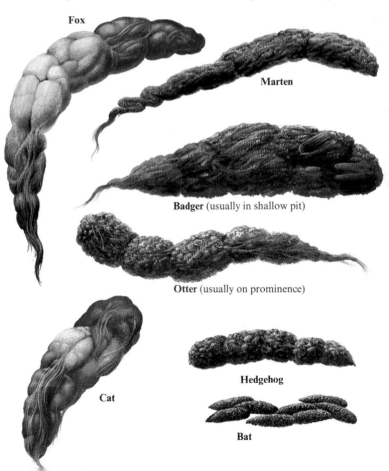

Fox

Marten

Badger (usually in shallow pit)

Otter (usually on prominence)

Cat

Hedgehog

Bat

Skulls and teeth

Skulls and teeth are important in classifying and identifying mammals for a number of reasons. In the first place they are very complex structures which reflect, in a rigid measurable form, many of the important features of the animal's head – eyes, ears, nose, jaws etc. – that give each species its distinctive appearance. Skulls or jaws therefore tend to be more obviously distinctive than other parts of the skeleton. Skulls may be prepared by burying an animal that has been found dead, or, more messily and laboriously, by boiling until the flesh can be picked off. But being relatively resistant to decay, skulls can often be found already clean of flesh, for example on beaches, in caves, around carnivore dens and in the pellets or other feeding debris of birds of prey. Skulls, or more often fragments of jaws or isolated teeth, are also the most identifiable form in which mammals are found in a fossil state, including 'subfossil' specimens found in archaeological sites. The following illustrations show the principal forms taken by skulls; in many cases the finer distinctions between individual species are shown in the main text for the species.

Small skulls (actual size)

Horseshoe bat

Common shrew

Verspertilionid bat

Wood mouse

Mole

Field vole

Desman

Small skulls, under 4 cm in length or with tooth-rows of under 15 mm, will belong to bats, shrews, moles, desman, weasel or the smaller rodents. Bat skulls have continuous rows of sharply pointed teeth with prominent fang-like canines above and below, preceded by very small incisors. In horseshoe bats the incisors are separated from the canines on a slender bone that easily becomes detached and there is a characteristic hump in the nasal region. Shrews have long slender skulls with continuous tooth-rows and the *first* teeth greatly enlarged. Rodents have a long gap between the first, chisel-shaped incisor teeth and the cheek-teeth. The latter are reduced to three, occasionally four, in all small rodents. In all rodents the incisors continue to grow throughout life; in some, for example in most voles, the cheek-teeth or molars are also ever-growing, with flat grinding surfaces showing complex patterns of alternating triangles that are usually distinctive of the species. In mice the molars are rooted and have rounded cusps on the surface. Weasel skulls are like those of stoats (see below) but smaller, usually under 4 cm.

Medium-sized skulls ($\times \frac{1}{2}$)

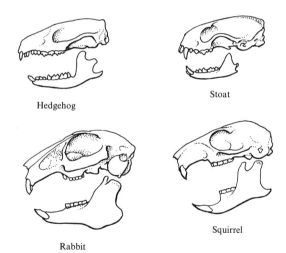

Hedgehog

Stoat

Rabbit

Squirrel

Medium-sized skulls, in the range 4 to 15 cm, comprise the hedgehogs, the larger rodents, the rabbit and hares, and most of the carnivores. The hedgehogs have continuous tooth-rows but no enlarged canines. The lagomorphs – rabbit and hares – have incisors like those of rodents but there is a second smaller pair close behind the prominent upper ones. The cheek-teeth, following a long gap, are transversely elongated. The carnivores all have prominent fang-like canines and most have one of the cheek-teeth in each row, known as the carnassial,

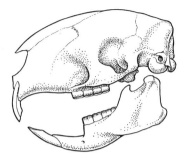

Porcupine ($\times \frac{1}{3}$)

enlarged, with prominent cutting edges. The outline of a carnivore skull in top view is usually distinctive of the species, but it should be noted that the longitudinal 'sagittal crest' along the top of the brain-case, to which the principal 'temporal' jaw muscles are attached, increases in prominence with age and may be almost absent in a very young animal.

Large carnivore skulls ($\times \frac{1}{3}$)

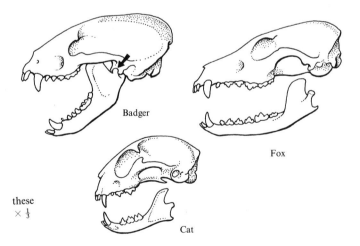

Badger

Fox

these
$\times \frac{1}{3}$

Cat

Amongst the larger carnivore skulls, that of the badger is unusual in lacking carnassials and in having the lower jaws locked on to the skull so that they cannot be detached without breaking them. Fox skulls have very elongated muzzles; those of dogs are similar but usually have the teeth more crowded and

Large carnivore skulls ($\times \frac{1}{2}$)

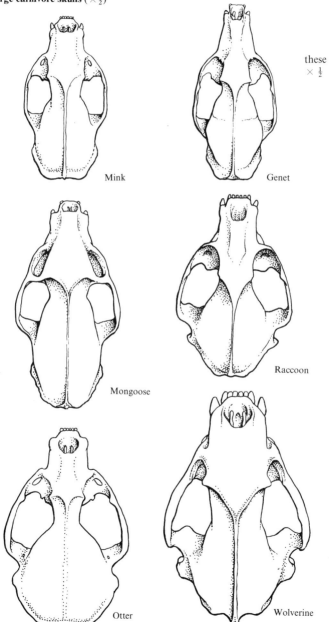

these $\times \frac{1}{2}$

Mink

Genet

Mongoose

Raccoon

Otter

Wolverine

of course are very variable in size. Cats have very short skulls and those of wild and domestic cats cannot always be distinguished.

Seal skulls are like those of carnivores but the cheek-teeth are rather uniform in size and simple in shape, without distinctive carnassials.

Skull of Common seal ($\times \frac{1}{4}$)

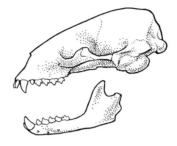

Amongst the ungulates, pigs are distinctive in having tusks and almost continuous rows of low-crowned teeth, some very complex, without long gaps. All the other even-toed ungulates – the deer, goats, sheep and cattle – have very distinctive skulls with no incisors in the upper jaws, four pairs of incisor-like

Ungulate skulls ($\times \frac{1}{10}$)

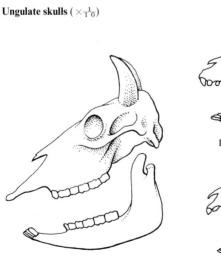

Cow

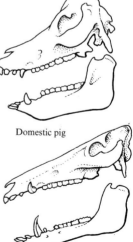

Domestic pig

Wild boar

Skull of Roe deer ($\times\frac{1}{6}$)

teeth below and six high-crowned cheek-teeth in each row, preceded by a long gap. Horses have a rather similar dentition but upper incisors are present and there are only three pairs of lower incisors.

Skull of Horse ($\times\frac{1}{10}$)

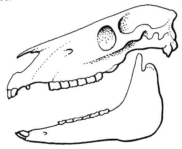

Skulls of whales are usually identifiable as such by their sheer size. Those with teeth have either a single tusk-like tooth in each jaw or rows of numerous identical conical teeth. In the smallest species, the Porpoise (the one most often found on beaches), each tooth is slightly flattened and spade-like; in the dolphins they are conical and pointed.

Skull of Porpoise ($\times\frac{1}{5}$)

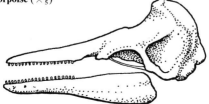

Antlers and horns

The antlers of deer are shed and grow anew each year. They are composed of solid bone, covered while growing with a short-haired skin known as 'velvet'. They grow from permanent, bony knobs or 'pedicels' on the skull so that skulls of males can be recognized as such with or without antlers. The antlers become more complex each year until the animal is in its prime but the degree of development varies greatly amongst individuals and according to local conditions so that age cannot be accurately assessed from the antlers.

Antlers of a red deer in four successive years

The horns of sheep, goats, cattle and other 'hollow-horned ruminants' are permanent structures, consisting of a horny sheath on a bony core and they are always unbranched. After death the horn may work loose and become detached from the core.

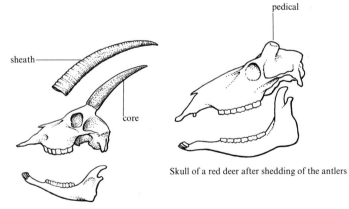

Skull of a goat with the horny sheath detached from the bony core

Skull of a red deer after shedding of the antlers

MARSUPIALS: order Marsupialia

No indigenous European species, but one wallaby has been introduced.

RED-NECKED WALLABY *Macropus rufogriseus* **Plate 10**
Identification. This wallaby is about the size of a hare but has a long tail, short ears and a bounding bipedal gait which are distinctive. It is diurnal but can be very secretive and difficult to locate. Its droppings are fibrous, ovoid with rounded ends, and *c.* 2cm long. The very widely spaced tracks made by an animal hopping in snow are unmistakable.
Range. Native in eastern Australia and Tasmania; at least two feral populations are found in England: in the Peak District and in Sussex. They are commonly kept in zoos and parks from which animals may escape.
Habitat. Woodland and scrub.
Habits. Red-necked wallabies are solitary or live in small groups. They are diurnal, grazing and browsing on a wide variety of plants including heathers. The young are born singly and are carried in the mother's pouch for about nine months.

INSECTIVORES: order Insectivora

This group of terrestrial, subterranean and aquatic animals comprises the hedgehogs, moles, desmans and shrews. They feed upon insects, worms and other invertebrates. In all of them the snout is rather elongate, the teeth are in continuous rows and there are five digits on each foot.

HEDGEHOGS: family Erinaceidae

Hedgehogs are terrestrial animals with a dense covering of spines. Nocturnal, but slow moving, they are usually easy to find with a torch. They can often be located by the grunting and snuffling noises they make as they forage. Very vulnerable to road accidents, they are frequently found killed on roads. The three European species are very similar to each other but they only overlap in very limited areas.

WESTERN HEDGEHOG *Erinaceus europaeus* Plate 1

Identification. The only hedgehog in most of its range. In the zone of overlap with the Eastern hedgehog the absence of a white breast-patch in the Western species is the only easily observed difference but its skull is also distinctive. In southern Spain this species is very pale, with many wholly white spines, and is best told from the very similar Algerian hedgehog by the very narrow spine-free parting on the crown.

Range. Most of western Europe, including Britain and Ireland. The zone of overlap with the Eastern hedgehog runs from the Baltic to the Adriatic and is about 200km wide in Czechoslovakia. Also present in northern Russia and western Siberia.

Habitat. This hedgehog is found in woodland wherever there is ground vegetation, but it is also abundant in grassland, especially when adjacent to woodland, hedgerows or scrub, including urban gardens, parks and playing fields, meadows and dune slacks. In the Alps it can be found to a height of 2000m in the dwarf pine zone, but not above the tree-line.

Habits. Hedgehogs live on the surface of the ground, without burrowing or climbing to any extent. Predominantly nocturnal, they are sometimes out by day, especially in autumn. They respond to disturbance by rolling into a tight ball. A nest of dry leaves is used for rearing young and for hibernation. It is usually made on the ground under dense shrubs, such as bramble, and also in garden sheds and similar situations. Hibernation is from October until April but hedgehogs are occasionally active during winter. During hibernation the body temperature drops to that of the environment (but not usually below 4°C), the pulse falls to about 20/min and the breathing to about 10/min.

Most young are born from June to September, with some females having two litters per year, each of about four or five babies. The young spend about three weeks in the nest but often stay together with the mother for several weeks after that, especially in the autumn. They feed on insects, earthworms, slugs and similar creatures.

EASTERN HEDGEHOG   *Erinaceus concolor*   **Plate 1**
Identification. The East European species has a white breast which contrasts with its otherwise dark underparts. In other respects it is like the Western hedgehog but its skull is distinctive.
Range. Eastern Europe, overlapping with the Western hedgehog in a zone from western Poland to the Adriatic. This is the only hedgehog on Crete and some other Greek Islands. It extends to Israel and Iran.
Habitat and habits. As for the Western hedgehog.

ALGERIAN HEDGEHOG   *Erinaceus algirus*   **Plate 1**
Identification. This species is paler than most examples of the other European hedgehogs, but note that the Western hedgehog is equally pale in southern Spain. The best guide to identification is the spine-free 'parting' on the crown of the head which is wider than in the other species – wide enough for a pencil to be inserted without difficulty.
Range. Malta, Balearic Islands, south and southwestern coasts of France and some parts of Spain (probably introduced from its main range in northwestern Africa).
Habitat and habits. As for the Western hedgehog, but the Algerian hedgehog does not hibernate and sometimes nests in a burrow.

MOLES: family Talpidae, genus *Talpa*

These subterranean animals have cylindrical bodies, greatly enlarged front feet, long sensitive snouts, no projecting ears, extremely small eyes and velvety black fur. They are rarely seen above ground but are sometimes active in leaf-litter in woodland and can always easily be detected by hills of earth pushed up from below the ground. The three European species are difficult to distinguish but the areas of overlap are very limited.

Section of mole tunnels with nest mound (*left*) and normal 'hill' (*right*)

NORTHERN MOLE   *Talpa europaea*   **Plate 1**
Identification. This is the only European mole except in the Mediterranean region. It can be distinguished from the two southern species by the fact that its eyes, although very small, can be opened (although it requires very careful study with a lens to observe this). The Northern mole is larger than the Blind mole and has a narrower muzzle than the equally large Roman mole (width of skull

across cheek-bones 11–13mm – see figure). The upper incisor teeth form a U and the largest (first) are less than twice the size of the smallest (third).

Range. Most of Europe, including Britain but not Ireland, and ranges east to central Siberia. It overlaps with the Blind mole on the south side of the Alps and in Iberia. This species occurs at higher altitudes but both species tend to be montane in the south.

Habitat. The Northern mole lives mainly in grassland and deciduous woodland, rarely in coniferous forest or heathland. It occurs in mountains up to 1000m in Scotland and 2000m in the Alps, provided that there is sufficient depth of soil for it to tunnel.

Habits. The mole spends its life almost permanently underground, except when young animals are dispersing. Each animal lives in its own system of tunnels which is continually being extended. Digging is done by using the spade-like front feet alternately, to scrape the soil and push it back past the body. Periodically the loose soil is pushed up a shaft in the same way to form a molehill. The position of the nest can sometimes be determined by the presence of a particularly large hill. Its voice is a gentle twitter, with louder squeaks when fighting. Moles are active day and night throughout the year. They usually give birth to a single litter of three or four young in the spring. They feed on earthworms, insect larvae and other invertebrates.

BLIND MOLE *Talpa caeca*   Plate 1
Identification. The Blind mole is smaller than the Northern and Roman moles. Careful measurement of the hind foot (without claw) is probably the best guide to identification: it is usually under 17mm long. Its eyes are permanently closed by a thin membrane which cannot be separated without damage. The upper incisor teeth form a V shape, the largest (first) being more than twice the size of the smallest (third).

Range. Mediterranean region, mainland only.

Habitat and habits. As for the Northern mole.

Northern   Blind

Upper incisors of moles

ROMAN MOLE *Talpa romana*   Not illustrated
Identification. The Roman mole is the only mole in most of its range and can be distinguished from the adjacent Blind mole by its larger size (head and body over 130mm, hind feet over 17.5mm) and from the Northern mole by its permanently closed eyes (as in the Blind mole) and by its wider muzzle (width of skull across cheek-bones 13.5–15mm – see figure).

Range. Southern Italy, southern Yugoslavia, Greece; overlapping in parts with the Blind mole but rarely with the Northern mole.

Habitat and habits. As the Northern mole.

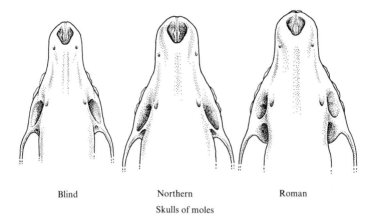

Blind   Northern   Roman

Skulls of moles

PYRENEAN DESMAN *Galemys pyrenaicus* (family Talpidae)   **Plate 1**
Identification. At close quarters or in the hand the long spatulate muzzle of the
Pyrenean desman is unique. This animal is the size of a mole, but distinguished
by normal front feet, large webbed hind feet and a long tail. It is about twice the
size of a water shrew and distinguished from the aquatic rodents by its long
muzzle.
Range. Pyrenees, northwestern Spain and northern Portugal.
Habitat. Mountain streams and clear canals, from 300 to 1200m.
Habits. The Pyrenean desman swims competently, propelling itself with its hind
feet. It nests in holes in the banks of streams or in crevices under rocks and tree
roots. One litter of about four young is produced in spring. Its food is mainly
aquatic invertebrates found on the river bed.

SHREWS: family Soricidae

Mouse-sized animals, shrews can be distinguished from true mice by their
slender, pointed muzzles. They are usually abundant wherever there is sufficient
ground vegetation to provide cover, and are often detectable by their highly-
pitched squeaking. They make shallow tunnels in light soil and litter, but rarely
climb. They are very active by day and night, summer and winter, feeding on
insect larvae and other invertebrate prey. They can frequently be found under
logs, planks etc. Their skulls are often abundant in owl pellets and corpses are
regularly discovered in discarded bottles from which they have been unable to
escape. The different species are very similar and close examination of the teeth
may be necessary for precise identification, especially the simple, conical,
unicuspid teeth of the upper jaw immediately behind the large, hooked first
tooth (see plates 2 and 3). These can be seen with a lens by opening the side of
the mouth in a living or freshly dead animal. Young animals are virtually fully
grown when they leave the nest; size is therefore a useful guide in identification.

TYPICAL RED-TOOTHED SHREWS: genus *Sorex*

These shrews all have red-tipped teeth (but so do water shrews, *Neomys*, and the red may almost disappear with wear in aged animals), 5 unicuspid teeth on each side (the last sometimes very small) and the first lower tooth with a wavy upper margin (unless very worn). Young animals, predominating in late summer and autumn, have well-haired tails; by the following spring and summer, when they breed, their tails are almost naked. Adult males have a prominent scent gland on each flank, marked by a line of pale hair (present also in the female Alpine shrew).

COMMON SHREW *Sorex araneus* Plate 2

Identification. The Common shrew can be recognized by its three-coloured coat with a distinct band of intermediate colour on each flank between its dark brown back and its pale belly. The upper parts vary from medium brown in juveniles to very dark brown in adults. The unicuspid teeth are rather large, the second equal to the first, thereafter decreasing uniformly. It is noticeably larger than the Pygmy shrew but only distinguishable from Millet's shrew and the Spanish shrew by very careful measurement of skull proportions or by examination of chromosomes.

Range. Europe including Britain and the Pyrenees but absent from Iberia, most of France and Ireland. This species overlaps slightly with Millet's shrew in a zone from the Netherlands to Switzerland. It extends eastwards as far as Lake Baikal.

Habitat. The Common shrew can be found in almost all habitats with the necessary minimum of ground cover: woodland, hedgerows, heaths, dunes, rough grassland and scree. In mountains it may live up to the summer snow-line.

Habits. These shrews are very active by day and night but rarely leave thick cover. Juveniles are territorial: breeding is usually delayed until the second year. A nest may be made under a log, or grass tussock etc.; several litters of 5–7 young are born during the summer. Shrews feed on insects, spiders, woodlice, snails etc.

MILLET'S SHREW *Sorex coronatus* Not illustrated

Identification. This species is not clearly distinguishable from the Common shrew except by chromosomes, but it is slightly smaller, and detailed measurements of skull and lower jaw enable most animals to be identified.

Range. Northern Spain to the Netherlands, south-western Germany and Switzerland, overlapping slightly with the Common shrew; it replaces the Common shrew on Jersey.

Habitat and habits. As the Common shrew.

SPANISH SHREW *Sorex granarius* Not illustrated

Identification. The Spanish shrew is like the Common shrew but slightly smaller and with the muzzle rather short and broader. It cannot be distinguished with certainty without making detailed measurement or chromosome examination.

Range. Mountains of central Spain, probably not overlapping with either Millet's shrew or the Common shrew.

APPENNINE SHREW *Sorex samniticus* Not illustrated
Identification. Similar to the Common shrew but the tail is distinctly shorter (usually less than 40mm). The first upper tooth has the concavity between the two cusps widely rounded in contrast to the sharp, V-shaped notch in the Common shrew (see figure).
Range. Southern Italy, overlapping with the Common shrew in the Appennines.
Habitat. This species has been recorded up to 1160m where it coexists with the Common shrew but it also occurs on low ground in the absence of the Common shrew.

Upper front teeth of Common and Appennine shrews; note difference in notch of first tooth

PYGMY SHREW *Sorex minutus* **Plate 2**
Identification. The Pygmy shrew is distinctly smaller than the Common shrew and is two-coloured. The back is medium brown at all ages. In length and thickness the tail is about equal to that of the Common shrew, and therefore appears much larger relative to its body. The third unicuspid tooth is larger than the second (distinguishing the Pygmy from all other European shrews).
Range. Throughout Europe, but only at high altitude in the south. Widespread in Britain and Ireland, including most small islands. Ranges eastwards to the Himalayas.
Habitat. The Pygmy shrew can be found in the same habitats as the Common shrew but is more widespread, tolerating even shorter vegetation such as that of mountain heaths.
Habits. Similar to those of the Common shrew but the Pygmy shrew is less subterranean and usually less abundant.

LAXMANN'S SHREW *Sorex caecutiens* **Plate 2**
Identification. This species is intermediate in size between the Common and the Pygmy shrews. It is two-coloured but darker above than the Pygmy shrew. In juveniles the tail is especially well tufted. Its unicuspid teeth are well-spaced and rather small.
Range. Scandinavia and Poland eastwards to Japan.
Habitat. Forest and tundra.

LEAST SHREW *Sorex minutissimus* **Plate 2**
Identification. This species is exceedingly small (comparable to the Pygmy white-toothed shrew, p. 127, but their ranges are separate). The hind feet

measure less than 9mm, distinguishing this species from the Pygmy shrew which is the next smallest species. The small size of the skull is also distinctive – the tooth-row measures less than 6mm.
Range. Scandinavia and Estonia eastwards to Japan. The species is known from rather few localities but is probably overlooked elsewhere.
Habitat. Wet coniferous forest.

DUSKY SHREW   *Sorex sinalis*   Plate 2
Identification. Similar in size to the Common shrew, the Dusky shrew is distinguished by an underside almost as dark as the upper. Its unicuspid teeth decrease in size very uniformly from front to back.
Range. Scandinavia and Finland eastwards to China.
Habitat. Mainly wet coniferous forest.

ALPINE SHREW   *Sorex alpinus*   Plate 2
Identification. The Alpine shrew is slightly larger than the Common shrew. It is slatey grey above and only slightly lighter below. Its tail is longer than that of any other European shrew, being about equal to the combined length of the head and body. The fifth unicuspid tooth is larger than in other *Sorex* and the second lower tooth is more clearly two-pointed.
Range. Mountains of central Europe to the Pyrenees and Balkans. Between 600 and 1500m in the Alps, down to 180m in southern Germany.
Habitat. Coniferous forest, especially near water.

WATER SHREW   *Neomys fodiens*   Plate 3
Identification. This species and the next are the largest and darkest of the European shrews. The upperside is almost black and the underside is very variable, sometimes pale silvery-grey but usually suffused with brown and occasionally entirely black. The tail has a prominent keel of stiff silvery hairs extending for the whole length of the underside and the hind feet have similar fringes. The teeth are red-tipped, as in species of *Sorex*, but there are only four unicuspids on each side and the first lower tooth has the upper margin smooth.
Range. Most of Europe except Iceland, Ireland, most of Iberia and other parts of the Mediterranean zone, ranging eastwards to the Pacific.
Habitat. This is the most aquatic of the European shrews, found especially on well vegetated banks of rivers, streams and lakes, but also in small ditches, ponds, marshes, water-cress beds and on boulder-strewn sea shores. Occasionally they are found far from water, in woodland for example. In the Alps they have been recorded up to 2500m.
Habits. Water shrews habitually swim and dive, capturing prey of insect larvae and other invertebrates underwater as well as on land. They have venomous saliva which is capable of paralysing prey such as small fish and frogs. On land, water shrews behave like other shrews, using runways in dense vegetation, but they also make burrows in river banks.

MILLER'S WATER SHREW   *Neomys anomalus*   Plate 3
Identification. This species differs from the Water shrew mainly in the lesser development of a keel of specialized hairs under the tail. Such a keel is either

absent or confined to the terminal third of the tail. The underside of the body is more consistently pale than in the Water shrew. The skull is difficult to distinguish from that of the Water shrew but the unicuspid teeth tend to have rather long bases and small cusps.

Range. Discontinuous in the mountains of west and central Europe, but more continuous on low ground in eastern Europe.

Habitat. Found mostly near water as in the Water shrew – the two species may occur together on the same stream. It also occurs in wet woodland and grassland away from open water.

Habits. As for the Water shrew.

WHITE-TOOTHED SHREWS: genera *Suncus* and *Crocidura*

These shrews lack any pigment on the teeth, even when young, and have very characteristic whiskers on the tail – scattered long hairs protruding at right angles far beyond the normal short clothing hairs. The coat is usually greyish-brown with a slightly frosted appearance lacking in *Sorex* and *Neomys*. The unicuspid teeth in the upper jaw number three in *Crocidura* and four in *Suncus* (but the fourth is very small and may be difficult to detect). These are the common shrews of the lowlands of southern Europe but they overlap extensively with the more northern red-toothed shrews.

PYGMY WHITE-TOOTHED SHREW *Suncus etruscus* **Plate 3**
Identification. This is by far the smallest shrew in its range (and one of the smallest mammals in the world), with the head and body less than 45mm. It is paralleled in size only by the Least shrew (p. 125) of the far north and northeast. The very small hind feet (7–8mm) distinguish it from the young of the larger species, which in any case, if so small, would not likely be out of the nest. In colour and in the whiskery tail it resembles the other white-toothed shrews. The skull is easily distinguished by the four unpigmented unicuspid teeth on each side and the very small size (tooth-row 5–6mm).

Range. Mainly confined to the Mediterranean lowlands, but also on the Atlantic coast of France. Also in North Africa and much of southwestern Asia.

Habitat. Grassland, scrub, gardens etc., often found under stones and logs. It has been recorded up to a height of 1000m in Italy and 630m in France.

Habits. Little is known about this animal in the wild. In spite of its small size it preys upon insects up to the size of grasshoppers and crickets.

GREATER WHITE-TOOTHED SHREW *Crocidura russula* **Plate 3**
Identification. Generally the commonest of the white-toothed shrews, this species is distinguished from the Bicoloured white-toothed shrew by the paler colour of the back, which merges gradually into the even paler underside. It is more difficult to distinguish from the smaller Lesser white-toothed shrew (details under that species). The skull can be distinguished (with difficulty) from those of the other white-toothed shrews by the rather elongate, narrow unicuspid region and the relatively large third unicuspid tooth when compared with the adjacent cusp of the next tooth (but this is difficult to apply if the teeth are very worn).

Range. South and central Europe. Also on the islands of Alderney, Guernsey and Herm of the Channel Isles, and in North Africa.

Habitat. Grassland, woodland, hedgerows etc., especially on dry ground. This species is frequently found in gardens, outhouses and farm buildings. It usually lives below 1000m, occasionally up to a height of 1600m in the Alps.

Habits. Similar to those of the Common shrew. It is active day and night with peaks of activity after dusk and around dawn. Breeding may extend from February to November in the south.

LESSER WHITE-TOOTHED SHREW
Crocidura suaveolens   **Plate 3**

Identification. Very similar to the Greater white-toothed shrew and only distinguishable by careful measurement. Externally the tail (about 35mm) and the hind feet (11mm without claws) are the most practical, compared with 40 and 12mm in the larger species. The total length of the skull is 15–18mm and the upper tooth-row is 6–8mm, compared with 18–22 and 7–9mm in *C. russula*. The second unicuspid tooth is more distinctly smaller than the third than in *C. russula*.

Range. Rather sparse in France and Iberia but more widespread in southeastern Europe. It is present on the Scilly Isles, Jersey, Sark, Ouessant and Yeu, but not on the British or Irish mainlands. Also found in North Africa and east to Japan.

Habitats and habits. As for the Greater white-toothed shrew.

BICOLOURED WHITE-TOOTHED SHREW
Crocidura leucodon   **Plate 3**

Identification. Similar in size to the Greater white-toothed shrew but rather darker above and with a sharp demarcation between dark upper and pale underparts. The tail is also clearly two-coloured. The skull is distinguishable from that of the Greater white-toothed shrew by the shorter deeper rostrum with more crowded unicuspid teeth, the last of which is rather small in relation to the adjacent cusp of the first large tooth.

Range. Central and eastern Europe but absent from Iberia, much of France and from the British Isles. Found eastwards to the Caspian Sea.

Habitat and habits. As for the Greater white-toothed shrew. This species in particular has been recorded 'caravanning', behaviour in which an adult leads its part-grown young, each holding in its mouth the tail of the one in front. This may occur only when a nest is disturbed and has also been recorded more sporadically in some other species of shrews.

BATS: order Chiroptera

Bats are the only mammals that are capable of true flight as distinct from gliding. They normally fly only at night and usually, even when they are seen in good light at dusk, it is impossible for observers without considerable experience to identify the species in flight with any certainty. Both by day and during hibernation in winter bats spend their resting time in a more or less torpid state in dark cavities such as caves, hollow trees, attics and cellars. At rest many can be identified with ease without handling, although measurement is often necessary for confirmation. Handling should be kept to an absolute minimum, especially in winter, for a bat's survival can be jeopardized by the loss of energy in awakening, when no food is available to replace it.

The following features are of particular value in identification:

the presence or absence of complex folds of skin on the nose;

size, as measured by the length of the forearm (although care must be taken to exclude young animals, in which the wing-bones are separated by cartilage which appears translucent when viewed against a light);

whether the ears make contact on top of the head or are clearly separated;

the presence and shape of a lobe, the tragus, arising from the base of the ear;

the position on the leg, ankle or foot at which the edge of the wing membrane is attached;

the presence and length of a cartilaginous spur, the calcar, arising from the ankle and supporting the edge of the tail-membrane;

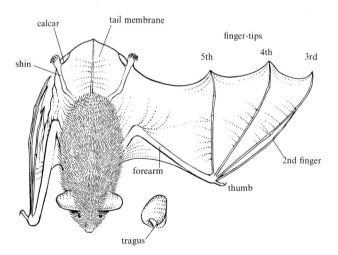

A pipistrelle bat

the amount of hair on the surface or margin of the tail-membrane;
the extent to which the tail protrudes beyond the membrane;
whether the body fur is uniform in colour from root to tip or two-coloured;
the way in which the wings are folded or envelope the body at rest.

The breadth of the wing relative to the length can be judged by the length of the fifth finger relative to the second.

All European bats feed on insects. They navigate and locate prey by a form of echo-location, emitting pulses of ultrasonic sound through the mouth or nose (depending upon the species) and building a picture of the environment from the echoes received. The signals emitted have frequencies and patterns (constant or descending pitch etc.) that are characteristic of the species and portable 'bat detectors' are available that convert the ultrasonic pulses into audible sound and allow some degree of identification of flying bats.

Migratory movements occur but little information is available. Winter and summer roosts are commonly separate. Females usually form segregated breeding colonies in summer. The young are usually born singly or as twins and remain in the roost for about three weeks before flying. They are fully grown by five or six weeks, but many do not breed until they are two or three years old. Their life-span may run from about 10 to 20 years.

HORSESHOE BATS: family Rhinolophidae

This group is distinguished from all other European bats by the presence of complex lobes on the face around the nostrils, which are associated with the emission of the ultrasonic pulses used in echo-location. The various species differ in the details of these nose-leaves, especially in the central lobe or 'sella' as seen from below and from the side, and also in the uppermost projection or 'lancet'. Horseshoe bats roost in colonies, in the winter usually in caves, mines or cellars. They differ from all other European bats in the way they wrap their wings tightly around the body when roosting. They hang freely from the roof rather than in crevices. Their flight is generally low and fluttering and they appear rather pallid.

LESSER HORSESHOE BAT   *Rhinolophus hipposideros*   **Plate 4**
Identification. The smallest horseshoe bat in Europe, this species can be distinguished from the next smallest – Mediterranean and Blasius's – by its slightly darker colour above and by the profile of the noseleaf, which lacks a prominent upper projection on the central sella. The sella appears conical when seen from the front.
Range. Southern and central Europe, including Britain. It is the only horseshoe bat in Ireland. Also in North Africa and east to Kashmir.
Habitat. Mainly wooded country, roosting in caves, tunnels and cellars in winter; breeding colonies in attics and farm buildings in summer.
Habits. Lesser horseshoe bats form large colonies in summer but are more dispersed in winter. Their flight is erratic and fluttering. They emerge about half an hour after sunset. Movements up to 150km have been recorded.

GREATER HORSESHOE BAT   *Rhinolophus ferrumequinum*   **Plate 4**
Identification. Its large size distinguishes this species from all but Mehely's
horseshoe bat. The lancet of the noseleaf is not so abruptly narrowed as in
Mehely's and the sella is constricted in the middle (as seen from the front).
Range. As for the Lesser horseshoe bat but absent from Ireland and seriously
declining in the north of its range, e.g. in England. Outside Europe it extends
from North Africa to Japan.
Habitat. As for the Lesser horseshoe bat.
Habits. As for the Lesser horseshoe bat, but its flight is less erratic and rather
butterfly-like. Breeding colonies are noisy with constant squeaking and
chattering.

MEDITERRANEAN HORSESHOE BAT
Rhinolophus euryale   **Plate 4**
Identification. This species is easily distinguished from the two preceding
horseshoe bats by its intermediate size and the slender pointed projection above
the sella (as seen in profile). It is more difficult to distinguish from Blasius's
horseshoe bat – the best characters to look for are the parallel sides of the lower,
forward-facing part of the sella (front view) and the rather narrow horseshoe.
Range. Southern Europe and from North Africa to Iran.
Habitat and habits. As for the Lesser horseshoe bat. Sometimes the Mediterranean horseshoe bat is found in very large colonies, roosting in closely packed
groups. It does not envelope its body with its wings when at rest.

BLASIUS'S HORSESHOE BAT   *Rhinolophus blasii*   **Plate 4**
Identification. This bat is very similar in size, colour and noseleaf to the last
species. It is most easily distinguished by the lower part of the sella, looking
from the front and below – it tapers to a blunt point above in this species but is
parallel-sided in the last. The sides of the lancet are concave and the horseshoe is
rather broad.
Range. South-eastern Europe. Also found in most of Africa and southwestern
Asia.
Habitat. This bat lives mainly in caves.
Habits. Little known.

MEHELY'S HORSESHOE BAT   *Rhinolophus mehelyi*   **Plate 4**
Identification. A rather large, pale species with noticeably large ears, Mehely's
horseshoe bat is most easily distinguished by the shape of the uppermost part of
the noseleaf, the lancet. Seen from the front this narrows abruptly and ter-
minates in a long slender point. The upper projection of the sella (in profile) is
longer than in the Greater horseshoe bat but shorter and less slender than in the
Mediterranean and Blasius's horseshoes.
Range. Mediterranean region, including North Africa and east to Iran.
Habitat. Mainly in caves.
Habits. Little known.

VESPERTILIONID BATS: family Vespertilionidae

Most European bats belong to this family. There are no appendages on the nose and the long tail is wholly contained within the tail-membrane or protrudes by only one or two vertebrae. All the species have an appendage, the tragus, extending upwards within the conch of the ear, the shape and size of which is valuable for identification.

MYOTIS BATS: genus *Myotis*

This group of eleven species is characterized especially by the tragus which is long, slender, pointed and rather straight. The muzzle is relatively long and slender with six cheek-teeth on each side above and below (i.e. six small teeth behind the long prominent canines).

DAUBENTON'S BAT *Myotis daubentoni* Plate 5
Identification. A small bat, sharing with the following three species very large feet (distinctly more than half the length of the shin), long calcar (reaching two-thirds of the distance from the ankle to the tail-tip) and pale, pinkish brown muzzle and ears. The size overlaps that of the Long-fingered bat but this species has the back a richer, reddish brown and the shins and adjacent membranes are scantily haired. The ears are relatively short and the tragus is about half the length of the ear.
Range. Most of Europe, including Britain and Ireland, and east to Japan.
Habitat. Wooded country, roosting in trees and buildings in summer, often in caves in winter.
Habits. In winter they are usually dispersed, roosting in small crevices, sometimes amongst scree on the floor of a cave or mine. In summer the nursery colonies may be large. They emerge about half an hour after sunset and usually fly along regular beats, for example the edge of a wood.

NATHALINA BAT *Myotis nathalinae* Not illustrated
Identification. This species is very similar to Daubenton's bat from which it has only been distinguished since 1977. It is slightly smaller on average (forearm 33–36mm) and slightly greyer, but precise identification requires microscopic examination of the teeth and genitalia.
Range. So far only known from Spain, France and Switzerland but it possibly occurs elsewhere.
Habitat and habits. Little known. In Spain they have been found in an abandoned mine, dispersed in small groups along with Greater horseshoe bats.

LONG-FINGERED BAT *Myotis capaccinii* Plate 5
Identification. This species is very similar to Daubenton's bat but is a little larger and is most easily distinguished by the much greater amount of hair on the shin and on the adjacent parts of the membrane. The wing membrane meets the leg at or above the ankle. The overall colour is paler and greyer than in the other species of *Myotis*.

Range. Most of the Mediterranean region, including North Africa and the Middle East.

Habitat. Frequently found near water, this species occurs in caves in summer and winter.

Habits. This is a gregarious species, sometimes found in colonies of several hundred and often associated with other species of bats such as the Greater mouse-eared and Schreiber's bat.

POND BAT *Myotis dasycneme*   Plate 5

Identification. This is another close relative of Daubenton's bat but it is considerably larger although overlapping a little in size with the Long-fingered bat. The upper side is a more yellowish brown than in the two preceding species, rather sharply demarcated from the pale brownish grey underparts. The shin and adjacent membranes are almost naked and the wing membrane meets the leg at the ankle.

Range. An eastern species, reaching its western limit in northeastern France, and extending eastwards to the River Yenesei. Absent from Britain and Ireland.

Habitat. Like the preceding species, the Pond bat is found especially in wooded country near water. In winter they roost mainly in caves while breeding colonies in summer are frequently in roofs of buildings.

Habits. At least some colonies migrate up to several hundred kilometres between their winter and summer quarters. In summer they emerge well after sunset and commonly hunt low over the surface of water, sometimes picking insects from the surface.

BRANDT'S BAT *Myotis brandti*   Plate 5

Identification. This and the following species are the smallest members of the genus *Myotis* and together are distinguished by the dark colour of all the naked skin, especially noticeable on the muzzle. The feet are relatively much smaller than in the four preceding species and the coat is rather dark. Brandt's bat is distinguished from the Whiskered bat by being more reddish brown above and a brighter buff below but juveniles are grey and indistinguishable from whiskered bats. Adult males can be distinguished by a club-shaped penis. The skull differs from that of the Whiskered bat by the presence of an extra cusp on the first large cheek-tooth in the upper jaw (visible with a lens on a living animal – see figure).

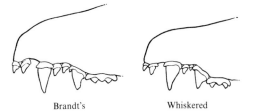

Brandt's   Whiskered

Upper front teeth of Brandt's and Whiskered bats

Range. Probably widespread in central and western Europe but the limits are still uncertain because of confusion with the Whiskered bat. Found in Britain but not confirmed in Ireland.

Habitat. Found mainly in caves in winter and in buildings in summer.

WHISKERED BAT *Myotis mystacinus*   Plate 5

Identification. The Whiskered bat is fairly easily recognized amongst the species of *Myotis* by its small size, small feet, dark skin and dark greyish coat, the last point distinguishing it from the very similar Brandt's bat (but note that young Brandt's bats are also very grey). In adult males the penis is thin and of even width, not bulbous as in Brandt's bat. The first large cheek-tooth in the upper jaw lacks the small anterior cusp that is characteristic of Brandt's bat (see figure).

Range. Widespread, except for the far north, and present in Britain and probably Ireland. Outside Europe found from North Africa to Japan.

Habitat. Wooded country. In summer it is found in trees and buildings sometimes forming large nursery colonies; in winter in caves but usually dispersed in small numbers.

Habits. This bat emerges fairly early in the evening and sometimes flies by day. The flight is rather slow and fluttering. Marked individuals have been known to survive for almost 20 years.

GEOFFROY'S BAT *Myotis emarginatus*   Plate 6

Identification. This is a small bat most easily distinguished by a deep notch in the hind margin of each ear (but note that a shallow concavity is present in this position in some other species, especially in Natterer's bat). Otherwise it is rather similar to Natterer's bat although it is more reddish. In this as in the following four species the margin of the wing membrane meets the foot at the base of the outer toe. The margin of the tail membrane is much less hairy than in Natterer's bat.

Range. Most of southern Europe, north to northern France and Czechoslovakia.

Habitat. Geoffroy's bats are found in caves and mines in winter, and mainly in trees and buildings in summer.

Habits. This is a colonial species, both in summer and winter. Breeding colonies may contain up to 200 females and are often associated with Greater horseshoe bats.

NATTERER'S BAT *Myotis nattereri*   Plate 6

Identification. Natterer's bat is very similar to Geoffroy's bat but the notch in the hind margin of the ear is much less distinct. A dense fringe of short hairs on the margins of the tail membrane, between the end of each calcar and the tail-tip, is the most distinctive feature. The ears are rather thin and translucent and the tragus is particularly long, slender and pointed, distinctly over half the length of the ear.

Range. This is one of the most widespread of European bats, present in Britain and Ireland and absent only from most of Scandinavia and the southeast. It also occurs in North Africa and east to Japan.

Habitat. Mainly in open but well-wooded country, often associated with water. They roost in trees, buildings and caves.

Habits. In summer breeding colonies may be quite large, but in winter Natterer's bats are more solitary, being found singly or in small groups in small rock crevices as well as deep caves and mines.

BECHSTEIN'S BAT   *Myotis bechsteini*   **Plate 6**

Identification. Bechstein's bat is easily distinguished from all other species of *Myotis* by its very long ears, reaching far beyond the tip of the nose when they are laid forwards (but still much shorter than those of the long-eared bats [p. 140], and clearly separated from each other). The coat and the membranes are rather reddish brown.

Range. Central and eastern Europe, becoming rather scattered in the west, including southern England. East to the Caucasus.

Habitat. Forest and woodland.

Habits. Bechstein's bat is an elusive species, usually roosting in small numbers in tree-holes in both summer and winter, although it is occasionally found in houses and in caves. They emerge shortly after sunset and hunt with a rather slow flight amongst trees.

GREATER MOUSE-EARED BAT   *Myotis myotis*   **Plate 6**

Identification. This is by far the largest species of *Myotis* and the largest of the vespertilionid bats except for the very rare Greater noctule. The narrow, pointed tragus distinguishes it clearly from the Noctule and Serotine which both approach this species in size. It is less easily distinguished from the Lesser mouse-eared bat as described under that species.

Range. Most of Europe except in the north, but only very marginally established in southern England. East to Asia Minor and Israel.

Habitat. Mainly in open, lightly wooded country. They roost in caves and in buildings at all times of the year.

Habits. Mouse-eared bats are highly colonial, especially in summer when several hundred females may occupy one breeding site. In winter they are more dispersed, often hanging fully exposed from the roof of a large cave, although large congregations sometimes occur. Some colonies are migratory. Marked individuals from a breeding colony south of Moscow have been found as far away as northern Greece. Large beetles and moths form the principal part of their diet.

LESSER MOUSE-EARED BAT   *Myotis blythi*   **Plate 6**

Identification. Although smaller than the Greater mouse-eared bat this species is much larger than any other *Myotis*. It can be difficult to separate from the Greater mouse-eared bat – apart from the smaller size, the tragus is narrower, especially at the base, and the muzzle is more slender and pointed. There is some overlap in the size of the forearm of the two species, although 59mm separates most individuals into one or the other species. Careful measurement of the skull and teeth provides a more precise identification, this species having the total length of the skull under 23mm and the upper tooth-row from canine to last molar under 9.5mm.

Range. Southern Europe, mainly in the Mediterranean lowlands, and on most of the Mediterranean islands. Also found in North Africa and east to China.
Habitat and habits. As for the Greater mouse-eared bat.

NOCTULES AND ALLIES: genus *Nyctalus*

These are large bats with rather long slender wings – the fifth finger, representing the width of the wing, is especially short in relation to the others. The muzzle is short, the ears are short and rounded and the tragus is very short and kidney-shaped, quite different from the narrow pointed tragus of *Myotis* bats.

NOCTULE   *Nyctalus noctula*   Plate 7
Identification. The Noctule is a large bat with a rich golden-brown fur (the same colour to the roots of the hairs) which is quite distinctive except for the even larger but rare Greater noctule. First year juveniles are much duller but nevertheless of a richer colour than other species.
Range. Widespread except for the far north. It occurs in Britain but not Ireland, and east to Japan.
Habitat. Mainly in woodland, roosting in trees.
Habits. Noctules are colonial bats, often roosting in large colonies in hollow trees, but also in small cavities such as old woodpecker nest-holes where they compete with starlings. In summer occupied trees can often be located by the noisy squeaking, especially on hot days. In winter they roost in trees and buildings (usually in external fissures) but seldom in caves. They emerge early in the evening, sometimes even before sunset, flying high and overlapping in their activity with swifts and swallows. Migrations of up to 1600km have been recorded.

LEISLER'S BAT   *Nyctalus leisleri*   Plate 7
Identification. Leisler's bat (or Lesser noctule) is similar in structure to the Noctule but it is distinctly smaller and duller with a greater difference between the dark upperside and lighter underside. The hairs are much darker towards the roots than at the tips.
Range. This is a rare species with a rather scattered distribution in most of Europe. It occurs in Britain and Ireland, on Madeira and the Azores, and extends east to the Himalayas. It is a migratory species and vagrants have been recorded in places, such as the Shetlands, far from known breeding colonies.
Habitat. Woodland, roosting mainly in tree-holes, occasionally in buildings.
Habits. Similar to those of the Noctule. Breeding colonies may comprise several hundred females. They occasionally fly by day, especially in the autumn, and on the Azores, where they are the only species of bat, they are predominantly diurnal.

GREATER NOCTULE   *Nyctalus lasiopterus*   Plate 7
Identification. This rare species is only clearly distinguishable from the Noctule by its larger size, but the difference is considerable – forearm 62–69mm compared with 46–55mm in the Noctule. It is the largest bat in Europe.

Range. A rare species, known from widely scattered localities north to central France and southern Poland, and east to the Urals.
Habitat and habits. A woodland species, probably similar to the Noctule but little known.

SEROTINE *Eptesicus serotinus* Plate 7

Identification. The Serotine is a large dull-brown bat most easily distinguished by the tail-tip which projects beyond the edge of the membrane to the extent of about one and a half vertebrae. Compared with the similar-sized Noctule, the wings are broad, the ears are rather longer and the tragus is also longer although still shorter and more round-tipped than in the species of *Myotis*. The areas of naked skin are particularly dark.
Range. Widespread except in Scandinavia. It occurs in southeastern England but not in Ireland. Outside Europe it occurs in North Africa and east to Korea.
Habitat. Mainly a woodland species, roosting in tree holes but also frequent in towns and villages, roosting in buildings and occasionally in caves.
Habits. Serotines usually emerge well before it is dark. They feed on large moths and beetles such as cockchafers, sometimes landing on trees to capture an insect. Breeding colonies in buildings contain up to 50 females while males usually roost alone in summer. Movements of up to 300km have been recorded between summer and winter quarters.

NORTHERN BAT *Eptesicus nilssoni* Plate 7

Identification. The Northern bat is distinctly smaller than the Serotine and therefore more easily confused with some of the pipistrelles and *Myotis* bats, but useful distinguishing features are the projecting tail-tip and the relatively short tragus, as in the Serotine. The fur of the upper parts has a characteristic yellow sheen due to the rather short pale tips to the otherwise dark hairs.
Range. As the name implies this is the most northerly bat in Europe, extending beyond the Arctic Circle, but it also occurs in the mountains of central Europe.
Habitat. Mainly forest but also around farms, up to 2000m in central Europe. It roosts in trees and buildings, occasionally in caves.
Habits. Northern bats frequently fly by daylight, not only during the light summer nights of northern Europe but also in spring and autumn. They are most often found roosting in wooden buildings, in colonies of up to 50, but also in tree-holes. The central European populations are resident, not migrants from Scandinavia as was once suspected.

PARTI-COLOURED BAT *Vespertilio murinus* Plate 7

Identification. This bat is easily recognized by the distinctive fur – very dark brown with white tips above, giving a frosted appearance, contrasting rather sharply with pale underside. Otherwise it is very similar to the Serotine and Northern bat. The tail projects a very small distance beyond the membrane, by about one vertebra, while the ears and traguses are very broad and rounded, as in the Noctule. All the naked skin is very dark.
Range. Widespread in eastern Europe (and east to the Pacific) but rather rare and local in the west. It is migratory and vagrants have occurred in the North Sea and Britain.

Habitat. Woodland and farmland, and frequently in towns. In summer roosts are in trees, buildings and fissures of rock, in winter in deeper caves and cellars.
Habits. Parti-coloured bats emerge late in the evening and return early, rarely being seen in daylight. This species is unusual amongst bats in that in summer colonies of males are more frequently found than of females, the latter presumably breeding singly or in small dispersed groups. They are unusually noisy in flight, making shrill squeaking calls. Migrations of 130km have been recorded between summer and winter sites in France and up to 850km in Russia.

PIPISTRELLES: genus *Pipistrellus*

Pipistrelles are small bats, closely related to the noctules and serotines and sharing with them rather short, rounded ears with short, blunt traguses and a lobe of membrane on the outer edge of the calcar (the spur from the ankle supporting the tail membrane). These features enable them to be distinguished from the equally small species of the genus *Myotis*. The species of pipistrelle are difficult to distinguish and it may be necessary to examine the upper teeth with a lens. With care this can be done on a living bat by gently pushing back the upper lip at one side of the mouth.

COMMON PIPISTRELLE   *Pipistrellus pipistrellus*   **Plate 8**
Identification. This is the most widespread and abundant bat in Europe as well as the smallest. The colour is very variable, from light greyish brown through quite rich reddish brown to very dark brown, but in any one individual the upper surface is very uniformly coloured with no 'frosting'. There is no pale margin to the wings which are relatively narrow (length of fifth finger about 40mm). The thumb is short (about equal to the width of the wrist). The small tooth immediately behind the large upper canine tooth is visible from the side but is partly concealed by the canine.
Range. Widespread except for the far north, and present in Britain and Ireland. It also occurs in North Africa and east at least to central Asia.
Habitat. A very wide range, including woodland, open farmland and moorland with few trees, but usually near water. Roosts are mostly in buildings and trees at all seasons, sometimes in caves in winter.
Habits. Common pipistrelles roost in confined crevices rather than in large cavities, for example under the tiles of a roof or in a cavity wall. This is the most abundant bat in Europe and very large colonies may be formed. Summer breeding colonies of females may number several hundred for example in the roof of a house. These are normally formed in June and deserted in August when all the young are flying. At this time males are scattered and roost singly or in small groups. Winter roosts usually contain both sexes and may be in buildings or in caves. Almost 100,000 have been estimated in one cave in Rumania, probably derived by migration from distant breeding colonies. At summer breeding colonies pipistrelles usually emerge about half an hour after sunset. Before giving birth females make one flight per night, of about four hours, but when they have young in the roost they make two flights, one just after dusk and one before dawn. The single young (occasionally twins) remains in the roost until it can fly at about three weeks old. Common pipistrelles feed

on a great variety of small insects which are usually caught and eaten in flight. They fly later in the autumn than most bats, sometimes not entering their hibernation site until December, and small bats seen flying in winter are most likely to be this species.

NATHUSIUS'S PIPISTRELLE   *Pipistrellus nathusii*   **Plate 8**

Identification. This species is very like the Common pipistrelle but the colour of the upper parts is slightly less uniform. The wing is broader (fifth finger about 45mm) and the length of the thumb is distinctly greater than the width of the wrist. The small tooth between the canine and the large premolar is larger than in the Common pipistrelle and does not overlap the adjacent teeth. All the teeth are relatively long and slender.

Range. Widespread in eastern Europe, more scattered in the west. There are only two records for Britain, of single bats, perhaps vagrants, in southern England. It occurs eastwards to the Urals.

Habitat. Mainly woodland.

Habits. As for the Common pipistrelle but probably more migratory. Movements of up to 1600km have been recorded in Russia.

KUHL'S PIPISTRELLE   *Pipistrellus kuhli*   **Plate 8**

Identification. This species is generally rather light in colour but otherwise very similar to the Common pipistrelle. The thumb is short. The extreme hind margin of the wing membrane, especially between the foot and the tip of the nearest finger, is white (but this may occur to a lesser extent in other species of pipistrelle). In this and the next species the small tooth behind the upper canine is very tiny and crowded inwards so as to be scarcely visible from the outside and the large teeth are virtually in contact. The front teeth are very different in size, the two outer ones being very much smaller than the central pair.

Range. Confined to southern Europe and the west of France. It also occurs throughout Africa and east to Pakistan.

Habitat and habits. As for the Common pipistrelle.

| Common | Nathusius's | Kuhl's | Savi's |

Upper front teeth of pipistrelles

SAVI'S PIPISTRELLE   *Pipistrellus savii*   **Plate 8**

Identification. This species is most similar to Nathusius's pipistrelle in general appearance, but with a very pronounced contrast between dark upper and light underside and between the dark bases and the light tips of the hairs. The thumb is short. The teeth are as in Kuhl's pipistrelle but even more crowded so that the small premolar is quite invisible from the outside and is sometimes absent. The front teeth are more even, the outer pair just a little shorter than the central pair.

Range. Confined to the Mediterranean zone in Europe, but also in North Africa and most of temperate Asia.
Habitat and habits. As for the Common pipistrelle but found especially in montane country, extending to over 2000m in altitude in the Alps.

HOARY BAT   *Lasiurus cinereus*   Plate 8
Identification. A large bat, easily recognized by the dense fur covering the whole upper surface of the tail membrane and the very mottled, frosted appearance of the body fur.
Range. This is a common, migratory North American species that has been recorded as a vagrant in Iceland, mostly in October, and once in Scotland.

COMMON LONG-EARED BAT   *Plecotus auritus*   Plate 9
Identification. The enormous length of the ears is sufficient to distinguish this and the next species from all other European bats. The bases of the ears meet each other on top of the head. At rest the ears are folded back but the long slender traguses remain erect. The two long-eared bats are rather difficult to distinguish from each other. In this species the superficial colour of the back varies from yellowish brown to greyish brown (especially in young bats) but if the fur is parted the basal zone of the hair usually appears distinctly brown. The tragus is rather translucent. It is narrower (5mm at the widest point) and the thumb is longer (over 6mm) than in the following species.
Range. Widespread, including Britain and Ireland, and east through Asia to Japan.
Habitat. Wooded country, roosting in trees and buildings throughout the year, occasionally in caves in winter.
Habits. Long-eared bats usually wait until it is dark before emerging. Their flight is slow and fluttering. They hunt amongst trees, often hovering to take insects from the leaves, although they also catch prey in flight. Breeding colonies occur especially in roofs of houses. The bats roost mostly in crevices although they will also hang freely from the roof of the cavity when the temperature is high. The young are born, usually singly, in June and July and do not themselves breed until they are two or three years old. Some common long-eared bats migrate, as shown by records of animals found on light-ships in the North Sea and off Ireland.

GREY LONG-EARED BAT   *Plecotus austriacus*   Plate 9
Identification. This bat is very similar to the last but the fur of the upper surface is always very greyish. The basal zone of the hair, revealed by parting or blowing the fur, is dark slaty-grey. The tragus is grey and opaque. It is wider (about 6mm at the widest) and the thumb shorter (under 6mm) than in the Common long-eared bat.
Range. Southern Europe, north to the Netherlands and southern Poland, and including the south coast of England. Also found in North Africa and east to central Asia.
Habitat and habits. As for the Common long-eared bat, but more frequently in towns and villages, roosting mainly in buildings.

BARBASTELLE   *Barbastella barbastellus*   **Plate 9**
Identification. This is a small bat, easily recognized in the hand by the combination of short ears that nevertheless meet on top of the head, and very short dark snout, projecting very little in front of the inner margins of the ears. All the naked skin is very dark. The coat is very dark brown but with a distinct white frosting on the rear half of the back.
Range. Throughout most of central Europe. Local in England. Also found in North Africa and east to the Caucasus.
Habitat. Woodland, roosting mainly in trees and buildings.
Habits. Barbastelles are elusive bats, especially in summer when they are very dispersed, roosting in small numbers in crevices in trees, and generally avoiding the more obvious large cavities. They often fly low over water to feed. In winter, they are sometimes found in caves in cold weather and concentrations of up to 2000 have been recorded in eastern Europe.

SCHREIBER'S BAT   *Miniopterus schreibersi*   **Plate 9**
Identification. This is a medium-sized bat, superficially resembling a small Noctule or Leisler's bat. The muzzle is short and the head rather domed and covered with erect, velvety fur quite different from that on the back. The ears are very short and the wings very long and narrow at the tips. In the third (longest) finger the subterminal segment (the third counting from the wrist) is unusually long, about three times the length of the preceding segment. At rest this terminal part is folded back sharply against the rest of the wing.
Range. Southern Europe, north to central France and the Danube Basin. In the rest of the world this species has the widest range of any European bat, being found throughout Africa, southern Asia and Australia.
Habitat. This species generally prefers open country, roosting in caves and sometimes in buildings.
Habits. Schreiber's bat is a highly colonial species. In breeding caves several hundred young may be found in a compact mass and they appear to be fed indiscriminately by the females who roost in clusters separate from the young. Schreiber's bats emerge from their roosts early in the evening and sometimes fly long distances to their feeding areas, with a fast, swallow-like flight.

FREE-TAILED BATS: family Molossidae

Free-tailed bats constitute a large family found throughout the tropics but only one species occurs in Europe. They are easily recognized by the long tail extending far beyond the short tail-membrane.

FREE-TAILED BAT   *Tadarida teniotis*   **Plate 9**
Identification. This is the only bat in Europe in which the tail extends far beyond the membrane. The ears are equally distinctive, projecting forwards over the muzzle and joined across the top of the head. It is also one of the largest species in Europe.
Range. The Mediterranean zone of Europe, and from North Africa through central Asia to Japan.

Habitat. These bats live mainly in hilly country or on sea-cliffs but are also frequently found in towns. They roost in rock crevices and amongst stonework as well as in caves and mines.

Habits. Free-tailed bats fly high with a very direct flight, and sometimes associate with swifts at dusk. They are frequently active in winter and probably have only a very limited hibernation, depending upon the temperature.

SLIT-FACED BATS: family Nycteridae

One member of this mainly tropical family has occurred as a vagrant in Europe. Members of the family are easily recognized in the hand by a deep groove on the top of the head leading from the nostrils to a cavity on the forehead. Another unique feature is that the tip of the tail divides to provide a support for the membrane on each side of the tail-tip.

EGYPTIAN SLIT-FACED BAT *Nycteris thebaica* Not illustrated

Identification. This is the only species of slit-faced bat that occurs north of the Sahara and is therefore the only one likely to occur as a vagrant in Europe. Forearm about 42mm.

Range. One record from Corfu, Greece, in 1914. Found throughout Africa and in Israel.

RABBITS, HARES ETC.: order Lagomorpha

The lagomorphs are not closely related to any other living mammals. Besides the familiar rabbits and hares this order includes the pikas, a group of short-eared, short-legged animals found in northern Asia and America.

RABBITS AND HARES: family Leporidae

Rabbits and hares are amongst the easiest of European mammals to observe directly, for they frequent open ground and are at least partially diurnal. They can be distinguished from all other mammals by their long ears, long hind legs and short fluffy tails (see also introduced wallabies, p. 119). Their footprints are also distinctive. Rabbits and hares are most active at dawn and dusk, and feed by grazing and browsing. The three species are fairly easy to distinguish. The skulls of lagomorphs are easily recognized by their chisel-shaped incisors (as in rodents) with a small second pair of upper incisors close behind the first.

RABBIT *Oryctolagus cuniculus*   **Plate 10**
Identification. Rabbits can be distinguished from hares by their shorter ears, which lack black tips, their smaller size and shorter legs, which are especially noticeable when they run. The upper side of a rabbit's tail is brown, but usually only the white underside is visible as it scampers off. Black individuals are not uncommon in some districts. Rabbit burrows can usually be identified by the small spherical droppings outside the entrance. The rabbit's skull differs from that of hares in having a wider 'bridge' across the palate between the molar teeth.
Range. Rabbits can be found throughout Europe except in the far north and east. They were originally confined to Iberia (and north-west Africa) but are an introduction of long standing elsewhere.
Habitat. Rabbits favour grassland (natural and sown), especially where associated with woodland, scrub, hedges or rocks which provide cover. They are especially abundant on stable dunes and grassy sea-cliffs, and are commonly found up to 500m in Britain, 1000m in the Alps and 2000m in the Pyrenees but not on heather moors nor in coniferous woodland.

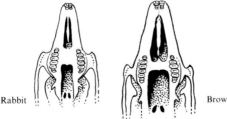

Rabbit   Brown hare

Palates of rabbit and hare

Habits. Rabbits are highly colonial, and their deep burrows are usually found in groups, often under shrubs or in a woodland bank. They are active mainly at night, but are also diurnal if undisturbed, and feed on grass, bulbs and bark in winter. They can be a serious pest in most crops, cereal and root, and in young tree plantations. Litters, usually of 4–6 young, are born underground throughout the spring and summer, and emerge at about 3 weeks. Rabbits make a warning sound, given by thumping the ground with the hind feet, but are otherwise silent except for squealing when attacked.

BROWN HARE *Lepus capensis*   Plate 10

Identification. The Brown hare is considerably larger than the Rabbit, its very long ears and legs being noticeable. Its ears have conspicuous black tips and its tail is black above, although when the hare is running away only the white underside may be seen. The overall colour of this species is a much warmer yellowish brown than in the Mountain hare. The skull is easily distinguished from that of a rabbit by its narrow palatal bridge and wide nasal passage.

Range. Throughout Europe, except for Iceland and northern Scandinavia but introduced and very local in Ireland.

Habitat. The Brown hare lives mainly on farmland, especially permanent pasture but commonly in cereal crops if pasture is also present. It is also found in open woodland, especially in eastern Europe, and up to heights of *c.* 1500m in the Alps, sometimes higher in the Pyrenees, but rarely above 500m in Britain.

Habits. Generally solitary and dispersed. The Brown hare feeds mainly at night but is often active at dusk. Hares do not burrow but rest and have their young (leverets) above ground, usually amongst long grass. When disturbed they crouch with ears flattened but run very fast if approached too closely. Spectacular chases and 'boxing matches' occur, especially in spring. The young, most often two in number, are born fully-furred and open-eyed.

Taxonomic note. It is possible that the hares of Iberia, Sardinia and the Balearic Islands, which are small with rufous thighs, belong to a different species from those of the rest of Europe. If this is so the name *Lepus capensis* should be applied only to the Iberian species and *Lepus europaeus* to the brown hares from the rest of Europe.

MOUNTAIN HARE *Lepus timidus*   Plate 10

Identification. The Mountain hare can be distinguished from the Brown hare by its noticeably shorter ears and all-white tail. Except in Ireland the summer coat is greyer than in the Brown hare and it turns more or less completely white in

Brown hare   Mountain hare

Rostrum of hares: note the curvature of the incisors

winter, except for the black ear-tips. In Ireland the summer coat is brighter and the Mountain hare remains brown in winter, making it more difficult to distinguish from the Brown hare (which has been introduced in parts of Ireland). Skulls of this species can be distinguished from those of Brown hares by the lesser curvature of the upper incisors (see figure).

Range. Northern Europe, the Alps, Scotland and Ireland (and introduced in Northern England). Eastwards through Siberia to Japan and also in North America.

Habitat. This species is found in montane grassland, heaths and open woodland; also lowland habitats including pasture and arable land where brown hares are absent. They may be present down to an altitude of *c.* 1300m in the Alps, and rather lower down the slopes in winter.

Habits. As for the Brown hare but mountain hares sometimes make short burrows for shelter. They feed on shrubs, such as heather and willow as well as on grass, sedges and rushes. More sociable than brown hares, they occasionally form large groups.

RODENTS: order Rodentia

Rodents are the most diverse and numerous small mammals in Europe. They all have a characteristic tooth structure, with a single pair of chisel-shaped incisor teeth, usually yellow or orange, in both upper and lower jaws, followed after a long toothless gap by a short row of grinding cheek-teeth. The external appearance is very varied but the small mouse-like ones can be distinguished from the similar-sized shrews by the shorter, blunter muzzle. Most rodents are basically seed-eaters but some, such as the voles, are specialized herbivores and many are very versatile, making use of buds, insects and seeds as they become seasonally abundant.

SQUIRRELS: family Sciuridae

Members of the squirrel family are very diverse in external appearance. The family includes the tree squirrels, flying squirrels, ground squirrels (sousliks) and marmots, all of which are represented in Europe. All but the flying squirrel are diurnal and relatively easy to watch. The tree squirrels and flying squirrel could only be confused with the much smaller and nocturnal dormice, and the ground squirrels only with the hamsters or mole-rats.

RED SQUIRREL   *Sciurus vulgaris*   Plate 11

Identification. This is the only native, diurnal tree squirrel in Europe – the only possible confusion is with the introduced Grey squirrel in Britain and Ireland. In the British Isles the Red squirrel is, with only rare exceptions, a rich reddish brown in summer with white underparts, but note that the Grey squirrel can show a certain amount of red. In autumn they moult to a duller, greyer brown and acquire prominent ear-tufts. The tail is the same colour as the back following the autumn moult but a peculiarity of the British and Irish race is that the tail progressively fades so that by the following spring and summer it becomes a light creamy brown or in extreme cases almost white. The ear-tufts do likewise but are virtually worn away by the following spring and are not replaced until autumn. In most parts of continental Europe there is a dark, sometimes almost black, form in addition to the red one. The two forms occur together in the same population and interbreed, although the ratio of dark to red animals varies from place to place. Continental animals do not show the seasonal fading of the tail but in northern Scandinavia the entire winter coat may be almost pure, pale grey.

Range. Throughout Europe wherever there are trees. In Britain the range of the Red squirrel has progressively declined during this century as the Grey squirrel has spread, and the Red is now absent from most of England. It occurs throughout Siberia and in northern Japan.

Habitat. The Red squirrel is found especially in coniferous forest but it also occurs in deciduous woodland, particularly beech. It reaches 2000m in the Alps and Pyrenees.

Habits. Red squirrels are active throughout the day but especially just after dawn and before sunset. They spend most time in the trees but also forage on the ground, carrying food up a tree before eating it. They can climb and leap with great agility and usually come down a tree trunk head first. They feed predominantly upon tree seeds, especially those of conifers, but beech mast is also important. Cones are held in the paws and the scales gnawed off to expose the edible seeds. Buds, tubers and fungi are also important items of their diet. Surplus food is stored rather haphazardly. Red squirrels do not hibernate. They build spherical nests (dreys), usually placed in a fork close to the main trunk, and there may be several within one squirrel's territory. Young are born mostly in spring and summer, with one or two litters of two to four young per year. The young begin to leave the nest when they are about seven weeks old. The most usual sound made by red squirrels is a sharp 'chuck-chuck-chuck . . .' that can be heard at all seasons.

GREY SQUIRREL *Sciurus carolinensis* **Plate 11**

Identification. Predominantly grey throughout the year, but always with some brown, especially in summer. Ear-tufts are never developed, distinguishing this species from the Red squirrel which may be predominantly grey in winter but then has prominent ear-tufts. The Grey squirrel is larger than the Red and the white fringes to the rather flattened tail are also characteristic.

Range. A north-American species introduced to Britain and Ireland and now the dominant squirrel in England and Wales. It is still extending its range and replacing the Red squirrel.

Habitat. Although primarily suited to life in broad-leaved forest this squirrel is very adaptable and is also found in conifers. They are common in urban parks and suburban gardens wherever there are suitable trees.

Habits. Grey squirrels are very similar in behaviour to red squirrels but they tend to spend more time on the ground. In autumn and winter they feed predominantly on tree seeds, such as acorns and beech mast, but they also strip cones in the same way as red squirrels do. They store acorns and other nuts by burying them separately or hiding them in crevices, finding them, later in the winter, by scent rather than memory. In spring and summer they feed mainly on buds and sappy bark. Nests are made of twigs and leaves, often on an exposed branch although cavities are also used. The most usual call is a harsh repetitive chatter, often accompanied by a rhythmic flicking of the tail.

FLYING SQUIRREL *Pteromys volans* **Plate 11**

Identification. Being strictly nocturnal this squirrel is very difficult to observe and can usually be located only by finding a nest in a tree-hole. On either side of the body a membrane extending from wrist to ankle is used in gliding through the air. These membranes are prominent when in use but not when the animal is at rest or climbing amongst the branches. Flying squirrels are noticeably smaller than red squirrels but could easily be confused with the Fat dormouse although the ranges overlap only very marginally.

Range. This is a Siberian species that reaches its western limit in Finland and Latvia where it is very rare and probably declining.

Habitat. Mixed forest, especially with mature birch trees.

Habits. Flying squirrels do not fly actively like bats but use their membranes to glide from tree to tree. They can change direction in flight by movements of the membranes. When landing they turn sharply head-up by raising the tail and arch the membrane like a parachute to act as a brake. They are active only at night and spend the day in a nest in a cavity, such as a woodpecker's hole, where they also rear their young. They feed mainly on seeds and buds and do not hibernate.

EUROPEAN SOUSLIK   *Spermophilus citellus*   Plate 11

Identification. In overall appearance sousliks resemble other burrowing rodents, such as the Water vole and Common hamster, more than they do the related tree squirrels but they are easily identified by the combination of large eyes, very short ears and short but well-haired tail. They move rapidly, live in colonies and often sit in an erect 'begging' position. This species differs from the Spotted souslik in lacking clearly-defined pale spots but the coat is not entirely uniform, usually showing a faint mottling or barring.

Range. A species of the Ukrainian steppes extending northwestwards as far as Czechoslovakia and the immediately adjacent parts of East Germany and Poland.

Habitat. Dry grassland including pasture and the margins of cultivated ground, up to 1300m in Czechoslovakia and 2200m in Yugoslavia.

Habits. Sousliks are colonial and diurnal, making complex networks of underground tunnels with numerous openings. They move quickly while foraging and give a sharp whistle before darting underground if danger threatens. They feed mainly on seeds which they carry underground in cheek-pouches. They store surplus food in autumn and fatten themselves on these stores underground before beginning a true hibernation which lasts until about the end of March. Breeding takes place soon after they emerge, a single litter of about six young being born in May or June.

SPOTTED SOUSLIK   *Spermophilus suslicus*   Plate 11

Identification. This souslik differs from the last species in having the back covered with pale spots which are much more prominent than the faint mottling sometimes visible in the European souslik. The tail is shorter and less hairy.

Range. From the central Russian steppes westwards as far as southeastern Poland and northeastern Rumania.

Habitat and habits. As for the European souslik but more frequently than that species on cultivated ground where it can survive ploughing. Sometimes a serious pest.

ALPINE MARMOT   *Marmota marmota*   Plate 12

Identification. Marmots are the largest of the ground squirrels, more than twice the size of the sousliks and clearly separated by habitat. They are easily observed by day and the short but well-haired tail distinguishes them from other large rodents, none of which are in any case likely to occur on the mountain pastures favoured by marmots.

Range. Alps and Tatra Mountains; reintroduced in several parts of the Pyrenees and in northern Yugoslavia.

Habitat. Open alpine pasture, especially on south-facing slopes where there is sufficient soil, or stabilized block scree, to provide deep burrows. Although they normally occur above the tree-line, between 2000 and 3000m, they also extend down to 800m in some areas in the absence of trees.

Habits. Marmots live in small family groups sharing deep burrows. They feed on grasses, sedges and other herbs and carry dry grass into their burrows for bedding. They move with a rather cumbersome lope but are very vigilant, frequently sitting upright to look for danger and giving a sharp whistle if alarmed. They hibernate in a deep part of the burrow, well-filled with hay, sometimes all the family together. Hibernation lasts from about October to April and breeding takes place soon after awakening. The young animals do not breed until they are about three years old.

Siberian chipmunk

SIBERIAN CHIPMUNK *Tamias sibiricus*

Identification. A small, diurnal squirrel with five bold dark stripes along the back and flanks, not easily confused with any native European species. The tail is shorter and less bushy than that of the tree squirrels but much longer than that of the sousliks. Head and body 15–22cm, tail 10–14cm.

Range. Colonies derived from escaped animals have become established in parts of France, West Germany, Netherlands and Austria. The native range is in northern Russia and Siberia.

Habitat. Forest with bushy undergrowth.

Habits. Chipmunks are active by day, spending much time on the ground but also climbing with great agility amongst shrubs and low trees. They make large hoards of nuts and seeds for use in the winter when they are less active than red squirrels but do not hibernate completely like the sou
sliks.

BEAVERS: family Castoridae

EUROPEAN BEAVER *Castor fiber*   Plate 12

Identification. The Beaver is the largest rodent in Europe, much larger than the other aquatic rodents – the Coypu, Muskrat and Water vole. In the water it is a more graceful swimmer than any of these and could be mistaken for an otter but it is much stouter and the very broad tail is distinctive. It is most easily located

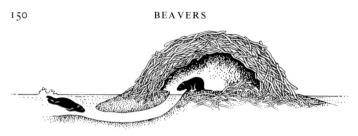

Beaver lodge

by finding evidence of tree-felling. Lodges, dams and canals are also distinctive but are not always present.

Range. Indigenous populations are now confined to Finland, Scandinavia, Poland, the Elbe and the Rhone, but successful reintroductions have taken place in parts of France, southern Germany and Austria. It also occurs in Russia and western Siberia.

Habitat. Beavers are confined to rivers and lakes with broad-leaved woodland on the banks.

Habits. Beavers are well known for making elaborate lodges and dams but these are only made under certain conditions, and in some areas, for example on the lower Rhone, beavers live very unobtrusively in burrows in the river bank entered by holes that are usually under water. They may create ponds with a constant water level by damming streams, and lodges may be built in such ponds, consisting of a pile of sticks with a central nesting chamber entered from under water and with a dry floor just above water level. In summer beavers feed on a great variety of vegetation but in winter they feed especially on bark and twigs. Small trees are felled and dragged into the water where they are stored. Beavers are active mainly at night but also by day in the absence of disturbance. They usually make little sound but they sometimes loudly slap the water with their tails as a warning signal. The young, two to four in a litter, are born in spring and stay with the parents for at least a year.

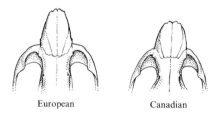

European　　　　　　　Canadian

Skulls of beavers

CANADIAN BEAVER *Castor canadensis* Not illustrated
Identification. Difficult to distinguish from the European beaver but darker, especially on the head. Skulls are readily distinguished by the short nasal bones with very convex margins (see figure).
Range. Introduced from North America to Finland where it is now more widespread than the European species but mostly occupying different areas.
Habitat and habits. As for the European beaver.

PORCUPINES: family Hystricidae

This family of Old-world porcupines comprises twelve species of large heavily spined rodents mainly in Africa and tropical Asia.

PORCUPINE *Hystrix cristata* **Plate 12**
Identification. This is one of the largest rodents. It is quite unmistakable by virtue of the enormous development of black and white spines and the crest of long stiff bristles. This species is distinguished from related porcupines which occasionally escape from zoos by having the crest on the head very long and predominantly white, and the short spines on the rump predominantly black.
Range. A northern African species found in Europe only on Sicily and in parts of mainland Italy, possibly as a result of introduction.
Habitat. Open woodland and scrub.
Habits. Porcupines live in small groups in large deep burrows or caves and are active only at night. They feed on roots, bulbs and bark and can be a serious pest in root crops, orchards and market gardens. The spines are a very effective defence. If attacked a porcupine will turn and reverse into its adversary. The spines are not barbed (as are those of the American porcupines) but they can inflict serious wounds. The tail-tip bears peculiar spines shaped like elongated goblets which produce a characteristic rattling sound when the tail is shaken. About two to four young are born underground in summer.

COYPUS: family Capromyidae

This family comprises the hutias of the West Indies as well as the South American Coypu which is now present in Europe as a result of introduction.

COYPU *Myocastor coypus* **Plate 12**
Identification. The Coypu is a large aquatic rodent intermediate in size between the Muskrat and the Beaver but with the tail cylindrical, not flattened vertically or horizontally as in these species. The large head and stout body contrast with the slimmer outlines of Muskrat and the very much smaller Water vole and Common rat. The hind feet are conspicuously webbed.
Range. A native of southern South America. Wild populations have become established in parts of Europe as a result of escapes from fur farms, but many colonies are short-lived since coypus are not very resistant to severe winters. Long-established populations persist in England (East Anglia) and parts of France.
Habitat. Marshes and drainage channels with dense aquatic vegetation.

Habits. Coypus are expert swimmers, propelling themselves mainly with alternate thrusts of the webbed hind feet. They are mainly nocturnal and crepuscular, resting by day in surface nests amongst thick vegetation or in burrows in banks. They feed on the leaves and stems of many marsh plants and in winter especially on rhizomes, for example those of reed mace. Breeding occurs throughout the year. A litter commonly consists of four to six young which are well furred and can swim soon after birth.

DORMICE: family Gliridae

Dormice are elusive, nocturnal rodents that are generally much less abundant than other mice. With one exception they have bushy tails but all are much smaller than squirrels. Much of their activity is above ground and nests can be found in shrubs, tree-holes and bird nest-boxes. They feed on buds, nuts and fruit, and hibernate throughout the winter, in this respect differing from all other mouse-like rodents except the birch mice. The five species are quite distinctive. Skulls of dormice are rare in raptor pellets but can be distinguished by the presence of *four* cheek-teeth above and below and usually by a characteristic perforation at the lower rear angle of the lower jaw. (See figure opposite)

GARDEN DORMOUSE　*Eliomys quercinus*　　　　Plate 13
Identification. The tail of this species is highly distinctive, with a flattened tuft at the tip, although the exact pattern of black and white on it is variable. The combination of black mask and large ears is also distinctive.
Range. Most of Europe except for the British Isles, Iceland, Scandinavia and the Low Countries. East to the Urals and in North Africa.
Habitat. Compared with the other dormice this species is less strictly arboreal and is often found on the ground in scrub and especially amongst rocks and stone walls. Although mainly found in woodland, both deciduous and coniferous, it also occurs in orchards and gardens and readily enters houses. It can be found as high as 2000m in the Alps and Pyrenees.
Habits. Like other members of its family the Garden dormouse is a very agile climber and almost totally nocturnal. Its nest is built in a tree-hole or in a cleft in a wall or amongst rocks. Hibernation takes place from October, or even September, until April, and a litter of usually four or five young is born in May or June, sometimes followed by a second litter later in the summer. In addition to autumnal fruits and nuts a great variety of other food is taken, including more animal food, such as insects, snails, eggs and nestlings of mice, than other dormice take. Garden dormice make a variety of chattering calls.

FOREST DORMOUSE　*Dryomys nitedula*　　　　Plate 13
Identification. The black mask distinguishes the Forest dormouse from the larger but similar Fat dormouse and the plain, although bushy, tail differentiates it from the Garden dormouse.
Range. An eastern species, reaching westwards to Poland and the Alps, and east to western China.
Habitat. Confined to deciduous woodland, especially where there is a thick shrub layer. Forest dormice live as high as 1500m in the Alps.

Habits. Compact nests of twigs are built in the canopy of tall trees as well as in shrubs. Forest dormice hibernate from October until April.

FAT DORMOUSE   *Glis glis*   **Plate 13**

Identification. This is the largest of the dormice. It is very much smaller than the Grey squirrel but could be mistaken for the Flying squirrel which, however, is a northern species that scarcely overlaps in range. The colour may be pure grey or may be suffused with yellowish brown.

Range. Most of eastern, central and southern Europe, but absent from most of Iberia. It has been introduced to England where it is confined to a limited area northwest of London.

Habitat. Mature woodland, requiring neither shrubs nor secondary growth. Fat dormice can be found up to 2000m in the Pyrenees but rather lower in the Alps.

Habits. The summer nest is often built high in the canopy of a tree, in a fork or hole, but as in most dormice the hibernation nest is generally lower, in a hollow trunk or even underground. Hibernation lasts from October until April. These dormice become very fat by feeding on nuts and seeds prior to hibernation. About four or five young are born in early summer and they may live for six or seven years.

HAZEL DORMOUSE   *Muscardinus avellanarius*   **Plate 13**

Identification. This is the smallest dormouse and the most distinctive in colour, being a bright orange-brown above and paler below, although juveniles are much duller and greyer. The bushy tail distinguishes it from the Harvest mouse which is of a similar size and colour with equally short ears, but with a slender, naked tail.

Range. Most of Europe except for the far north, Iberia, Ireland and Iceland. Also in Asia Minor.

Habitat. Deciduous woodland with a dense undergrowth of shrubs.

Habits. The Hazel dormouse spends most of its active time (at night) climbing amongst shrubs and low trees, travelling nimbly along slender twigs with its very prehensile feet. The summer nest is usually in shrubs, and is very often built of the stripped bark of honeysuckle, but also of grass, leaves and moss, with no obvious entrance (see plate). Nest boxes for birds are often used in summer and winter, although natural winter nest-sites are usually at ground level or below. Hibernation lasts from October until April. One or two litters per year may be produced, each of about four or five young. Hazelnuts are a favourite item of diet – nuts opened by the Hazel dormouse can be distinguished by the very neat,

Skull of a hazel dormouse

round hole with a smooth inner margin. Other mice and voles leave more ragged holes with tooth-marks all over the margin.

MOUSE-TAILED DORMOUSE *Myomimus roachi*   Plate 13

Identification. The short-haired tail of this species distinguishes it from all other dormice but could lead to confusion with some other mice and voles. The tail is a little shorter than the head and body and therefore longer than in most voles. The Balkan snow vole is most similar but is larger and has smaller eyes. The combination of pale grey coat and short ears distinguishes it from other long-tailed mice.

Range. In Europe confined to Bulgaria and Thrace but this is an elusive species and may occur also in adjacent countries. It occurs also in Asia Minor.

Habitat. Dry woodland and scrub.

Habits. Little is known about this species but it appears to be more terrestrial than other dormice.

HAMSTERS, VOLES, MICE and RATS: family Muridae

This very large family includes the true mice and rats along with the hamsters, lemmings and voles and, outside Europe, the gerbils and many other related rodents. All have only three cheek-teeth in each row. The family includes most of the dominant small rodents. They tend to breed quickly, with a succession of large, rapidly developing litters, and have a correspondingly high mortality and short life span. In Europe, the hamsters, the voles and lemmings, and the mice and rats constitute three very distinct groups, sometimes considered separate families, but worldwide these distinctions become very blurred.

HAMSTERS: family Muridae, subfamily Cricetinae

Hamsters are small burrowing rodents, adapted especially to the dry steppes of central Asia and eastern Europe. They have very short tails, moderate sized ears (larger than in voles and lemmings) and cheek-pouches. They feed mainly on seeds which they store underground. They are nocturnal and spend the winter in hibernation. Skulls of hamsters have three cheek-teeth in each row with the grinding surfaces simpler and much flatter than in the true mice and rats but much less angular than in the voles and lemmings. The familiar Golden hamster (*Mesocricetus auratus*) which is kept as a pet and as a laboratory animal does not occur wild in Europe although it may occur as an escape from captivity. In its original wild form it closely resembles the Rumanian hamster but lacks dark markings on the muzzle and nape. Most domesticated hamsters are paler than the wild form and many colour varieties have been bred.

COMMON HAMSTER *Cricetus cricetus*   Plate 14

Identification. The Common hamster is a large plump rodent about the size of a Common rat or Guinea pig. The pattern of black underside and pale patches on the flanks, neck and head is quite distinctive. The amount of black below is variable but there is always considerably more than in the Rumanian hamster which is always much smaller.

Range. An eastern species extending westwards through central Europe as far as the Netherlands and the extreme east of France, but it is rather rare and scattered in the west and has declined in some areas, in Belgium for example.

Habitat. Grassland. Originally a species of open steppes, the Common hamster has adapted to cultivation to a certain extent and is found in rough grass on the edges of fields, river banks etc. but not on closely grazed pasture. It does not occur at heights above about 500m.

Habits. Each animal occupies a system of burrows up to two metres deep containing separate sleeping and food storage chambers. Food, mainly seeds but also roots, potatoes etc., is carried in extensive pouches opening internally in the cheeks and stored underground. Such stores have been known to contain up to 15kg of grain. Hibernation lasts from October to March or April although they may awaken at intervals to feed on their stores. There are usually two litters produced during the summer, each of six to twelve young.

RUMANIAN HAMSTER *Mesocricetus newtoni* **Plate 14**

Identification. This species is like a smaller version of the Common hamster with much less black below. It differs from the very closely related Golden hamster in having a duller coat with usually dark marks in front of the eye and on the nape.

Range. Confined to the Black Sea coast and the lowlands of Bulgaria, Rumania and Ukraine.

Habitat and habits. As for the Common hamster.

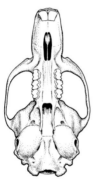

Skull of a Rumanian hamster (× 1¼)

GREY HAMSTER *Cricetulus migratorius* **Plate 14**

Identification. A mouse-sized animal, without the bold markings of the larger hamsters. It is distinguished from the voles by the slightly larger ears and eyes and the shorter tail.

Range. A widespread Asiatic species, reaching its western limit in scattered localities in Ukraine, Bulgaria and Greece.

Habitat. Cultivated and uncultivated grassland and also in open woodland.

Habits. This species stores food and hibernates just like the Common hamster.

GERBILS: family Muridae, subfamily Gerbillinae

Gerbils, also known as jirds, are small mouse- and rat-sized rodents that abound in great diversity in the steppes and deserts of central Asia, Arabia and Africa. None occur as indigenous animals west of the River Don in southern Russia, but the Mongolian gerbil, *Meriones unguiculatus*, is widely kept in captivity and escapes may be found. The combination of moderately long, well-haired tail, yellowish coat, white underside and grooved upper incisor teeth distinguish it from all indigenous European rodents (Plate 14).

LEMMINGS and VOLES: family Muridae, subfamily Microtinae

Lemmings and voles are the dominant small rodents of the more open grassy habitats of Europe, especially in the wetter areas. They are predominantly grass-eaters, making a complex system of paths – runways – at ground level, although some burrow extensively, some are partly aquatic and some climb amongst shrubs. Compared with mice they have blunt muzzles, short ears, small eyes, short legs and short tails. The grinding surfaces of the cheek-teeth (three in each row) form a continuous flat surface with a pattern of alternating triangles that is characteristic of each species. They breed rapidly and form an important part of the diet of many predators, both mammals – foxes, weasels, cats, etc. – and birds such as owls, harriers, and buzzards. Most species are active day and night and all remain active throughout the winter. There is no fundamental difference between lemmings and voles – the name lemming is usually applied to a few species with particularly short ears and tails.

NORWAY LEMMING   *Lemmus lemmus*   Plate 14

Identification. The bold yellow and black pattern of this species is quite distinctive although it varies in detail and in intensity.

Range. Confined to Scandinavia.

Habitat. Normally confined to the tundra and the corresponding open alpine zones farther south, but also in open birch and willow scrub and in 'lemming years' spreading into wooded and cultivated lowland habitats.

Habits. Lemmings make shallow burrows in summer and in winter they make extensive runways through the snow on the surface of the ground, their pattern often conspicuous when the snow melts. They feed on grasses, sedges and dwarf shrubs. Breeding is normally confined to summer but it sometimes continues in winter under the snow. The population density is notoriously variable, with a cycle of abundance and scarcity about every four years, occasionally reaching plague proportions. Mass emigrations then occur, with animals sometimes becoming channelled together as they move downhill. These wandering animals tend to be aggressive (to each other) and disorganized. If dense concentrations are formed at a water barrier they will attempt to cross, provided that it is calm and they can see the other side, but many drown. There is no reason to believe that they commit suicide as is commonly said. Emigrants may form breeding colonies in atypical habitats but these are usually short-lived.

WOOD LEMMING *Myopus schisticolor*   **Plate 14**
Identification. The dark slaty-grey coat of this small lemming is unique. A rusty-coloured streak in the centre of the lower back is always present but is not conspicuous. The skull is similar in size to those of many voles but it shares with the Norway lemming a characteristic transverse elongation of many of the elements of the cheek-teeth, with some of the junctions between adjacent elements at the extreme edge of the tooth.
Range. Confined to Scandinavia, Finland, northern Russia and Siberia, and rather local in its distribution.
Habitat. Confined to coniferous forest, especially wet areas with secondary growth.

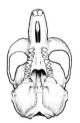

Skull of a wood lemming (× 1¼)

Habits. Burrows and runways are made in moss and this species is unique amongst European rodents in feeding predominantly upon mosses. Another unique characteristic is that males make up only about a quarter of the population and many females are only able to produce female offspring. Its numbers fluctuate but, unlike the Norway lemming, it never becomes conspicuously abundant.

RED-BACKED VOLES: genus *Clethrionomys*

This is a distinctive group of voles, with three species in Europe all with a russet coat, which is particularly characteristic, although this is less pronounced in juveniles. They are associated especially with shrubby ground, either in woodland or amongst dwarf willow, bilberry etc. on mountains and tundra. They feed on softer vegetation than other voles and associated with this the cheek-teeth develop roots and wear away after about one and a half years, unlike most other voles in which they continue to grow indefinitely with little change in appearance.

BANK VOLE *Clethrionomys glareolus*   **Plate 15**
Identification. The Bank vole has larger eyes and ears than species of *Microtus* and *Pitymys* and the tail is longer, fairly well-haired and clearly darker above than below. The pattern of the cheek-teeth is less sharply angular than in species of *Microtus* and *Pitymys*. The pattern of the third upper tooth is very variable, even in a single population.

Range. Throughout Europe, except in the extreme north and south, and east to Lake Baikal. It has probably been introduced in Ireland where it is still spreading.

Habitat. This is the vole most adapted for a woodland habitat although it is found wherever there are dense shrubs such as bramble, rose or bilberry and also in bracken. It is found to heights of 2000m in the Alps and Pyrenees and to 800m in Britain.

Habits. Bank voles use runways at ground level and underground tunnels but they also climb on fallen trees and amongst shrubs and are therefore easier to watch than most small rodents. Like most voles they are active day and night and throughout the winter. They feed on buds, leaves, seeds and fruit as well as some insects and other invertebrates. Nests are made under logs or tree roots and several litters of usually three to five young are produced between spring and autumn. Breeding may also occur in winter if the population is low and food is abundant.

NORTHERN RED-BACKED VOLE *Clethrionomys rutilus*   **Plate 15**
Identification. This species is rather lighter and brighter than the Bank vole but is most easily distinguished by the shorter tail which is also more densely haired, the brush of terminal hairs reaching 10–12mm in length. The cheek-teeth are similar to those of the Bank vole but they tend to be rather short and broad and the last upper tooth is always similar to the complex extreme found in the Bank vole.

Range. Northern Scandinavia to Siberia and arctic North America, replacing the Bank vole.

Habitat. Mainly in open birch woodland and willow scrub.

Habits. Similar to those of the Bank vole. They enter houses and farm buildings readily in winter.

GREY-SIDED VOLE *Clethrionomys rufocanus*   **Plate 15**
Identification. The chestnut colour characteristic of species of *Clethrionomys* is confined to a narrower zone of the back than in the other species and the flanks are greyish. (But note that very young individuals of the other species may have various admixtures of grey and russet when they are moulting.) This is the largest *Clethrionomys* and the tail is relatively longer than in the other two. The cheek-teeth are more angular and develop roots later in life. The last upper tooth always resembles the simple form in the Bank vole.

Range. A northern species extending from the tundra zone southwards in the mountains of Scandinavia and eastwards to Japan.

Habitat. Open woodland of birch and pine and on open mountain and tundra wherever there are dwarf shrubs.

Habits. Similar to the other species of *Clethrionomys*. Grey-sided voles feed especially on the shoots of dwarf shrubs such as bilberry and crowberry.

BALKAN SNOW VOLE *Dinaromys bogdanovi*   **Plate 15**
Identification. This is a distinctive long-tailed vole with a soft, pale grey coat. It most closely resembles the Snow vole but there is even less brown in the coat and the tail is longer (about three-quarters of the length of the head and body and usually over 75mm). The large hind feet (over 22mm) are also diagnostic. The

cheek-teeth develop roots late in life but otherwise closely resemble those in species of *Microtus*.

Range. Confined to the Balkans.

Habitat. This is a montane vole, found especially on rocky slopes above the tree-line between 600 and 2000m.

Habits. Nests are made in crevices of rock or under stones. The litter size of two or three is smaller than in most voles and the gestation period is longer, about four weeks instead of three as in most voles and mice.

GRASS VOLES: genus *Microtus*

These are the dominant voles in grassland where they make a network of runs on and just below the surface, often identifiable by the presence of piles of olive-green droppings covered with chopped fresh grass. They feed predominantly upon grasses and sedges and have ever-growing cheek-teeth with a sharply angular pattern of triangles on the grinding surfaces. The eyes and ears are smaller than in the red-backed voles but larger than in the pine voles. The identification of species by external appearance is very difficult without practice or specimens for comparison. Skulls are often abundant in raptor pellets and can be identified if both upper and lower tooth-rows are present although individual variation can cause difficulty.

FIELD VOLE   *Microtus agrestis*   **Plate 16**

Identification. Compared with the Common vole this species has the coat rather long and shaggy, especially in winter, and the ears are well-haired with hair extending a little way inside at the base. The tail is clearly darker above than below. The skull can be recognized by the second upper cheek-tooth which has an additional lobe on the inner side at the hind end, not found in any other European vole (except occasionally in Günther's grass vole).

Range. Throughout the continent, except southern Europe, and eastward to Lake Baikal. Present in Britain but not Ireland.

Habitat. This vole is found in all grassy habitats provided the grass is long enough to provide cover – open woodland, hedgerows, meadows, marshes, river banks etc. It does not survive in closely grazed pasture and conversely can become very abundant when all grazing is excluded as when ground is fenced prior to afforestation. It extends up to the snowline wherever there is enough vegetation or loose rock to provide cover.

Habits. This species makes a network of runways on the surface of the ground amongst grass and also uses shallow tunnels below the surface. The nest of finely shredded grass may be in a tussock of grass or below ground. They are active by day and night and are commonly the principal prey of raptors such as the Barn owl, Short-eared owl, Kestrel and Hen harrier. Several litters of four to six young are produced from spring to autumn. The population density fluctuates with a cycle of about four years and pastures may be badly damaged in peak years.

COMMON VOLE   *Microtus arvalis*   **Plate 16**

Identification. This species is very similar to the Field vole but its coat is shorter and its ears are less hairy, the inside of the conch being almost naked right to the base. The colour is generally lighter and the tail is only faintly darker above than below. The teeth differ from those of the Field vole in the absence of the extra lobe on the second upper cheek-tooth.

Range. Throughout Europe except for the Mediterranean lowlands and the far north. It is absent from Scandinavia and the British Isles except for the Orkney Islands and Guernsey. There is an introduced population on Spitzbergen.

Habitat. Grassland, including short, grazed pasture.

Habits. This vole is more of a burrower than the Field vole and can therefore survive on ground with very little cover, such as closely grazed pastures. In other respects it closely resembles the Field vole.

SIBLING VOLE   *Microtus epiroticus (M. subarvalis)*   Not illustrated

Identification. This species is not distinguishable from the Common vole except by chromosomes and by dissection of the genitalia.

Range. Overlapping with the Common vole in much of eastern and central Europe but the limits are not yet known.

ROOT VOLE   *Microtus oeconomus*   **Plate 16**

Identification. Very similar to the Field vole, but where both species occur together the Root vole, with practice, can be recognized by its slightly larger size and longer tail. The first lower cheek-tooth is distinctive, with a simple structure shared only by the Snow vole amongst species of *Microtus*.

Range. An eastern species reaching west to Norway and the Baltic coast of Germany, with an isolated population in the Netherlands. It occurs throughout Siberia and in Alaska.

Habitat. Grassland, but often in wetter areas than other grass voles, including sedge swamps.

Habits. The Root vole makes extensive tunnels but in wet ground the nest may be above ground, for instance amongst the basal stems of a clump of sedge or rushes. Otherwise its habits are as for the Field vole.

SNOW VOLE   *Microtus nivalis*   **Plate 16**

Identification. This is the most distinctive of the European grass voles, with a relatively long pallid tail (about half the length of the head and body) and a very greyish brown coat. The whiskers are especially prominent. The first lower cheek-tooth is characteristic, with few triangles and a double-sided lobe at the front, whilst the last upper tooth tends to be rather simple and elongate. (See also Balkan snow vole, p. 158.)

Range. Confined to Spain, Portugal and the French Pyrenees.

Habitat. Mainly lives on open mountain slopes above the tree-line, especially amongst scree or shrub and ranging to a height of over 4000m on Mont Blanc. However it also occurs on low hills with dry woodland in southern France.

Habits. Although all the grass voles are active by day and night this species is particularly diurnal and can be seen basking in the sunshine on rocky slopes. Snow voles feed on a variety of alpine plants as well as grass; shrubs such as bilberry are important items of their diet.

GÜNTHER'S VOLE   *Microtus guentheri*   **Plate 16**
Identification. Most similar to the Common vole but distinguishable by the very short tail, about a quarter the length of the head and body. The tail and the hind feet are very pale. The tooth pattern is the same as in the Common vole but the triangles on the grinding surface tend to be well separated from each other and the second upper cheek-tooth sometimes has an extra loop on the inner, rear corner, as is regular in the Field vole. The bony capsules enclosing the inner ears are larger than in other voles.
Range. In Europe this species is confined to the extreme south-east: southern Yugoslavia, Greece, Bulgaria and Thrace. It also occurs in Asia Minor, Israel and Libya.
Habitat. Dry grassy ground, including pastures and crops where it may do considerable damage.
Habits. As other grass voles.

CABRERA'S VOLE   *Microtus cabrerae*   Not illustrated
Identification. A large vole, very similar to the almost equally large Iberian race of the Common vole. The one distinctive external feature is the presence of many long, protruding dark hairs on the hind quarters, considerably longer than the similar 'guard hairs' that occur throughout the coat in all voles. The upside is rather darker than in the Common vole and the grey of the underside is more strongly suffused with buff. The skull has an unusual arched profile (see figure) and the cheek-teeth are very similar to those of the Common vole although with the posterior loop of the upper row and the anterior loop of the lower row less developed.
Range. Confined to Spain, Portugal and the French Pyrenees.
Habitat and habits. On the whole this vole occupies lower ground than the Common vole in Iberia, from coastal marshes in southern Portugal to as high as at least 1500m in central Spain. In the hills it is found especially in open woodland with shrubby undergrowth such as bramble, sometimes in company with the Common vole.

Cabrera's   Common

Skulls of Cabrera's and Common voles

PINE VOLES: genus *Pitymys*

The pine voles are very similar to the grass voles but they have even smaller eyes and ears and short fur, in keeping with their more subterranean habits. A further distinction is the presence of only five pads on the sole of each hind foot, compared with six in the grass voles. The skulls are less angular than in *Microtus* and the first lower cheek-teeth are distinctive, with one pair of triangles confluent with each other but separated from those in front and behind (see figure). The number of species in Europe is still uncertain and critical identification is beyond the scope of this guide. However it is rare for more than two species to occur together and locality is therefore a good guide to probable identity.

First lower left molars of a grass vole, *Microtus* (*left*) and a pine vole, *Pitymys* (*right*)

COMMON PINE VOLE   *Pitymys subterraneus*   **Plate 17**
Identification. This pine vole occurs with grass voles rather than other species of pine voles. It can be distinguished from the grass voles by the smaller eyes and ears, and small hind feet (under 15mm) with only five pads. This species, along with *P. multiplex, P. bavaricus, P. tatricus* and *P. liechtensteini*, has the last upper tooth more complex than in the remaining pine voles, with four lobes on the inner side.
Range. From France through central and eastern Europe south of about 52°N.
Habitat. Most kinds of grassland, including short pasture as well as open woodland, up to heights of 2000m in the Alps.
Habits. Common pine voles resemble common (grass) voles in many ways but are distinctly more subterranean and obtain much of their food underground in the form of rhizomes, bulbs and roots. They are active mainly at night and excavate extensive tunnels just below the surface of the soil. The litter size, usually about three or four, is smaller than in the grass voles and the number of nipples is correspondingly fewer – only two pairs (in the groin) compared with four pairs in most other groups of voles.

ALPINE PINE VOLE   *Pitymys multiplex*   Not illustrated
Identification. Scarcely distinguishable from the Common pine vole but with clearer yellowish and reddish tones in the coat. It is slightly larger on average (hind feet 15–16mm) and the last upper tooth has the two sides of the second element more sharply separated from each other.
Range. Confined to the Juras and the southern side of the Alps, up to a height of 2000m.
Habitat and habits. More diurnal than the Common pine vole but similar in other respects.

BAVARIAN PINE VOLE   *Pitymys bavaricus*   Not illustrated
Identification. Distinguishable from the Common pine vole only by chromosomes and small differences in the skull and teeth.
Range. Bavarian Alps.

TATRA PINE VOLE   *Pitymys tatricus*   Not illustrated
Identification. This local species can be distinguished from the Common pine vole, with which it coexists, by its slightly darker colour, larger eyes (1.5–3mm in diameter), and larger size (head and body 100–110mm, tail 30–45mm, hind feet 17–18mm).
Range. Confined to the Tatra Mountains in eastern Czechoslovakia and the adjacent part of Poland.
Habitat. Coniferous forest from 1500 to 2300m.

LIECHTENSTEIN'S PINE VOLE
Pitymys liechtensteini   Not illustrated
Identification. This pine vole is only separable from the Common pine vole by chromosome differences and small details of the skull and teeth.
Range. Northwestern Yugoslavia.

MEDITERRANEAN PINE VOLE
Pitymys duodecimcostatus   **Plate 17**
Identification. Compared with the other pine voles, this species, along with its close relatives *P. lusitanicus* and *P. thomasi*, is distinctly lighter and more yellowish above and a paler silvery-grey below. The fur is particularly soft and dense and the tail is very short. The last upper tooth in this and all the species following is simpler than in the preceding species, with only three inner ridges, but it differs from Savi's pine vole in having the outer ridges very uneven in size.
Range. Confined to southeastern France and eastern and southern Spain.
Habitat and habits. As for the Common pine vole.

LUSITANIAN PINE VOLE   *Pitymys lusitanicus*   Not illustrated
Identification. Slightly smaller than the Mediterranean pine vole, this species can safely be distinguished from it only by cranial measurements.
Range. Portugal, most of Spain, except for the south and east, and extreme southwestern France.

THOMAS'S PINE VOLE   *Pitymys thomasi*   Not illustrated
Identification. This is very similar to the Mediterranean pine vole and only distinguishable from it by its chromosomes and cranial proportions.
Range. Southern Yugoslavia to Greece.

SAVI'S PINE VOLE   *Pitymys savii*   **Plate 17**
Identification. This species is not clearly distinguishable from the Common pine vole externally. The skull can be distinguished by the last cheek-tooth which has a simple form as in the Mediterranean pine vole but with the external ridges of equal size.
Range. The area in which this pine vole can be found comprises three separate segments which may represent distinct species: southwestern France and north Spain (*gerbii* or *pyrenaicus*), Italy and Sicily (*savii*), and southern Yugoslavia (*felteni*).

WATER VOLES: genus *Arvicola*

Water voles are the largest indigenous European voles (exceeded only by the introduced Muskrat). They are very similar to the grass voles (*Microtus*) but have longer tails. Although they are usually associated with water they are not conspicuously adapted for swimming, having neither a flattened tail nor webbed feet, and in some areas they live in normal dry habitats. The two species are very similar but they differ in size in those areas where they occur together.

NORTHERN WATER VOLE *Arvicola terrestris* Plate 17

Identification. Very similar to the Field vole but almost twice its size and with the tail proportionately longer, about half the length of the head and body. In the north of Scotland most animals are completely black and elsewhere black individuals occur sporadically. Young water voles can be distinguished from grass voles of similar size by the disproportionately large hind feet. In the water they are noticeably smaller than muskrats, coypus or beavers, but can easily be mistaken for the Common rat which is frequently seen swimming but has a much longer tail. The teeth of water voles closely resemble the simpler patterns found in the grass voles.

Range. This species is found over most of Europe except for the south and west of France, and Iberia, but note that there is an apparently isolated population in the Pyrenees.

Habitat. In most areas this species is closely associated with fresh water, in sluggish rivers and lakes with well-vegetated banks and in marshes, but in the south of its range it tends to be less aquatic, occupying grassland far from water.

Habits. Water voles swim and dive competently although they are much less agile and graceful in the water than the more specialized rodents like the Coypu and Beaver. They swim by paddling rapidly with all four feet. When disturbed they dive and usually surface under cover of vegetation. They are frequently active by day, but especially around dawn and dusk. They make extensive burrows in the banks of rivers and ditches, opening above or below water level.

Burrow of a water vole

Where they occur away from water, for example in southern Germany, they make extensive burrows, with mounds of earth at the entrances the size of mole-hills but distinguishable by the presence of a hole. Water voles feed on grasses, sedges and other vegetation including roots (and root-crops) in winter. Litters of about four to six young are born throughout the summer.

SOUTHWESTERN WATER VOLE   *Arvicola sapidus*   **Plate 17**
Identification. This species is scarcely distinguishable by external appearance from some northern forms of the Northern water vole but it is much larger and somewhat darker than the southern forms with which it coexists in parts of France and the Pyrenees. The tail is also proportionately longer, usually over 11cm. Skulls can be distinguished especially by the broader nasal bones, usually over 5mm, and longer tooth-rows, usually over 10mm.
Range. Iberia and most of lowland France, overlapping with that of the Northern water vole in the Pyrenees, middle Rhone and the Paris Basin.
Habitat. This water vole always lives in aquatic habitats, by rivers, canals, lakes and marshes where waterside vegetation provides cover.
Habits. As for the aquatic forms of the Northern water vole.

MUSKRAT   *Ondatra zibethicus*   **Plate 18**
Identification. This is a close relative of the voles and lemmings although it is much larger than any other species of the group, fully twice the size of the water voles. It is usually seen swimming and can be distinguished from the even larger Coypu and Beaver by the tail which is flattened in the vertical plane. The feet are not webbed. The coat is particularly soft and dense and is used commercially as musquash.
Range. A North American species, established in much of Europe through escapes from fur-farms. It occurred in Britain in the 1930s but was successfully eradicated.
Habitat. This species lives always by fresh water, in rivers, lakes, ponds and marshes with well-vegetated banks.
Habits. Muskrats are more accomplished swimmers than the water voles, using both the hind feet and the tail. They dive if alarmed and can swim long distances under water, usually surfacing in cover. They are especially active in the early morning. Nests are sometimes built on the surface amongst aquatic vegetation, consisting of a platform and a domed roof built of grass, reeds or sedge, sometimes as much as a metre high and resembling a beaver lodge. They also make extensive burrows in river banks, usually entered from under water. Their food is mainly aquatic vegetation. Muskrats are as prolific as their smaller relatives, with the potential to produce several litters of up to eight young during the summer.

MOLE-RATS: family Muridae, subfamily Spalacinae

Many different groups of rodents throughout the world have become adapted for a subterranean life but none to such an extreme degree as members of this group. They lack all external sign of eyes, ears or tail. There is a line of stiff bristles on either side of the head. The incisor teeth are very prominent and are used for digging, but the feet are normal, without enlargement of the front feet such as is found in moles. They live almost permanently underground, in extensive networks of tunnels, generally on drier ground than is occupied by moles. In contrast to the 'insectivorous' moles they feed entirely on vegetable matter such as roots, rhizomes and bulbs. Plants may be seen to disappear into the ground as they are pulled down by the roots into an underground tunnel. The two species are difficult to distinguish and both are very variable in colour. Size, especially of the hind feet, is the best external guide.

GREATER MOLE-RAT   *Spalax microphthalmus*   **Plate 18**
Identification. This is the larger species of mole-rat, up to 31cm in length and with the hind feet usually over 25mm. The skull can be distinguished from that of the Lesser mole-rat by the wide rostrum (behind the upper incisors) and the absence of small perforations beside the posterior opening.
Range. From southern Russia and the Ukraine to Rumania, Bulgaria and northern Greece.
Habitat. Grassland and cultivated ground.
Habits. Mole-rats dig primarily with the teeth, pushing the soil backwards with the feet and also using the head to push through soft soil. They are mainly nocturnal. Each animal occupies its own system of tunnels, which contains a nest as well as storage chambers. There is only one litter per year, of about four or five, born in spring. The young may travel above ground to disperse but apart from that mole-rats rarely emerge from their tunnels. Where they are abundant they can be a serious agricultural pest.

Greater   Lesser

Skulls of mole-rats

LESSER MOLE-RAT   *Spalax leucodon*   **Plate 18**
Identification. This species is smaller than the Greater mole-rat – usually under 26cm, hind feet under 25mm. The skull has characteristic perforations on either side of the posterior opening and the anterior rostrum is relatively narrow.
Range. From Yugoslavia and Greece to the Black Sea coast. Also found from Asia Minor to Libya.
Habitat and habits. As for the Greater mole-rat.

RATS and MICE: family Muridae, subfamily Murinae

Compared with other rodents of their size, the true rats and mice have long thin tails, prominent ears, rather pointed muzzles, large eyes and sleek fur. Their dentition – only three cheek-teeth in each row – and lack of hibernation distinguish them from the superficially similar birch-mice (p. 173–4) and the Mouse-tailed dormouse (p. 154). Like other members of the Muridae rats and mice are prolific breeders and are usually abundant and dominant in their habitats. Although primarily seed-eaters they are versatile feeders. However the rooted teeth, with numerous rounded cusps, are not adapted for grazing. Half-grown rats can be distinguished from mice by the disproportionately large hind feet.

COMMON RAT *Rattus norvegicus*   Plate 18
Identification. When it is seen clearly this species could be confused only with the Ship rat. The long tail and large ears serve to distinguish it from the similar-sized water voles but it should be remembered that this species, like the water voles, is frequently seen in water and is a competent swimmer. Compared with the Ship rat it has a shorter, thicker tail (a little shorter than the head and body), shorter ears and blunter muzzle, and generally presents a more bulky, less athletic appearance. The colour is usually brown above and grey below but black individuals occasionally occur. The skull, provided it is adult, with fully developed teeth, differs from that of the Ship rat in being more angular, with the top of the braincase flanked by approximately parallel ridges.
Range. Almost ubiquitous as an introduction of long standing from southern Asia.
Habitat. Common rats are found in almost all man-made or man-influenced habitats, from city sewers, rubbish dumps, warehouses, cellars, industrial sites and railway embankments to gardens, arable fields, farmyards and farm build-ings. They are also common on many coasts, especially of estuaries, and on the banks of lowland rivers, but rarely occur in truly undisturbed inland habitats.
Habits. Common rats make extensive burrows, often conspicuous in hedgerows or on river banks. Although they are competent climbers they are less inclined to climb than ship rats and are more often associated with water. Although primarily nocturnal they are fairly often seen by day and often live in close proximity, reaching considerable densities. They are very versatile feeders, concentrating upon grain and weed seeds when available, but capable of exploiting an enormous range including root-crops, sewage, kitchen waste, shellfish, earthworms, carrion, eggs, buds and fruit. Breeding may take place throughout the year if food remains abundant, or may cease in winter. Litters can be produced at intervals of three to four weeks and average about seven or eight young, with as many as twelve not uncommon. The Common rat is the ancestor of the white rats and other colour varieties used as laboratory animals.

SHIP RAT *Rattus rattus*   Plate 18
Identification. From the Common rat this species is distinguished by its longer tail, usually a little longer than the extended head and body, large rounded ears and more pointed muzzle. It is also a little smaller, with a more slender and

167

athletic 'jizz'. The colour is extremely variable. Three principal varieties occur but all may be found together and are interfertile, although usually one form is predominant in any colony. In northern urban populations the dominant colour is black or dark grey all over; further south the brown varieties are more frequent, with the underside either grey or white. The skull differs from that of the Common rat in its more rounded contours, especially in the curved ridges on either side of the braincase.

Range. Ubiquitous in southern and central Europe but scattered and mainly confined to seaports in the British Isles and northern Europe. Originally from southeast Asia.

Habitat. Almost confined to disturbed habitats, in the north primarily in buildings such as warehouses, further south also on farms. It is less associated with water than is the Common rat.

Habits. Similar to those of the Common rat but this species climbs more readily and the nest is frequently above ground, for example amongst rafters or in a wall cavity. As the name implies this is the more frequent species on ships.

WOOD MICE AND ALLIES: genus *Apodemus*

These are the most abundant mice in natural habitats throughout most of Europe, especially in woodland. They have large eyes and ears, long thin tails and rather long, slender, pale hind feet. They are agile, nocturnal and very prolific. Although they are easily trapped, identification of live-trapped animals can be difficult, especially in eastern Europe. In all species the young on leaving the nest are darker and greyer than the adults. Skulls are usually abundant in owl pellets but the species are not easily distinguished. They can sometimes be identified by characteristics of the teeth but these are at best subtle and at worst unusable due to wear.

WOOD MOUSE   *Apodemus sylvaticus*   Plate 19

Identification. This is the commonest mouse in most parts of Europe. The upperparts are yellowish brown slightly suffused with grey whilst the underside is a pale silvery grey. There is usually a small streak of yellowish brown in the centre of the chest. This is sometimes absent and sometimes extends as a line backwards towards the belly but it never extends sideways as in the Yellow-necked mouse.

Range. Ubiquitous apart from northern Scandinavia and Finland.

Habitat. The Wood mouse is usually the dominant small rodent in woodland, even where ground vegetation is scarce or absent, but it also occurs in many other habitats, such as gardens, hedgerows, scrub and cliffs. It frequently enters houses and farm buildings. Its normal altitudinal limit is the tree-line but it will follow human activity higher.

Habits. Wood mice are very agile, whether on the ground or climbing in shrubs and trees. They readily cross open ground and are less restricted to runways in thick vegetation than are the voles and shrews. They are predominantly nocturnal, spending the day in a nest in an underground tunnel or in a crevice amongst tree roots or under a log. They feed mainly on seeds which are often stored underground. In woodland acorns, beech mast and hazel nuts are important. Animal food such as snails, earthworms and insects is regularly taken and in

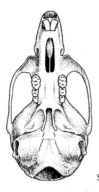

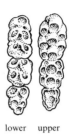

lower   upper

Skull and molar teeth of a wood mouse

spring seedlings and buds are important. Breeding takes place from spring to autumn and may continue through the winter if food is abundant, for example after a heavy crop of acorns. Litters usually consist of four to seven young and they leave the nest just before they are three weeks old. Wood mice are preyed upon by all the woodland owls as well as by foxes, cats and weasels.

YELLOW-NECKED MOUSE   *Apodemus flavicollis*   **Plate 19**
Identification. This mouse is very similar to the Wood mouse but slightly larger, a slightly richer colour above and even paler below. There is always a yellowish brown mark on the chest, usually considerably larger than in the Wood mouse and extending sideways, often joining with the dark upperside to form a complete collar.
Range. Widespread in eastern and central Europe but missing from much of France and the Low Countries, and confined to mountains in most of the Mediterranean zone. Yellow-necked mice are patchily distributed in England and Wales.
Habitat. Mainly woodland, including orchards and wooded gardens. It is less frequent than the Wood mouse in scrub and open habitats, but enters houses more readily. It is more common than the Wood mouse in alpine coniferous forests and occurs up to the tree-line.
Habits. As for the Wood mouse, but probably more frequently found above ground. They have been trapped in the upper canopy of tall forest trees.

PYGMY FIELD MOUSE   *Apodemus microps*   **Plate 19**
Identification. Very similar to the Wood mouse but slightly smaller – the hind feet in particular are a useful guide, being under 20mm, and the ears, under 15mm. The chest spot is small or absent. The Pygmy field mouse is easily confused with pale forms of the House mouse and with the Steppe mouse but it can be distinguished by the longer hind feet (over 16mm) and the normal upper incisor teeth, lacking the notch found in most species of *Mus*.
Range. The lowlands of eastern Europe from Bulgaria to Czechoslavakia.
Habitat. Mainly in open habitats such as long grass, scrub and crops.
Habits. As for the Wood mouse.

ROCK MOUSE   *Apodemus mystacinus*   **Plate 19**
Identification. This mouse is larger and much greyer than any other species of *Apodemus* (but note that young animals of the other species are much greyer than the adults). It can be easily distinguished from a young rat of similar size by the hind feet which would be disproportionately large in a young rat. There is no chest spot in this species.
Range. Confined to northern Greece, Albania and the coastal mountains of Yugoslavia. It also occurs on the island of Corfu.
Habitat. The Rock mouse is found in dry woodland and on more open rocky hillsides with scrub, overlapping to some extent with the Wood mouse and the Yellow-necked mouse.
Habits. As for the Wood mouse.

STRIPED FIELD MOUSE   *Apodemus agrarius*   **Plate 19**
Identification. The Striped field mouse closely resembles the Wood mouse but has a distinctive bold dark stripe along the whole length of the back from the nape to the rump. The ears are rather smaller than in the Wood mouse and the tail slightly shorter than the head and body, the latter point distinguishing it from the similarly striped birch mice which have much longer tails (p. 174).
Range. Eastern Europe, west to southern Denmark and northeastern Italy.
Habitat. This species is found in scrub, hedgerows and the edges of woods, overlapping the Wood mouse in these habitats but not following the Wood mouse into dense woodland.
Habits. The Striped field mouse is less strictly nocturnal than the other species of *Apodemus* but in other aspects of behaviour it closely resembles the Wood mouse.

HARVEST MOUSE   *Micromys minutus*   **Plate 20**
Identification. The Harvest mouse is the smallest mouse in Europe and is readily recognized by its very small ears and rich orange-brown coat. The tail is slender and slightly prehensile. This is an elusive species, most easily detected by the distinctive summer nests – these are spherical balls of grass woven into stems of growing grass or other herbs, usually between 20 and 50cm above ground level. The skull is easily identified by the extremely short tooth-rows (under 3mm) and short rostrum.
Range. Widespread except for Scandinavia and much of the Mediterranean zone.
Habitat. Harvest mice are found especially in long grass, for example on roadsides, edges of fields, marshes, riverbanks and amongst scrub. They also occur in cereal crops and on the edges of reed beds.
Habits. Harvest mice are agile climbers, using their slender feet to grip twigs and twisting their tails loosely around stems as a safety harness rather than as an active support. In summer they spend much of their time above ground, foraging especially for seeds. The young, usually four to six in a litter, are reared in a nest anchored to stems of grass or herbs, often where the grass stems are supported by shrubs such as rose or bramble. In winter they spend more time at and below ground level and the above-ground nests are usually abandoned (but the empty nests are much easier to find in winter when the grass has withered). Although mainly nocturnal harvest mice are more active by day than most

other mice, especially in winter. However, since they usually keep within thick cover, they are not easily observed.

HOUSE MICE AND THEIR ALLIES: genus *Mus*

These mice are very similar to those of the genus *Apodemus*. The House mouse is usually identifiable by its dark colour but its outdoor relatives are more difficult to recognize. They are all rather small, with smaller eyes, ears and, especially, hind feet than mice of the genus *Apodemus*. There is never a yellow chest-spot. The tail is almost naked, with conspicuous scaly rings, and in those species that most closely resemble *Apodemus* it tends to be distinctly shorter than the head and body. The skull can be recognized by a notch in the wearing surface of the upper incisors as seen in profile (except in the Algerian mouse) and the very small size of the last cheek-tooth in each row. All the species are especially associated with the works of man, either indoors or on farmland, and are predominantly nocturnal. The classification of the European forms of *Mus* is still very provisional. The two forms of the House mouse are sometimes treated as separate species, and it is likely that the out-door *Mus* in Greece and adjacent regions represent a further species, *Mus abboti*.

Harvest mouse   House mouse

Skulls and teeth of mice

HOUSE MOUSE   *Mus musculus*   **Plate 20**
Identification. The western form (subspecies *M. m. domesticus*) is darker and greyer than any other European mouse, being dark brownish grey above and only slightly lighter below without a clear line of demarcation. The tail appears rather thick and naked compared with that of the Wood mouse and is about equal in length to the head and body. The eastern form (*M. m. musculus*) is browner, much paler below and has the tail slightly shorter than the head and body. In all forms the hind feet are noticeably smaller than in the Wood mouse and its allies, and there is a very characteristic notch in the upper incisor teeth (see figure).
Range. Throughout Europe. The western race occurs in Britain and Ireland and on the continent west and south of a line from Denmark through Austria to the Balkans. The eastern race occurs in Scandinavia as well as northeast of that line. The House mouse occurs almost throughout the rest of the world wherever there is human occupation.

Habitat. This is predominantly an indoor mouse, being found in and around houses, farm buildings, warehouses and factories. It is also found on farmland and in gardens, and in the absence of other mice (for example on small islands) often on sea-cliffs, scrub and other natural habitats.

Habits. House mice are very versatile. Out of doors they make extensive burrows and use runways at ground level, making nests of shredded grass underground or under stones or other debris. Indoors they occupy wall cavities, under-floor cavities and roof-spaces, making bulky nests of paper, cloth or similar soft material in crevices. Although primarily grain-eaters they can survive on a wide variety of food. Almost all stored human food may be attacked, much more being wasted by damage to containers than is actually consumed. House mice may breed throughout the year if food is abundant. There are usually about five or six young in a litter, and litters may be produced at intervals of three to four weeks. They are highly territorial and when the population density is high only a few dominant males hold territories and breed while young animals remain subordinate and fail to breed.

The House mouse is a major pest of agriculture and stored products and a serious carrier of disease. It is also the ancestor of the white mice which are used as laboratory animals and which have played a dominant role in the study of genetics and in medical research, especially into cancer.

ALGERIAN MOUSE   *Mus spretus*   Plate 20
Identification. This is a small, short-tailed, pale-bellied, out-door mouse, differing clearly in all these respects from the House mouse with which it coexists. The upperside is yellowish brown suffused with grey, with an almost pure yellowish brown line bordering the white or pale grey underside. The feet are entirely white. This species differs from all other European *Mus* in having normal upper incisors, without a notch in the wearing surface. The cheek-teeth are relatively large compared with those of the (larger) House mouse.

Range. Spain, Portugal and the Mediterranean coast of France, east to the Rhone Delta. Also found in northwestern Africa.

Habitat. Cultivated ground, gardens, scrub and open woodland, especially in wetter habitats.

Habits. Although this species appears to be very similar in many ways to the Steppe mouse it is less colonial and does not build storage mounds.

STEPPE MOUSE   *Mus hortulanus*   Not illustrated
Identification. This species, which closely resembles the Algerian mouse, over-laps with the House mouse in southeastern Europe just as the Algerian mouse does in the southwest, but in the southeast the difference between the two species is much less. The colour is much as in the Algerian mouse, with sharply contrasting upper and lower colour. However, the House mouse in the southeast is also rather pale, but with less sharply contrasting upper and under surfaces. The tail in the Steppe mouse is only slightly shorter than the head and body. The incisor teeth are notched as in the House mouse but the cheek-teeth differ from those of the House mouse by being broader and more rectangular, the first upper tooth in particular lacking a deep concavity on the inner/front margin.

Range. Southeastern Europe, west as far as Austria. Similar mice in Greece may

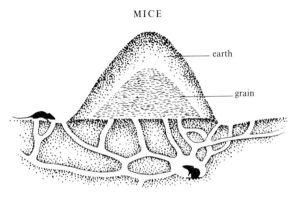

Storage mound and tunnel system of a steppe mouse

belong to a separate species, *Mus abboti*.

Habitat. Grassland and cultivated ground.

Habits. This species of mouse resembles the out-door forms of the House mouse in many respects but it is more colonial and regularly makes stores of food. These are placed in mounds of earth and have been known to contain as much as 10kg of grain. Live-trapped steppe mice are much more docile than wild house mice in similar circumstances.

CRETAN SPINY MOUSE   *Acomys minous*   **Plate 20**

Identification. In this species the whole of the upper surface from the neck backwards is covered with stiff spiny hairs, making it noticeably unique amongst European mice when in the hand. However, the spiny nature of the coat is not obvious at a distance when this species could be mistaken for a Wood mouse. The colour of the back is a little more yellowish than that of a Wood mouse and the underside and feet are white without a chest-spot such as is found in most *Apodemus*. The ears are large and the tail rather thick and scaly. The tail is very easily broken and many animals are found with only short stumps.

Range. Confined to Crete; spiny mice (the species cannot yet be clearly defined) also occur throughout Africa and southwestern Asia.

Habitat. The natural habitat of this species is dry scrub, especially on rocky hillsides, but it readily enters houses, especially in winter.

Habits. Spiny mice feed on seeds and live much as other species of mice. They are however unusual in having small litters of well-developed young, usually about two or three, following a long gestation of about six weeks. In captivity it has been found that other females act as midwives at a birth.

BIRCH MICE: family Zapodidae

Birch mice are superficially like Wood mice but have even longer tails. A dark stripe along the centre of the back prevents confusion with all except the Striped field mouse (p. 170) which has a particularly short tail for a mouse. Birch mice are nowhere abundant and they hibernate throughout the winter. They are mainly insectivorous although seeds are also eaten. Skulls are scarce in raptor pellets and are distinguishable from those of true mice by a small tooth preceding the three large cheek-teeth above but not below. (Dormice have this extra tooth above *and* below.)

NORTHERN BIRCH MOUSE   *Sicista betulina*   Plate 20

Identification. A narrow black stripe from the crown of the head to the base of the tail distinguishes this species from all other mice except the next species and the Striped field mouse (p. 170). The tail is about one and a half times the length of the head and body, much longer than in any other European rodent.

Range. Widespread in northern Russia and southern Finland but elsewhere in Europe occurring in isolated pockets, mainly in the northeast but west to Norway and Denmark and south to Austria and Rumania.

Habitat. Birch mice are found in woodland, especially of birch in the north, where there is a dense undergrowth and particularly in wet areas. In the south they are mainly montane.

Habits. Birch mice are nocturnal animals, spending the day in burrows and foraging at night. They move on the ground with a bounding gait and climb with great agility amongst shrubs. They hibernate from October until April in a nest built underground or in a rotten tree stump. Birch mice have only a single litter per year, of about three to five young, born in May or June. They feed mainly on insects and other creatures, especially those found in rotting logs, but they also eat seeds and fruit, especially before hibernation.

SOUTHERN BIRCH MOUSE   *Sicista subtilis*   Plate 20

Identification. This species has a central dark stripe like the Northern birch mouse but it is bordered on either side by a stripe that is slightly paler than the surrounding coat. The tail is shorter than in the northern species – about one and a third the length of the head and body – but still relatively longer than in any other European mouse.

Range. This is a species of the steppes of southern Russia. It extends into Rumania, and scattered populations occur west as far as eastern Austria. It extends eastwards to Lake Baikal.

Habitat. Rough grassland, scrub, open woodland and the margins of cultivated ground, found mainly at low altitudes.

Habits. As for the Northern birch mouse.

PRIMATES: order Primates

The primates comprise the lemurs, monkeys, true apes and Man. Apart from Man the only species in Europe is the Barbary ape of which there is a colony, probably introduced, on Gibraltar. In spite of its name this is a true monkey, of the family Cercopithecidae (which includes all the monkeys of Africa and Asia), and is not closely related to the true apes such as the Chimpanzee and Gorilla.

BARBARY APE *Macaca sylvanus*   Plate 21

Identification. The Barbary ape is a typical monkey except that it lacks a tail, and could not be confused with any other European mammal. Like most monkeys it has a short muzzle, large, forward directed eyes, short ears and long legs with prehensile hands and feet. It is closely related to the Rhesus monkey which is used in large numbers in medical research, but the Rhesus has a prominent tail.

Range. In Europe found only on the Rock of Gibraltar. Otherwise confined to Morocco and Algeria. The Gibraltar animals were probably introduced originally from Africa and the colony has at times been augmented by fresh introductions.

Habitat. Dry rocky hillsides with scrub.

Habits. The apes on Gibraltar number 30–40 and are maintained in two groups on the upper part of the rock by artificial feeding at two sites to keep them away from the town. They are tame but unconfined. Each group has a hierarchical social structure. Young are born singly in summer and they live for about 15 years.

CARNIVORES: order Carnivora

Carnivores vary greatly in size and shape – bears, weasels, cats and dogs are all carnivores – but most are predators, adapted especially for capturing and feeding upon relatively large prey, in particular prey that cannot be swallowed whole. They all have continuous rows of teeth, each row sharply demarcated into three small incisors, a large, conical canine or fang, and a variable number of cheek-teeth of which one, known as the carnassial, is usually especially large and blade-like, for shearing flesh. The coat is generally soft and dense, and most species have been extensively hunted and trapped for their fur. Many species have also been seriously depleted through persecution in the interests of farming stock or, more often, game preservation. Some, such as the Red fox and the Stoat, have withstood these pressures and remain abundant, but many carnivores are amongst the rarest and most endangered of European mammals. Most carnivores are secretive and nocturnal and, even when unmolested, live at much lower population densities than their prey. They are consequently difficult to detect and observe. Indirect signs such as footprints and droppings are useful for locating regular paths and dens.

BEARS: family Ursidae

Bears are the largest carnivores in Europe. Their tails are generally invisible and their feet are plantigrade, the entire sole and heel making contact with the ground.

POLAR BEAR *Thalarctos maritimus*   Plate 21
Identification. The habitat, the very large size – about two metres in length – and the entirely white (or creamy white) coat make the Polar bear unmistakable.
Range. Confined to the high Arctic. In the European sector polar bears are only resident at Spitzbergen, but they wander extensively on the sea ice. Animals from Spitzbergen occasionally reach the north coast of Norway and animals from Greenland occasionally reach Iceland.
Habitat. Sea ice and sea coasts, as far north as there is open water.
Habits. Polar bears are marine animals, hunting predominantly on the sea ice or in the sea. They prey mainly upon seals and to a lesser extent upon fish. Seals are usually killed as they emerge to breath at a hole in the ice, the bear striking a lethal blow with a front paw. Female polar bears make a den in the snow where they hibernate and have their young (usually one, occasionally twins) in February. The young bear emerges from the den when it is about a month old and stays with its mother for about a year. Males are solitary and nomadic and usually do not hibernate.

BROWN BEAR *Ursus arctos*   Plate 21
Identification. Adults are unmistakable by virtue of their very large size (about two metres long), heavy build, short rounded ears and the absence of a tail.

Their colour varies from pale fawn to dark brown. Young animals often have a pale collar, and the absence of a visible tail distinguishes them from wolverines (plate 25). Their footprints are distinctive – about the same size as those of a man but broader and with prominent claw marks. Large scratch marks on trees are another sign of their presence.

Range. Brown bears survive in considerable numbers in European Russia, Finland, Sweden, the Carpathians and the Balkan countries, but elsewhere in Europe they have been reduced to very small isolated populations. These occur in eastern Czechoslovakia, eastern Poland, Italy, the French Pyrenees, north-western Spain and Norway. In most countries they are either totally protected or can only be shot under licence. Outside Europe brown bears are found throughout northern Asia and in much of North America.

Habitat. Mainly forest, but also extending to open tundra in the north and to open pastures above the tree-line in the mountains.

hind   fore

Footprints of a brown bear (right feet)

Habits. Brown bears are solitary and territorial, and are active mainly at night, especially where they have been persecuted. They feed on a great variety of items, both vegetable and animal, including tubers, bulbs, berries, fungi, carrion, fish, eggs and honey. In autumn they eat large quantities of berries, acorns and beech mast prior to hibernation in a den, usually in a cave or rock crevice. The young, often twins, are born in January or February and are remarkably small at birth, about the size of a Guinea pig and weighing only about 350 grams. The young stay with the mother for most of the following year but the father takes no part in rearing the family.

DOGS AND FOXES: family Canidae

Compared with other carnivores dogs and foxes tend to be fast runners with long legs, long muzzles and prominent ears. Domestic dogs were derived from the Wolf. Although domestic dogs live in a feral state in some parts of the world feral populations are not tolerated in Europe because of the threat they pose to farm stock and game, and the danger of rabies.

WOLF *Canis lupus*   **Plate 22**
Identification. Wolves could be mistaken only for certain large domestic dogs, especially Alsatians, and, in southeastern Europe, for jackals. A wolf differs

from an Alsatian especially in having the chest shallower and the head broader, exaggerated by a ruff of long hair behind the cheeks. The neck is short and thick and the head is usually held low. The ears are always erect and the tail droops (in contrast with huskies and other northern breeds of dogs in which the tail is curled upwards). The colour is rather uniform in any individual but varies from a pale greyish brown to a darker yellowish brown.

Range. Wolves occur throughout Russia and extend from there into eastern European countries to some extent. Completely isolated populations occur in Spain and (in very small numbers) in Italy. Individuals may roam far beyond the normal range. Wolves are protected in some degree in most of Europe (totally in Norway, Sweden and Italy). They also occur throughout Siberia, south to Arabia and India, and in North America.

Habitat. Mainly open woodland and tundra, but also found in dense forest, especially when persecuted.

Habits. Wolves generally live in family groups, the young, frequently three to five in a litter, remaining with the parents for almost a year. Sometimes larger packs may be formed by the combination of two families or the addition of other individuals but packs over ten are rare. Typically wolves cooperate in hunting deer and other ungulates, especially in winter, but smaller items of prey such as hares, birds and rodents are also eaten as is carrion. Wolves make a characteristic mournful howl which is heard especially during the mating season in winter. The pack breaks up in spring when each breeding female prepares a den for the birth of her cubs – digging an earth, enlarging that of a fox or badger, or using a natural crevice. The male brings food for his mate and for the cubs when they are young. The Wolf is the ancestor of domestic dogs and many traits of the domestic dog such as tail wagging as a greeting, the bristling and growling of a dog asserting his dominance, and the flattened ears and tail-between-legs of a submissive animal are also found in wild wolves. Unprovoked attacks by wolves on people are almost unknown but they can do serious damage to live-stock.

JACKAL   *Canis aureus*   **Plate 22**

Identification. The Jackal is considerably smaller than the Wolf and also smaller than the average Alsatian dog. The colour is less variable than that of wolves and somewhat redder than most. It looks slender and agile compared with the Wolf.

Range. Confined to southeastern Europe, from Yugoslavia and Hungary southwards. Also to be found in most of southwestern Asia and northern Africa.

Habitat. Open country, including grassland, cultivated land and marshes.

Habits. Jackals are more solitary and nocturnal than wolves, spending the day in dense cover. They feed mainly on rodents, birds and carrion, but also scavenge for scraps around villages and farms. They frequently howl, especially at dusk – a clearer and less mellow sound than the howl of a wolf. A litter of four or five cubs is born in spring, usually in a burrow.

RED FOX *Vulpes vulpes* **Plate 22**

Identification. The Red fox is easily distinguished by its narrow muzzle, large erect ears and long, bushy tail, usually with a white tip. The coat is usually a rich reddish brown but it is rather variable. Dark markings on the neck and chest occur sporadically but the front surfaces of the fore legs are more consistently dark. The scent deposited in the urine is persistent and very distinctive.

Range. Throughout Europe, except Iceland, but including Britain and Ireland. Also occurs in North Africa, the whole of temperate Asia and much of North America.

Habitat. Red foxes live mainly in woodland but can also be found on open moorland and mountains, on farmland and increasingly in towns.

Habits. Red foxes are very versatile animals. They are mostly solitary and nocturnal but are quite often seen by day where they are undisturbed. They spend the day under shrubs, in a short burrow or earth dug by themselves, in a disused badger set or, in towns, under garden sheds or scrap. They feed mainly on rodents, but rabbits, birds, beetles, earthworms, eggs, carrion and refuse are also taken and, in autumn, fruit and berries. Surplus food is often buried. They make a variety of calls, especially a high-pitched bark. The young, usually about four or five, are born in a burrow in spring. They are active and weaned by about six weeks, but stay with their mother until the autumn. Silver foxes, frequently farmed for their fur, are a variety of the Red fox but do not occur in the wild in Europe.

ARCTIC FOX *Alopex lagopus* **Plate 22**

Identification. Arctic foxes vary considerably in colour but are never as reddish as the Red fox and are distinctly smaller. Most are greyish brown in summer and turn pure white in winter; a rarer variety, known as the 'blue fox' and comprising under five per cent of the population, is smoky grey throughout the year. The muzzle and ears are shorter than in the Red fox and the coat is very thick, especially in winter.

Range. The Arctic, including Iceland and Spitzbergen, and extending south in the mountains of Scandinavia.

Habitat. Tundra and open mountain country; also in open woodland in winter.

Habits. Arctic foxes behave much as red foxes but they are more sociable, both in summer, when several breeding burrows may be close together, and in winter when most animals move southwards or to the sea coast, sometimes travelling hundreds of kilometres. In summer, because of the short arctic nights, they normally hunt in daylight, feeding on voles, lemmings, birds and bird eggs. In winter carrion is more important and coastal animals also feed on shellfish. They sometimes follow polar bears to scavenge on the remains of their kills and may in this way find themselves far from land on the sea ice.

RACCOON-DOG *Nyctereutes procyonoides* **Plate 22**

Identification. The Raccoon-dog is a small, short-legged dog, more heavily built than a fox, with a distinctive black 'mask' across the face giving the head a close resemblance to that of a raccoon. It differs from a raccoon in its larger size, short, uniformly coloured tail and short ears.

Range. An eastern Asiatic species, introduced in Russia as a fur-bearer. It has spread steadily westwards and is found throughout Germany and as far as Switzerland and central Sweden. Not present in Britain or Ireland.

Habitat. Mainly woodland, especially by rivers and lakes.

Habits. Raccoon-dogs are solitary and nocturnal, behaving very much like foxes. They differ from other dogs and foxes in becoming relatively inactive in winter but this is not a complete hibernation and they emerge from their dens on mild nights. They are even more omnivorous than foxes, feeding on bulbs, fruit and nuts as well as rodents, frogs, earthworms and carrion.

WEASELS ETC.: family Mustelidae

The members of this family are very diverse. Most have long bodies and short legs and are very agile predators, adapted for pursuing small prey through dense vegetation. This group includes weasels, polecats, mink and martens. The larger members are more specialized and distinctive, for example Wolverine, Otter and Badger. Except for the badger they have typical carnivorous dentitions, with prominent canines and carnassials, and with the muzzle (and tooth-rows) intermediate in length between the elongate form seen in dogs and the short-faced condition of cats. Most mustelids are nocturnal but the smallest species, the Weasel and Stoat, are also active by day.

STOAT *Mustela erminea*   Plate 23

Identification. The Stoat can be distinguished from all but the Weasel by its reddish brown upper parts, white underside and small, slim body (not over 30cm). From the Weasel it differs in the longer, black-tipped tail and larger size although there is a little overlap. Males are considerably larger than females. In winter northern animals (for example in Scandinavia and northern Scotland) turn entirely white except for the black tail-tip. Further south they remain brown or turn partially white.

Range. Throughout most of Europe except for the Mediterranean lowlands. It is present in Britain and Ireland but not Iceland. The Stoat also occurs throughout temperate and arctic Asia and North America.

Habitat. The Stoat may be found in almost all terrestrial habitats, wherever there is the minimal cover necessary – woodland, hedgerows, long grass, scrub, marshes, cliffs, moorland, tundra and mountain scree.

Habits. Stoats are found singly or in family groups. They frequently hunt by day, usually keeping to cover amongst shrubs, long grass, rocks or dry-stone walls. They also climb trees. They are inquisitive and if one has been seen to disappear into cover it can often be enticed to show itself by making a squeaking noise. They prey mainly upon birds, mice, voles, rabbits and hares. Stoats will sometimes prance about to attract an inquisitive bird which is then pounced upon and killed with a bite on the neck. Stoats mate in summer but the development and birth of the young is delayed until the following spring. There are about six in a litter but up to twelve have been recorded and they may hunt in a family pack for several months before dispersing.

WEASEL *Mustela nivalis* **Plate 23**

Identification. The smallest carnivore. Weasels are the size only of a large vole or small rat but they are very much slimmer. They differ from stoats not just in their smaller size but also in having the tail short and without a black tip. The boundary between the brown and white on the flank may be straight or irregular. The size is very variable – males are much larger than females and southern animals are larger than northern ones, those in the Mediterranean lowlands (where stoats are absent) being as large as stoats. They turn white in winter only in the far north of Scandinavia and Russia.

Range. Throughout Europe except for Iceland and Ireland. Also found in North Africa and throughout Asia and North America.

Habitat. All terrestrial habitats, requiring very little cover.

Habits. Weasels hunt mainly amongst dense vegetation and are small enough to pursue rodents in their underground tunnels. They are active day and night and prey mainly on voles and mice although rats are also frequently killed and rabbits occasionally. Weasels are agile climbers and prey on birds and their eggs and nestlings in bushes and trees as well as on the ground. Weasels mate in spring and have one or two litters of about four to six young, without the delayed development found in stoats. They make a variety of hissing, chirping and trilling noises.

EUROPEAN MINK *Mustela lutreola* **Plate 23**

Identification. Both European and American mink are large but otherwise typical 'weasels', with long body, short legs and short ears. They are uniformly dark brown except for some white on the face, in the European species present on both upper and lower jaws. They are most readily confused with the Western polecat, but the coat is more uniformly dark and the white on the head is confined to the muzzle.

Range. Confined to eastern Europe (Finland to Rumania) except for an isolated remnant in western France, probably declining but little recent information is available. It extends eastwards to western Siberia and the Caucasus.

Habitat. Marshes and the banks of rivers and lakes.

Habits. European mink swim and dive competently although they have only partly webbed feet and are much less aquatic than otters. They are solitary and nocturnal, and prey upon water voles, musk rats, rats, waterside birds, frogs and fish. One litter of four or five young is produced in spring and the family disperses in late summer.

AMERICAN MINK *Mustela vison* **Plate 23**

Identification. Normal 'wild-type' animals are distinguishable from European mink by the presence of white only on the lower jaw and sometimes on the throat, never on the upper jaw. Many other colour varieties are bred on fur farms ranging from pure white through various shades of grey and brown and including patterns of dark lines on white. These may occur as escapes but rarely survive long in feral populations.

Range. Escapes from fur farms have established populations in Britain, Ireland, Iceland, Scandinavia, eastern Europe and elsewhere.

Habitat. Rivers, lakes and marshes.

Habits. As for the European mink.

WESTERN POLECAT   *Mustela putorius*   **Plate 24**
Identification. The Western polecat is dark brown all over except for white on
the tip of the snout and on the face between the eye and the ear. The dark hairs
forming the glossy outer surface of the coat are rather sparse so that the paler,
yellowish underfur shows through in places, giving a much less uniformly dark
appearance than in mink. Some feral ferrets (p. 183) closely resemble wild
polecats.
Range. Most of Europe except for Iceland, Ireland and northern Scandinavia.
In Britain the Polecat is now confined to Wales and the adjacent parts of
England. It extends eastwards only to the Urals.
Habitat. Western polecats live mainly in lowland wooded country, but are also
found on river banks and marshes, and frequently around farms.
Habits. Western polecats are mainly terrestrial, rarely climbing or swimming.
They are solitary and nocturnal. Scent glands, situated on either side of the
anus, produce a musk as in all mustelids, but in the polecats it is particularly
fetid and is released when the animal is alarmed as well as when it is marking
territory. Polecats feed upon rodents, rabbits, frogs, birds, earthworms, insects
and probably also upon carrion.

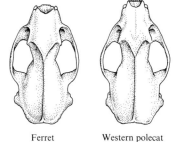

Ferret   Western polecat

Skulls of ferret and polecat ($\times$ $\frac{1}{2}$)

STEPPE POLECAT   *Mustela eversmanni*   **Plate 24**
Identification. The Steppe polecat closely resembles the Western polecat. It is
considerably paler above although the legs, feet and parts of the underside are
dark.
Range. Eastern Europe, from south Russia westwards as far as eastern Austria
and East Germany. Eastwards throughout central Asia to Manchuria.
Habitat. Grassland and farmland.
Habits. Steppe polecats resemble western polecats in their way of life except
that they more often live in burrows, either excavated by themselves or taken
over from sousliks or hamsters. They are also more often active in daylight.
Sousliks and hamsters are important items of diet where they occur but many
other kinds of prey are taken.

DOMESTIC FERRET *Mustela furo* **Plate 24**

Identification. Domesticated ferrets resemble polecats except in colour. They vary from albinos (usually a uniform creamy white, with or without pink eyes) through various shades of light brown, to a pattern and colour closely approaching that of the Western polecat. Since they are interfertile with wild western polecats, and often are interbred with them, every intermediate may occur. Most feral populations revert to a form that has the pattern of the wild Western polecat but in a rather dilute, faded form. Skulls of pure-bred ferrets differ from those of western polecats, but resemble those of steppe polecats, in having a narrower central 'waist' when viewed from above – under 15mm in ferrets, over 15mm in western polecats (see figure).

Range. Established feral populations resulting from escaped domestic ferrets are found in parts of Britain, especially on islands (Anglesey, Man, Lewis, Arran) and also on some Mediterranean islands (Sardinia, Sicily). They are not likely to persist as separate, recognizable forms where wild polecats occur.

Habitat and habits. Domestic ferrets are widely kept, especially for the control of rabbits. Feral animals behave as polecats.

MARBLED POLECAT *Vormela peregusna* **Plate 23**

Identification. The Marbled polecat closely resembles the Western and Steppe polecats in size and form but has a unique mottled coat, creamy-brown flecked with dark brown on the back and almost uniformly black below. It has a black and white facial pattern and the ears are more prominent than in the other polecats. The tail is bushy and black-tipped.

Range. In Europe found only in the extreme southeast, in Rumania, Bulgaria, Thrace and northern Greece. It extends eastwards through southern Russia and Turkestan to eastern China.

Habitat. Dry grassland, scrub and open woodland.

Habits. Similar to the Steppe polecat.

PINE MARTEN *Martes martes* **Plate 24**

Identification. The Pine marten is about the size of a small domestic cat but with the longer muzzle, short ears and short legs of the weasel family. It could be mistaken for a mink but is larger, with more prominent ears and a large and conspicuous pale patch on the throat and chest. This patch varies in colour from dull orange to cream but is never pure white as in the otherwise similar Beech marten.

Range. Most of Europe except for the extreme southeast and southwest. Present but local in Britain and Ireland. It extends eastwards to western Siberia, beyond which it is replaced by the closely related Sable.

Habitat. Mainly coniferous or mixed forest but also in deciduous forest and sometimes on open rocky ground and cliffs. Not usually above the tree-line on mountains, up to about 2000m in the Alps and Pyrenees.

Habits. Pine martens are solitary and hunt mainly at night or around dusk and dawn. Although they travel mostly on the ground they are extremely agile climbers and can move at great speed through the tree-tops. They prey mainly upon rodents, including voles, mice and squirrels, and birds. The den is usually in a hollow tree or rock crevice. Mating occurs in late summer and a single litter of about three young is born in the following spring. The young remain with the mother until the autumn.

BEECH MARTEN *Martes foina*   Plate 24
Identification. The Beech marten is very similar to the Pine marten, differing mainly in the throat patch which is pure white without any trace of yellow. The pale patch is variable in extent but usually less extensive than in the Pine marten and often divided by a dark strip in the centre. On Crete it is reduced to a small fleck or may be absent.
Range. Found throughout southern and central Europe but absent from Scandinavia and from Britain and Ireland. Its range extends into Asia east to the Altai and Himalayas.
Habitat. The Beech marten lives in deciduous woodland and also on open rocky hillsides, up to 2400m in the Alps, well above the tree-line. It is frequently found around buildings.
Habits. As for the Pine marten. Dens are often made in buildings, for example in farm lofts and ruins. Beech martens feed especially upon mice, shrews and birds, supplemented by berries in autumn.

WOLVERINE *Gulo gulo*   Plate 25
Identification. The Wolverine is the largest member of the weasel family, a little larger than a Red fox and more heavily built. It could be mistaken for a bear cub but differs in having short, weasel-like ears, a conspicuous tail and pale (but sometimes obscure) bands along the flanks and across the cheeks.
Range. In Europe confined to Scandinavia, Finland and northern Russia from where it extends eastwards throughout Siberia, Alaska and Canada.
Habitat. Forest and tundra.
Habits. Wolverines live mainly on the ground although they sometimes climb. They are solitary and nocturnal. In summer they feed on a variety of rodents, birds, eggs and invertebrates as well as fruit and berries, occasionally tackling large prey up to the size of a reindeer, especially ones that are sick or injured. In winter they specialize in carrion, travelling long distances and gorging on carrion when they find a carcase (hence the alternative name of Glutton). Mating takes place in spring or summer and development of the young is delayed so that the litter of two or three is produced the following spring. The young stay with the mother during their first winter.

OTTER *Lutra lutra*   Plate 25
Identification. Otters have the slim build of the smaller mustelids, such as polecats and mink, but the long tail is unique, being thick and fleshy and tapering gradually to a point. All four feet are webbed. In the water otters can be distinguished from the plumper aquatic rodents, such as the Coypu and Beaver, and the much smaller Mink by the combination of speed, agility, large size and slender build. Their presence can be most easily detected by searching for the regular sites where droppings are deposited, for example on a prominent boulder in a river. The droppings usually contain many fish scales and bones and have a characteristic smell.

Droppings (spraint) of an otter on a river boulder

Range. Formerly throughout Europe except for Iceland, but now absent, or rare and seriously declining, in many lowland and especially industrial areas, for example in West Germany and the Midlands of England. Also in north-western Africa and throughout most of Asia.

Habitat. Rivers, lakes and sheltered sea coasts.

Habits. Otters are solitary, nocturnal and elusive animals. They spend the day in a den, often amongst tree roots on a river bank or under rocks. They run on land with a bounding gait but hunt mainly in water, swimming and diving with great agility. When swimming fast they hold the front feet against the flanks and propel themselves by vertical undulations of the body and tail, and powerful strokes of the hind feet. They prey mainly upon fish – many different kinds including eels, trout, perch and sticklebacks – but also take amphibians, cray-fish, water birds and water voles. On the coast crabs are commonly eaten. Young are born at any time of the year but mainly in spring. There are usually two or three in a litter.

BADGER *Meles meles* **Plate 25**

Identification. The Badger is a thickset animal about the size of a corgi dog. It is unmistakable if seen well, with a black longitudinal stripe along the side of the white head, grey upperparts, black underside and legs, and short grey tail. The burrows or 'sets' are fairly easily recognized in woodland or hedgerows, typi-cally having a number of holes several metres apart, each at least 20cm in diameter and with a large accumulation of soil in front (usually containing characteristic black and white hairs).

Range. Throughout Europe except for northern Scandinavia. Present on Brit-ain and Ireland but not in Iceland. Widespread in temperate Asia.

Habitat. Badgers are found in deciduous woodland but also on open pastures, being most abundant where there is a mixture of the two. They do not extend significantly above the tree-line on mountains.

Habits. Badgers are more sociable than other mustelids. They occupy extensive systems of underground passages – 'sets' – with several openings. These are used and often enlarged by successive generations, often resulting in very large spoil heaps accummulating in front of the entrances. Each set may be occupied by several animals and there may be several sets within the territory of a group. Badgers are nocturnal. They feed mainly on earthworms but a great variety of other food is taken, both animal (for example voles, moles, rabbits, frogs, grubs and carrion), and vegetable (for example bulbs, fruit and nuts). Well marked paths lead from the sets and regular dung pits are used. Badgers are less active in cold weather but do not hibernate. Mating takes place mainly in spring but development of the young is delayed and the litter, up to four, is born late in the following winter.

MONGOOSES and GENET: family Viverridae

This family includes a great variety of small and medium carnivores, including the civets, mongooses and genets, that tend to replace the mustelids in the Old-world tropics. Two mongooses and one genet occur in Europe, probably as a result of introduction.

EGYPTIAN MONGOOSE *Herpestes ichneumon*   **Plate 25**
Identification. The Egyptian Mongoose has the same build as the smaller members of the weasel family such as the polecats and mink, with short legs, short ears and elongate body, but it can be distinguished by the long tapering tail, and the uniform but rather coarse and grizzled coat.
Range. These mongooses are found in southern Spain and Portugal (probably as a result of an early introduction) and have been more recently introduced to the island of Mljet, Yugoslavia. They also occur in Asia Minor and most of Africa.
Habitat. Scrub, rocky hillsides.
Habits. Mongooses are mainly nocturnal but are also more active by day than most other carnivores of their size. They are rather strictly terrestrial. They prey upon rabbits, rodents, birds and reptiles, including snakes. They break eggs by throwing them backwards between their hind legs against a rock. They are solitary except that the young animals, usually two to four in a litter, remain with their mother for several months.

INDIAN GREY MONGOOSE *Herpestes edwardsi*   Not illustrated
Identification. This mongoose is slightly smaller than the Egyptian mongoose (head and body about 45cm), with a relatively longer tail, about equal to the head and body. The colour is a grizzled greyish brown and the tip of the tail is paler than the rest.
Range. A native of India and southwestern Asia, introduced in the 1960s to Italy about 100km south of Rome.
Habitat and habits. As for the Egyptian mongoose.

GENET   *Genetta genetta*   **Plate 25**
Identification. The Genet is like a small, slim cat with spotted coat, long banded tail, short legs, sharp muzzle and prominent ears.
Range. Iberia, including the Balearic Islands, and most of France except the north and east. Also in Israel, Arabia and most of Africa.
Habitat. Woodland and scrub, up to 2000m in the Pyrenees.
Habits. Genets are agile climbers, moving with remarkable ease even in thorny bushes and trees. They are solitary and nocturnal and prey mainly upon rodents, particularly wood mice, birds and, especially in southern Spain and the Balearic Islands, reptiles. Berries and insects are also eaten. Two or three young are born in the spring.

RACCOONS: family Procyonidae

A family of medium-sized carnivores in the Americas of which one species has been introduced to Europe.

RACCOON   *Procyon lotor*   **Plate 26**
Identification. The Raccoon is a cat-sized animal, easily distinguished by its black mask and banded tail. (The Raccoon-dog, plate 22, which has a similar black mask does not have a banded tail.) Useful signs of the presence of a raccoon include scratch marks outside tree-holes (*c*. 12–15cm diameter) and prints on muddy river banks which show five long, unwebbed toes on each foot.
Range. Germany (East and West) and parts of adjacent countries. The Raccoon was introduced from North America and is spreading rapidly.
Habitat. Woodland, especially close to water.
Habits. The Raccoon is nocturnal and usually spends the day in a den in a tree-hole, sometimes at a considerable height, or amongst rocks. It is an agile climber and a competent swimmer but forages mainly on the ground. An omnivorous animal, it feeds on a wide variety of animal prey – frogs, rodents, fish, crayfish, molluscs and insects – as well as on fruit, nuts and cereals. Its long fingers can manipulate food dexterously. Raccoons are inactive for long periods in cold winters. They breed in spring, producing a litter of three or four young which follow their mother through their first winter.

CATS: family Felidae

These elusive nocturnal predators are the most completely carnivorous of the carnivores. They feed especially on mammals, birds and frogs. Compared with other carnivores cats have short muzzles and powerful paws with retractile claws. Their footprints therefore lack any indication of the claws.

LYNX   *Felis lynx*   **Plate 26**
Identification. The Lynx is much larger than the Wild cat or domestic cats, and especially much longer in the leg. Its ears and cheeks are tufted and its tail is short. The spotting of its coat is variable, being least in the far north, more prominent in the Carpathians, and most marked in Iberia and the Balkans.

(Spanish animals are sometimes considered to represent a separate species, the Pardel lynx, *Felis pardina*.) Their footprints are about twice the size of those of Wild or domestic cats (plate 45) and are without claw marks.

Range. Scandinavia, eastern Europe (montane in south) and Spain. Also in most of northern Asia and Canada. Lynx are generally very scarce but are strictly protected in most countries. They have recently been reintroduced in Switzerland and Bavaria.

Habitat. The Lynx is found mainly in coniferous forest in the north and in mountains but in Spain it also lives in lowland scrub, such as in the Coto Doñana Reserve.

Habits. A solitary nocturnal predator, the Lynx hunts by stealth on the ground or pounces from a low branch. It preys mainly upon hares, but rodents, young deer and ground birds, such as grouse and woodcock, are also caught. It is generally silent except for a wailing call made by the male in spring. Lynx are active throughout the winter. They breed in spring, producing a litter of two or three kittens in early summer in a den amongst rocks or in a hollow tree. The kittens remain with their mother through their first winter.

WILD CAT   *Felis silvestris*   **Plate 26**

Identification. The Wild cat is the size of a large domestic cat and if only glimpsed in the wild may be difficult to distinguish from it. Intermediate forms occur, produced by the inter-breeding of wild cats with feral domestic cats, but these are rare and most wild cats can be distinguished by their rather short, thick, bushy tail which is marked with discrete dark rings, a coat pattern of obscure stripes without blotches and pale paws. Their footprints lack claw marks but are not distinguishable from those of a domestic cat.

Range. Southern Europe north to the Tatras and Carpathians; Scotland. Also throughout Africa and western Asia.

Habitat. Forest and scrub; wild cats are now mainly confined to montane forests in the north of their range.

Habits. The Wild cat is mainly solitary and nocturnal. It is an agile climber but hunts mainly on the ground by stalking and pouncing. Its prey consists predominantly of rodents but it also takes rabbits, birds and frogs, rarely fish. Its voice is the same as that of the domestic cat. Wild cats breed in the spring and usually produce one litter of three to five young in May; second litters may indicate hybridization with domestic cats. The young disperse in the autumn. In contrast to domestic cats, wild cats do not appear to play with live prey and they do not generally bury their droppings.

DOMESTIC CAT   *Felis catus*   **Plate 26**

The domestic cat was derived from the Wild cat (probably first in North Africa) and is interfertile with it. Feral cats occur throughout Europe in town and countryside alike, many of them virtually independent of human contact. Those most resembling Wild cats usually differ in having longer, more pointed tails, with less clearly marked rings, and many have some rounded blotches on the flanks rather than vertical stripes. They usually have second and third litters during the summer.

PINNIPEDES: order Pinnipedia

Of the three families of pinnipedes, the seals, walrus and sea-lions, the last (Otariidae) are not found in European waters, although Californian sea-lions (*Zalophus californianus* – the species usually kept in zoos and circuses) have been known to escape and survive for some time in coastal waters.

SEALS: family Phocidae

Seals are found mostly in coastal waters and may be seen resting ashore on rocky and sandy beaches at all times of the year. On land they move with a wriggling motion without help from the hind feet, which form flippers used only for swimming. Identification in the water is difficult since usually only the head is visible: on land it is easier but there is much confusing variation in colour and pattern. Young animals in particular often lack the distinctive features that enable adults to be identified. South and west of the Baltic only Common and Grey seals are likely to be found, with the Monk seal the only species in the Mediterranean.

COMMON SEAL   *Phoca vitulina*   **Plate 27**
Identification. The Common seal can be distinguished from the Grey seal by its smaller size (sexes about equal), short muzzle with concave profile between forehead and nose, and closely set nostrils forming a V ('V for *vitulina*') when seen from the front. Pups are usually dark-coated at birth, occasionally with a white coat which is shed within a day or two. The Ringed seal is very similar in appearance.
Range. North Sea and Atlantic coasts of the British Isles, Scandinavia, Iceland and the western Baltic. Also on the coasts of eastern North America and the North Pacific.
Habitat. Common seals are usually found in shallow coastal waters, in estuaries, sheltered bays and fjords, and are occasionally encountered entering rivers.
Habits. At low tide common seals will haul themselves out of the water on to the rocks and especially on to sand-banks, where they may be seen in groups of up to 100, but usually separate from other species. They feed on fish with some molluscs and crustaceans. When diving they usually stay down for 5–10 minutes in shallow water, but dives with a duration of up to 30 minutes and reaching a depth of 100m are possible. These seals are generally sedentary and usually silent but pups have a high pitched wail. They breed in midsummer. Single pups are born on a tidal rock or sand-bank and are able to swim and dive from birth. They may climb on their mother's back.

RINGED SEAL   *Phoca hispida*   **Plate 28**
Identification. This is the commonest and smallest seal of the Arctic. It is very similar to the Common seal but the spots that pattern its coat tend to be surrounded by light rings. In the centre of its back the spots usually join to form a uniformly dark band but pattern and colour are very variable. Its nostrils

are V-shaped. Pups have a creamy white coat for the first two or three weeks.

Range. The Ringed seal's breeding range is circumpolar and confined to the high Arctic, the Baltic and Lakes Saimaa (Finland) and Ladoga (USSR). Regularly found on the coasts of Iceland and Norway in winter, and vagrants have been recorded southward towards Scotland and the Netherlands.

Habitat. Inshore waters, in bays and fjords, entering fresh water readily.

Habits. These seals feed mainly on small crustaceans. Some southward migration occurs in autumn but most remain in the Arctic in winter, feeding under the ice and breathing at holes kept open by regular use. Freshwater populations are resident. Ringed seals breed on land-fast ice in spring, widely dispersed. The pups remain on the ice for about two months during which time they moult from a white to a dark coat.

GREY SEAL   *Halichoerus grypus*   Plate 27

Identification. This species is larger than the Common seal, with the males considerably larger than the females. A long muzzle and arched nose are especially characteristic of adult males; females and young have a nose of straighter profile but it is never concave as in the Common seal. The nostrils are widely separated. In males the pattern tends to consist of light blotches on a dark background, in females of dark blotches on a light background but this difference is not conspicuous. Young are white at birth and remain white for several weeks.

Range. Breeding colonies can be found in Iceland, the Faroes, Britain, Ireland, Brittany, the Baltic and northern Norway; young animals and non-breeding adults are more widespread. Also on the eastern coast of Canada.

Habitat. The Grey seal is entirely marine. Breeding colonies are established mostly on small rocky islands, generally on more exposed situations than those used by the Common seal.

Habits. Grey seals haul out on rocks and sand-banks. They are often noisy, making a variety of loud wailing and grunting noises. They feed mainly on fish and breed mainly in large colonies, on rocky shores in late autumn in most of their range but on ice in spring in the Baltic. Bulls defend territories for about a month. Pups moult from a white to a dark coat after 2 weeks. They stay on shore, being suckled two or three times per day for $2\frac{1}{2}$–3 weeks, and are then deserted.

MONK SEAL   *Monachus monachus*   Plate 27

Identification. This is the only seal likely to be seen in or near the Mediterranean and the Black Seas. It is a uniform brown with an irregular white patch below. Pups are completely black for several weeks before moulting.

Range. Mediterranean and Black Seas, also Atlantic coast of north-western Africa. This species is very rare and numbers are declining; their survival is seriously threatened by the disturbance of breeding beaches by holiday-makers and persecution by fishermen.

Habitat. The Monk seal is entirely marine. Its breeding colonies are established on secluded sandy beaches, for instance in caves or below cliffs.

Habits. This species breeds in autumn, in small colonies, the pups remaining ashore for about six weeks.

HARP SEAL   *Pagophilus groenlandicus*   **Plate 28**
Identification. The distinctive black and white pattern of the Harp seal is most clearly marked in adult males; in females the pigmented areas are more brownish and tend to be broken into spots. Pups are white at birth. Juveniles are easily confused with Common or Ringed seals but their spots are usually more sparse and head and flippers are darker than the body.
Range. Harp seals breed in the White Sea, and also around Greenland, Jan Mayen and in northeastern Canada. Most remain within the Arctic in winter, but vagrants occur as far south as Britain.
Habitat. Pack-ice and open sea.
Habits. These seals breed in large colonies on pack-ice in early spring. Pups are deserted at about two weeks when they moult from a white to a grey coat and enter the water in three to four weeks.

BEARDED SEAL   *Erignathus barbatus*   **Plate 28**
Identification. This is a large, rare, Arctic seal. Its uniform colour and very prominent whiskers are distinctive (but see also the Walrus, below). Pups are greyish brown at birth becoming slightly spotted at the first moult.
Range. Bearded seals breed on the Arctic coasts of Norway and the USSR, also Spitzbergen, Jan Mayen, Greenland and northern Canada. They are generally resident but vagrants occur south to the North Sea.
Habitat. Shallow coastal waters.
Habits. These seals feed mainly on molluscs. They are confiding and curious, approaching small boats without fear. They make loud whistling and wailing calls. Bearded seals go ashore on ice-free coasts in summer but breed on ice-floes in spring, without forming large colonies.

HOODED SEAL   *Cystophora cristata*   **Plate 28**
Identification. The adult male of this species is unmistakable, for it has a sac of skin on the nose which is normally slack and wrinkled and hangs down over the mouth. This sac is capable of being inflated to about the size of a football or more (see plate). Females have a less conspicuous sac. A pattern of irregular blotches gives this species a resemblance to the Grey seal but there is more white in the Hooded seal, especially on the flanks. Pups are silvery bluish grey above and white below, with the head dark ('blue-backs').
Range. Hooded seals breed at Jan Mayen and west to Baffin Island but they disperse to Iceland, Spitzbergen and Arctic Norway. Vagrants may be seen as far south as Britain.
Habitat. Drifting ice and open sea.
Habits. These seals are solitary or live in small scattered groups. They dive deeply. Pups are born on ice, suckled for two weeks, and remain on the ice for a further two weeks.

WALRUS: family Odobenidae

WALRUS   *Odobenus rosmarus*   **Plate 28**
Identification. Its large size, uniform colour and enlarged bristly upper lip distinguish the Walrus from all species of seals. Tusks are a prominent feature of adult males and some females. The coat of the Walrus is very sparse,

especially in adults. On land its hind feet point forwards and help to support the body.

Range. Arctic coasts, where walrus usually remain close to the edge of the ice. In the European sector they are only regularly seen around Spitzbergen but vagrants occur south to Iceland and Norway and rarely as far south as Britain.

Habits. The Walrus feeds mainly on bivalve molluscs; it is sometimes predatory on seals. A gregarious creature, it breeds on the ice in spring. Pups swim from birth but remain with their mothers for at least a year.

ODD-TOED UNGULATES: order Perissodactyla

This order comprises the horses, rhinoceroses and tapirs. There are no wild or truly feral representatives in Europe but in some areas horses and donkeys live in a semi-wild state.

HORSES: family Equidae

In all members of the horse family there is only one toe, with a large hoof, on each foot.

DOMESTIC HORSE   *Equus caballus*
The domestic horse was derived from the Wild horse or Tarpan, *Equus ferus*, which extended from eastern Europe through the steppe zone to Mongolia. The wild form became extinct in Europe by the early 19th century or earlier, but an eastern race known as the Przewalski horse (*E. f. przewalskii*) survived in Mongolia and adjacent parts of China until recently and many animals of this race that are almost or entirely pure-bred remain in captivity. These ancestral wild horses are a uniform light greyish brown, usually with faint transverse striping on the legs, a pale muzzle, no forelock and a short erect mane. In

Przewalski horse

various parts of Europe a number of localized primitive breeds of domestic horses survive that show some of these characters although all have drooping manes, for example the New Forest and Exmoor ponies in England and the Camargue horses in southern France. Attempts have been made to 'reconstruct' the wild Tarpan by selective breeding of primitive domestic breeds and crossing with Przewalski horses, and a semi-wild herd of this kind exists in Poland. In most of these free-ranging herds the breeding is controlled to some degree and surplus animals are used, for example as riding ponies.

Molar tooth of a horse

DOMESTIC DONKEY *Equus asinus*
The domestic donkey was derived from the wild ass of northern Africa, *Equus africanus*, which probably never occurred wild in Europe. It is commonly kept as a beast of burden in southern Europe where some semi-wild populations also occur. There are also many in Ireland where they were introduced from Spain in exchange for horses during the Napoleonic wars. Compared with horses, donkeys are small, with long ears, an erect mane, usually a narrow dark central stripe on the back and a vertical one on each shoulder, and the base of the tail short-haired.

Domestic donkey

EVEN-TOED UNGULATES: order Artiodactyla

This order includes most of the large, herbivorous mammals and all those with 'cloven hooves', that is with two central toes on each foot hooved and equally developed. All mammals with paired horns and antlers also belong here although not all even-toed ungulates are horned.

PIGS: family Suidae

All pigs have long snouts with continuous rows of teeth of which one in each row, the canine, is enlarged into a tusk. There is only one species in Europe.

WILD BOAR   *Sus scrofa*   **Plate 29**
Identification. The Wild boar is the ancestor of the domestic pig which it resembles in its heavy body, short neck and short, thin legs. The coat is dense and bristly and the snout is always long and tapering, never compressed as in the short-faced breeds of domestic pigs. Adult males have prominent angular tusks, those of the upper jaw curving upwards to lie against but inside the straighter lower ones. Females have the canines much smaller. The young at first have prominent longitudinal stripes of brown and cream.
Range. Wild boar are found in most of Europe except Britain, Ireland, Iceland and Scandinavia (but there are some introduced animals in southern Sweden and Norway). Their range also extends throughout central and southern Asia. Wild boars are extensively hunted for sport but are also persecuted as crop-raiders. They remain abundant in most countries with extensive forest.
Habitat. Deciduous woodland.
Habits. Wild boars live alone or in small groups, the males separate from the females except during the rutting season in winter. Adult females are usually accompanied by their young, sometimes of two successive litters. They are mainly nocturnal, often travelling extensively and foraging in cultivated ground at night. They eat a great variety of food, mainly vegetable but also animal. They dig for bulbs and tubers and in autumn and winter acorns and beech mast are important in their diet. They become very fat in autumn but remain active throughout the winter. The mating season is in winter and the young are born in spring or early summer, with any number up to ten in a litter. They remain in a rough nest for a few days before following their mother around.

CATTLE, SHEEP AND GOATS: family Bovidae

This is the largest family of even-toed ungulates. They are characterized especially by the presence of paired, permanent, unbranched horns, and by the habit of rumination or chewing the cud whereby food is returned from the stomach to the mouth for further mastication after partial digestion.

BISON   *Bison bonasus*   **Plate 29**
Identification. Bison could only be confused with domestic cattle. They are similar in size but adult males have a distinctive mane of long woolly hair on the shoulders and neck and the hind quarters are relatively slim. The coat is a uniform dark brown. Females and young more closely resemble domestic cattle but have the head rather short and the shoulders slightly humped. Both sexes have horns.
Range. The European bison became extinct in the wild by the 1920s but has been reintroduced from captive stock to parts of Poland, Rumania and Russia. The principal Polish herd, in the Bialowieza Forest, was established in the 1920s. Bison also occur in North America (where they are usually called buffalo) but the American ones differ slightly from the European form and are variously considered a distinct species or subspecies.
Habitat. Deciduous forest.
Habits. Mature bulls are usually solitary for most of the year but females and young live in herds of ten to thirty animals. They feed by browsing the leaves of trees and shrubs and also by grazing. In autumn they add acorns to their diet and in winter heathers and evergreens. The mating season or rut takes place in August when the bulls join the matriarchal herds and mark their rutting territories by churning the soil with their horns and scratching trees. The cows leave the herd in early summer to have their single calves which are weaned by the autumn.

DOMESTIC CATTLE   *Bos taurus*   **Plate 29**
Domestic cattle arose from the wild Aurochs, which lived in Europe and western Asia until, in the 17th century, it became completely extinct in the wild. No cattle are truly feral (that is wild and uncontrolled) in Europe but several localized breeds have been preserved little changed since medieval times and are therefore much closer to the ancestral form than are the modern improved breeds. Amongst these primitive breeds are a number of herds of pure-bred 'white park cattle' in Britain, for example that at Chillingham in Northumberland (plate 29).

DOMESTIC WATER BUFFALO   *Bubalus bubalis*
Both wild water buffalo, *Bubalus arnee*, and their domestic derivative *B. bubalis* are found in southeastern Asia, but domestic animals are used in parts of southern Europe, especially in Italy. They are a uniform dark grey, and differ from domestic cattle mainly in the form of the horns, which are flattened in section and curve backwards.

MUSK OX   *Ovibos moschatus*   **Plate 29**
Identification. Musk oxen are like small cattle but appear very short-legged because of a long shaggy coat. The head and neck are short and the horns arise in contact on top of the head and bend downwards following the contours of the head before turning outwards and upwards. Both sexes have horns, those of the females being only slightly smaller than those of the males.
Range. A native of the American Arctic (including Greenland), extinct in the Eurasian Arctic since the end of the last glaciation but reintroduced in Spitzbergen (in 1929) and in the Dovre Fjell of southern Norway (in 1932) from

Water buffalo

where they have spread into the adjacent part of Sweden.
Habitat. Tundra.
Habits. Musk oxen live in small groups in summer and these join to form larger herds in winter. These groups contain males and females throughout the year. The mating season is in summer and a single calf is born the following May. Musk oxen feed on most tundra plants including grass, sedge and dwarf shrubs. When threatened, for example by wolves, they have a characteristic defence behaviour, forming a dense circle with the adults on the circumference facing outwards.

SHEEP: genus *Ovis*

Sheep differ from goats in having very thick, tightly coiled horns, glands in front of the eyes and no beard. Domestic sheep usually have a long pendulous tail.

MOUFLON *Ovis musimon* **Plate 30**
Identification. Mouflon resemble rather slim domestic sheep but have a normal coat of hair, any wool being concealed beneath ordinary straight body hair. Fully adult males have heavy, curled horns and are reddish brown with a pale patch on each flank. In females there is no flank patch and the horns are small (the usual condition on Corsica) or absent (usual on Sardinia and most of the introduced populations in mainland Europe). The tail is dark, contrasting with white buttocks, as in some deer, but the shorter legs and neck should prevent confusion with deer. The muzzle is white, the amount of white increasing with age.
Range. Native or long-established on Corsica and Sardinia (and Cyprus); introduced from there to many parts of central and southern Europe as a game animal. Although the Mouflon is closely related to the wild sheep of western Asia it is possible that the populations on the Mediterranean islands owe their

origin to introduction by man of stock that was domesticated but little changed from their wild ancestors.

Habitat. On the Mediterranean islands mainly on open mountains around the tree-line and amongst scrub. Elsewhere in Europe in woodland, especially where there are clearings or adjacent grassland.

Habits. A gregarious species. The females and young form flocks throughout the year. Adult males form separate flocks, individuals joining the matriarchal flock during the rutting season in autumn. The lambs are born in spring, singly or as twins. Mouflon are mainly grazers, feeding principally at night on grasses and sedges and resting by day in thick cover.

Soay sheep

DOMESTIC SHEEP   *Ovis aries*

Domestic sheep differ from their wild relatives (mainly the Asiatic mouflon or Urial, *Ovis orientalis*, of Asia Minor and Iran) by having the coat dominated by wool and lacking the straight hair that normally conceals the winter wool of the wild forms. Some localized primitive breeds of sheep have survived, unaffected by the great diversification of improved breeds that has occurred especially since the 18th century. One of the best known is the Soay sheep, feral on the island of Soay in the St Kilda group, Scotland, and now introduced also to the main island of St Kilda (Hirta) and widely kept in parks and zoos. Like many primitive breeds it is a uniform dark brown, with the build of a mouflon but with a coat of pure wool.

GOATS: genus *Capra*

Goats tend to have longer, less tightly curved horns than sheep, they lack facial glands and generally have a beard under the lower jaw (sometimes confined to males). Domestic goats commonly have the tail short and erect, in contrast to sheep; in wild forms the tail normally droops.

ALPINE IBEX   *Capra ibex*   **Plate 30**

Identification. A stocky goat found only at high altitude. Adult males have horns that sweep back in a single curve, diverging only slightly, with regular, prominent, closely-spaced ridges on the otherwise broad, flat front surface. The face is uniformly coloured (compare Chamois, p. 200). Females have very much smaller horns.

Range. In Europe Alpine ibex are confined to the Alps where they have been extensively reintroduced after reduction to a single herd in Gran Paradiso National Park in Italy. They are also found on the mountains of central Asia, the Himalayas, Arabia and northeastern Africa. In Europe they are strictly protected.

Habitat. On mountains, remaining above the tree-line all year, extending to the snow-line and usually considerably higher than chamois.

Habits. Ibex are extremely agile and sure-footed on steep rocks. Females and young form small herds in summer, with the males solitary or in small bachelor groups, often on higher ground. The rut takes place in winter and the kids are born in early summer, usually singly but occasionally twins. Ibex feed on many kinds of alpine vegetation – dwarf shrubs, grass, sedge and lichens.

SPANISH IBEX   *Capra pyrenaica*   **Plate 30**

Identification. The Spanish ibex is similar to the Alpine ibex but with the horns less prominently ribbed and spiralling outwards and upwards as well as back-wards, with the tips more divergent than in the Alpine ibex. The females have short horns. There is considerable variation in the shape of the horns between the various populations and it is possible that some, or even all, of the charac-teristics of the Spanish ibex are due to interbreeding with domestic goats at some time.

Range. Several isolated mountain groups of this species are found in Spain, modified to some extent by transplantation of animals, for example from central Spain to the southern side of the Pyrenees.

Habitat and habits. As for the Alpine ibex.

WILD GOAT   *Capra aegagrus*   **Plate 30**

Identification. This is the ancestor of the domestic goat which it resembles in many ways, but it can be distinguished from most domestic animals, and from the similar Alpine and Spanish ibexes, especially by the shape of the horns. These sweep back in a single gentle curve, only diverging slightly, and have a narrow keel on the front surface and obscure, widely spaced transverse ridges. Adult males have a beard, a dark stripe along the centre of the back and another across the shoulders. The females have short horns and more obscure markings. The tail is short and drooping (except during courtship, when the male holds the tail erect and pressed forwards).

Range. It is doubtful that any truly indigenous, pure-bred wild goats survive in Europe, but on Crete and some other Greek islands there are populations which, although probably introduced in antiquity, have been little affected by domestication or interbreeding with domestic stock. Similar populations also survive in many parts of southwestern Asia.

Habitat. Rocky hillsides and scrub.

Habits. Wild goats live in loose flocks, the males remaining separate except during the rut in late autumn or winter. They feed by browsing on trees and shrubs, often standing on their hind legs to reach high branches, as well as by grazing.

DOMESTIC GOAT   *Capra hircus*   Plate 30

Feral populations of domestic goats are found in Scotland, Wales, Ireland and on many Mediterranean islands, generally on rocky hills or cliffs. Many are of especial interest because they were derived from primitive domestic stock before it was affected by the development of modern breeds. Domestic goats generally differ from the ancestral wild goat, *Capra aegagrus*, in having an additional spiral twist to the horns so that they turn outwards and upwards rather than simply backwards. The British feral goats are mostly long-haired and many are piebald. They are generally smaller than modern milk breeds and the females usually carry small horns. Their ecology and behaviour are similar to those of ibex and wild goats.

CHAMOIS   *Rupicapra rupicapra*   Plate 30

Identification. The Chamois is a goat-like animal confined to mountains but rather smaller and more slender in build than the ibexes. The sexes are similar, having small erect horns with a sharp backward-pointing hook at the tips, and a bold black and white pattern on the head. The coat is a light brown in summer changing to dark brown in winter.

Range. Found only on the mountains of mainland Europe north to the High Tatras, in a large number of isolated populations.

Habitat. Chamois live around the tree-line, moving up to the higher open slopes in summer and down into forest in winter, descending to about 800m in places.

Habits. Chamois are gregarious, the females and young forming small groups which may combine in winter to form herds of a hundred or more. The mature males live alone, joining the groups during the rutting season in late autumn or early winter. The males display to each other by erecting the hair along the midline of the back, making them look large and shaggy. The young are born singly in spring. Chamois feed mainly by day, grazing and browsing on a great variety of plants, including conifers in winter. They make a sharp whistle when alarmed and the young animals bleat like goats.

DEER: family Cervidae

Deer are the principal large browsing and grazing animals of Europe and are ruminants like the bovids, with complex stomachs adapted for 'chewing the cud'. Most are found especially in woodland, often resting in secluded areas of dense growth by day and emerging to feed in glades or on adjacent grassland or cultivation at night. The males of all deer, except the introduced Chinese water deer, have antlers, which are also borne by female reindeer. Antlers are formed of bone and are shed annually, usually in spring. While they are regrowing they are covered with shortly-haired skin, known as velvet. Antlers of mature males are distinctive but those of young animals are less diagnostic. The pattern of the rump and tail is distinctive in most species and is similar in both sexes.

CERVINE DEER: genus *Cervus*

These are large sociable deer. The females and young form matriarchal herds that are joined by the males only during the autumnal mating season, known as the rut. The antlers are shed in the spring and regrown by early autumn. The young calves are spotted.

RED DEER   *Cervus elaphus*   Plate 31

Identification. This is the largest deer in most of Europe (exceeded in size only by the Elk). The pale patch around its tail is buff, never pure white as in Sika and Fallow deer, and there is no black on the rump nor on the tail, which is quite prominent (see also Roe deer, p. 204). In most fully mature males (stags) the antlers have *two* points directed forwards from the lower part of the main stem. These points are very close together and widely separated from the third point. This pattern is unique to Red deer – but young stags usually lack the second point, so that their antlers are not always distinguishable from those of a mature Sika, although in Red deer the first point tends to make a right angle with the main stem (an acute angle in the Sika). Some stags, known as hummels, fail to develop antlers beyond small knobs. During the autumnal rutting season stags develop a mane of longer hair on the neck and this persists during the winter. The Red deer's coat is reddish brown in summer, greyer in winter.

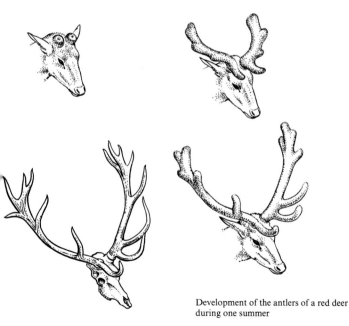

Development of the antlers of a red deer during one summer

Range. Most of Europe except Iceland and northern Scandinavia, but the distribution is scattered and many populations are the result of introductions, translocations or escapes from captivity in parks. Red deer also occur in North Africa, on most of the mountain ranges of central Asia and in western North America, where they are known as elk or wapiti.

Habitat. Red deer originally lived in open deciduous woodland, but now frequently are found on open moorland and mountains, in Scotland for example.

Habits. These gregarious deer form large herds when living in open country, but in woodland groups are smaller. Mountain populations show seasonal movement between alpine pasture in summer and valley bottoms or forest in winter. The autumnal rutting call of the stags is a loud roar or bellow. Stags wallow in mud or peat during the rut. A single calf is born in early summer. Red deer feed by grazing and browsing, their diet including heather and conifers in winter.

SIKA DEER   *Cervus nippon*   Plate 32

Identification. Sika are considerably smaller than red deer and a little smaller than fallow. The rump and tail pattern is the best guide to recognition: the rump is pure white with dark edging (as in the fallow deer) but the tail is short and white, with at most a diffuse greyish streak on the upper surface. The coat is usually clearly spotted in summer but almost unspotted, and much more grey, in winter. Antlers of mature males (bucks) resemble those of a young red deer stag, with never more than two, widely separated, points on the front of the main stem, each making an acute angle with the stem. Both sexes have a prominent white glandular patch on the hind legs, just below the central joint (the hock).

Range. A native of eastern Asia (Japan, eastern China, Taiwan), commonly kept in parks and now established in the wild in many parts of western Europe, including Britain and Ireland. In places a small amount of hybridization with Red deer has taken place, for example in northwestern England and southeastern Ireland.

Habitat. Woodland, including conifer plantations with clearings or adjacent open ground.

Habits. Sika live in small groups, usually keeping to thick cover by day and emerging at dusk to feed. The rutting call of the bucks is a sharp whistle. In other respects the life-cycle resembles that of the Red deer.

FALLOW DEER   *Cervus dama*   Plate 23

Identification. Fallow deer are intermediate in size between Red and Sika deer. They are usually boldly spotted in summer and unspotted and more grey in winter but the colour is very variable – dark grey and pale cream forms, lacking distinct spots, predominate locally. The tail pattern is distinctive, with the rump black and white, as in Sika, but the tail very long with a bold black line down the centre. The antlers of mature males (bucks) are usually distinctively flattened (palmate), a condition never found in Red or Sika deer, but the flattening may be poorly developed and inconspicuous. The lower part of the antlers is as in Sika, never with the additional point found in Red deer. There is a glandular patch on the hind leg, as in Sika but less conspicuous.

Range. The species is probably indigenous in the Mediterranean region but introduced populations of long standing occur through most of Europe including Britain and Ireland. This is the deer most frequently kept in parks.

Habitat. Mainly open woodland.

Habits. Fallow deer graze more than other deer but like all woodland deer they feed extensively on acorns and beech mast in autumn and winter. During the rutting period in autumn the bucks make a rhythmic barking or grunting sound. They also make scrapes in the ground with their antlers and urinate in them to establish territorial rights.

SPOTTED DEER *Cervus axis*   Plate 32

Identification. Spotted deer are boldly spotted at all seasons. The tail is long and dark-striped as in the Fallow deer but there is less white on the rump, without a black margin. The antlers have never more than three points which tend to be long and slender and are never flattened.

Range. An Indian species introduced and established in a few places in Europe, for example in Istria (Yugoslavia).

Habitat. Woodland.

Habits. Similar to Fallow deer. The rutting call of the bucks is a harsh bellow.

ELK *Alces alces*   Plate 33

Identification. Elk are by far the largest deer, with particularly long legs and high shoulders. They are generally dark without any light pattern on the rump or tail. The antlers of mature males (bulls) are usually flattened and palmate, with the hind margin smooth and numerous branches pointing forwards and upwards. They are much simpler in young animals and some adults retain a simple, branched form with little flattening. The muzzle is inflated and overhangs the mouth. The calves are unspotted.

Range. Scandinavia, Finland, northern Russia and eastern Poland. Also found throughout Siberia, Alaska and Canada (where they are known as Moose).

Habitat. Elk are most abundant where there is a mixture of forest and open ground, especially along river valleys and around lakes.

Habits. Elk are less gregarious than other large deer, most animals being seen singly. In summer they browse on deciduous trees such as willow and also on herbaceous waterside vegetation, often wading deeply in rivers and lakes. In winter they eat shoots and bark of trees and the foliage of conifers. The males make a bugling call during the rutting period in September and often spar. They shed their antlers in winter and the new ones are regrown and clear of velvet by August. Elk are kept as domestic animals in Russia.

REINDEER *Rangifer tarandus*   Plate 33

Identification. Reindeer are the only deer in which both sexes carry antlers although those of the females are usually smaller than those of the males. The males are usually without antlers during the winter but the females retain theirs until the early summer. The brow-tine – the lowest, forward projecting branch of the antler – is itself branched, a characteristic unique amongst deer. Colour and size are very variable. The wild tundra form in southern Norway and parts of Lappland is pale grey in winter (almost white in the north), darker greyish brown in summer and rather small. Domesticated animals are small and very variable in colour and pattern.

Range. Wild reindeer are now found on the mountains of southern Norway, on Spitzbergen and from eastern Finland through northern Siberia and arctic America (where they are known as Caribou). There is an introduced population on Iceland. A domesticated form is kept widely in Lappland and there is a herd of introduced domestic reindeer living in a semi-wild state in the Cairngorms in Scotland.

Habitat. Montane and arctic tundra, and (in Finland) open woodland.

Habits. Reindeer are gregarious, forming large matriarchal herds of females and young, although the adult males remain solitary. They join the herds during the autumn rutting season and leave again during the winter movements. In summer reindeer feed on a great variety of tundra plants, including grasses and sedges, but in winter they specialize on lichens, scraping the snow with their large hooves to expose the plants. Lowland reindeer (in Finland) migrate southwards in winter but the montane herds in Norway make only local seasonal movements. The young are born, usually singly, in May or June, and they can run with the herd within a few days of birth.

WHITE-TAILED DEER   *Odocoileus virginianus*   Plate 33

Identification. White-tailed deer are about the size of Fallow deer but are unspotted, reddish brown in summer, greyish in winter. The tail is broad and dark on the upper side, almost concealing the white rump when held low but exposing a conspicuous amount of white on the underside of the tail and on the rump when the tail is raised in flight. The main beam of the antlers slopes backwards then abruptly forwards with erect branches on the hind margin. Young fawns are spotted.

Range. The most widespread deer in North America, introduced and established in southwestern Finland.

Habitat. Woodland.

Habits. Similar to Red and Fallow deer. Moderately gregarious.

ROE DEER   *Capreolus capreolus*   Plate 34

Identification. The smallest native deer in Europe, usually seen singly in woodland. It is unique in having virtually no tail. The coat is a rich reddish brown in summer, with an obscure, pale rump patch; in winter it is greyish brown with a conspicuously white rump. The antlers have a very rough ring or 'coronet' around the base and never have more than three points. They are fully developed by May and are shed in early winter. The fawns are spotted.

Range. Generally abundant throughout Europe except for the far north but it is scarce in the Mediterranean lowlands. Present in Britain but absent from Ireland and Iceland. It also occurs across northern Asia to China.

Habitat. Woodland of all kinds, especially where there are clearings or plenty of low vegetation.

Habits. Roe deer tend to form small groups during the winter but otherwise are usually solitary. They are active mainly at night, spending the day in thick cover and often emerging at dusk to feed on adjacent open ground or in clearings. They browse on shrubs, especially bramble and bilberry and also on most broad-leaved trees. The rutting season is in July and August when the bucks mark their territory by 'fraying' small trees, rubbing the bark with the antlers until it is tattered and the wood is exposed. The fawns are born in early summer and twins are common. Both sexes make a sharp bark.

MUNTJAC *Muntiacus reevesi*   **Plate 34**

Identification. The smallest deer in Europe, not much larger than a fox. It has a characteristically rounded back and the male carries very small simple antlers pointing backwards from the end of permanent projections or 'pedicels'. The male also has a pair of slender tusks in the upper jaw, just visible when the mouth is closed but much less conspicuous than in the Chinese water deer and not usually detectable at a distance. The tail is short and broad, the same colour as the back when lowered but conspicuously white below when raised as it is when the animal is alarmed. The fawns are chestnut brown with buff spots.

Range. An eastern Chinese species, introduced and well established in much of southern England.

Habitat. Woodland with thick undergrowth.

Habits. Muntjac are elusive, solitary deer, active mainly at night but also by day if they are undisturbed. The bucks shed their antlers in early summer and regrow them by the autumn, but there is no clearly defined breeding season and fawns may be born at any time of year. In England muntjac feed mainly upon the leaves of bramble and other shrubs, but also eat fruit and acorns. They make a remarkably loud bark, usually repeated over long periods at regular intervals of four or five seconds.

CHINESE WATER DEER *Hydropotes inermis*   **Plate 34**

Identification. Chinese water deer are the only deer in Europe that never have antlers. They are small deer, intermediate in size between Muntjac and Roe, with a rather uniform yellowish-brown coat, large broad ears and no conspicuous pattern on the tail nor rump. The males have long slender protruding tusks in the upper jaw, up to 8cm long and visible under good field conditions. The fawns are spotted.

Range. Native in eastern China, introduced and well established in eastern England.

Habitat. Grassland, marshes and open woodland.

Habits. Chinese water deer are solitary and elusive, active mainly at night. The bucks make a whistling call during the rutting season in early winter and they also bark sharply. The young are born in May or June. Twins are most frequent but this species is unusual amongst deer in that litters of three or four are not uncommon and as many as six have been recorded.

WHALES, DOLPHINS AND
PORPOISES: order Cetacea

The whales and their smaller relatives the dolphins and porpoises are commonly referred to as cetaceans. There is no clear-cut difference between the three – large ones are generally called whales, small ones dolphins. In British usage the word porpoise refers only to the common porpoise and a few similar, non-European species, but in America it is commonly used for many species here called dolphins. Cetaceans are entirely aquatic, never going ashore voluntarily, and, except for a few in tropical rivers, entirely marine. They are more extremely adapted for an aquatic life than the seals – they completely lack hind limbs, the skin is naked, the tail is expanded into a horizontally flattened 'fluke' which provides the main propulsive force, there is no neck and the nostrils are situated on top of the head, usually far back from the tip of the snout. Cetaceans need to breath air at the surface of the sea. Some species can stay under water for up to an hour before surfacing to take a series of deep breaths, although usually they will 'blow' more frequently. In the big whales the moisture in the exhaled air usually condenses to produce a visible cloud whose characteristics can sometimes help in identifying the species concerned.

Field identification of cetaceans is usually very difficult since only brief, intermittent glimpses are obtained as the animal breaks the surface to breath. However dolphins sometimes leap clear of the water and larger whales occasionally do so. Useful characters to look for are the size, shape and position of the fin on the back, the shape of the head, including the presence or absence of a 'beak' and any pattern of light markings on the usually dark surface. Most species are gregarious so that if one is seen it is likely that there will be others nearby.

Cetaceans sometimes become stranded on beaches when they rarely survive for more than a few hours. In such animals a careful study of the teeth, or of baleen plates in the mouth of the toothless whales, is valuable in arriving at a precise identification. In Britain the legal position relating to the ownership and the responsibility for disposing of stranded cetaceans is complex and any find should be reported at once to the local Coastguard Officer.

There are two very distinct groups or suborders of cetaceans, the baleen whales (suborder Mysticeti) and the toothed whales (suborder Odontoceti).

BALEEN WHALES: suborder Mystaceti

These are mostly large whales. They have no teeth but the upper jaws bear numerous triangular horny plates, known as baleen, set transversely and close together, and hanging down into the mouth cavity. The inner edge of each baleen plate is frayed into a hairy fringe which serves to strain small food items from the water as the whale takes a mouthful of water then raises the floor of the mouth to squeeze the water between the baleen plates and out through the sides of the mouth. The food consists mainly of shrimp-like crustaceans – 'krill' – and to a lesser extent small fish. The large whales have all been seriously over-exploited by commercial whalers and are very rare in European waters. They mostly migrate seasonally between warm temperate waters, where they breed in winter, and the colder northern waters, where the best feeding grounds are located in summer.

In stranded animals the size and colour of the baleen is a useful guide to identification. Any variation in colour from front to back and on either side of the mouth should be noted.

RORQUALS and HUMPBACK WHALE:
family Balaenopteridae

The rorquals are slim, streamlined, fast-swimming whales. They all have a small fin on the back, well behind the middle. The head is narrow and pointed and the throat has numerous longitudinal grooves allowing expansion and contraction when feeding. The paired flippers are narrow and pointed. The blow is erect and appears single (plate 36). The Humpback whale belongs to the same family although it differs in being plump and slow-moving.

FIN WHALE *Balaenoptera physalis*   Plate 35
Identification. The Fin whale is dark above and white below but the pigment on the head is asymmetrical, being more extensive on the left side than the right. The asymmetry also extends to the baleen: the front plates of baleen on the right side are white, the remainder are banded with yellow and grey. In the water the small back fin is the main distinction from the very similar Sei whale.
Range. Worldwide in temperate and polar waters. In the European sector of the Atlantic they occur especially around Iceland, the Faroes and Norway and some at least migrate southwards, usually just beyond the edge of the continental shelf. This is the only large baleen whale likely to be seen in British and Irish waters, mostly between July and September. It also occurs in the western Mediterranean at all seasons. They are hunted in most of the Atlantic, the International Whaling Commission having set a quota of 701 from the North Atlantic for 1981.
Habits. Fin whales are gregarious. They feed close to the surface, almost entirely on 'krill' of the species *Meganyctiphanes norvegica* which reaches about 6cm in length, occasionally on shoals of small fish, especially capelin, *Mallotus*

villosus. Fin whales reach maturity between five and ten years and a single calf is
born every two years. The maximum life-span is believed to be about 80 years.

BLUE WHALE   *Balaenoptera musculus*   **Plate 35**
Identification. The largest of all the whales. The back fin is relatively very small.
The upper and under surfaces are similar, being dark bluish grey with pale
flecks, and there is no contrasting pattern of black and white as in the other
large rorquals. The baleen is entirely black and up to 80cm long.
Range. Worldwide but very rare. In the eastern North Atlantic blue whales
migrate between the Cape Verde Islands in the south and Spitzbergen in the
north, following especially the edge of the continental shelf. The population in
the whole North Atlantic is likely to be in the order of a few hundred animals. It
is not regular in the Mediterranean. No hunting has been approved by the
International Whaling Commission since 1960.
Habits. As for the Fin whale.

SEI WHALE   *Balaenoptera borealis*   **Plate 35**
Identification. This is a large baleen whale that is very similar to the Fin whale. It
is less slim and the back fin is rather larger with a backward projecting point.
The body is black above and white below with the pigmentation symmetrical.
The baleen plates are black with pale fringes.
Range. Worldwide in temperate and polar waters. In the Atlantic it is less
frequent than the Fin whale on the European coast but is sometimes moderately
common around Iceland in summer, although it is less regular in its appearance
than the Fin whale. It is not regular in the Baltic nor in the Mediterranean. The
Sei whale is hunted in Icelandic waters, the quota for the North Atlantic set by
the International Whaling Commission for 1981 being 100.
Habits. Sei whales are usually seen alone or in pairs. In the North Atlantic they
feed mainly on very small crustaceans, especially *Calanus finmarchicus*. Females
probably breed only every three years.

MINKE WHALE   *Balaenoptera acutorostrata*   **Plate 35**
Identification. This is the smallest of the baleen whales in the Atlantic, reaching
only about ten metres. It is black above and white below with a small back fin
and a very characteristic large white patch in the centre of each flipper. The
baleen is creamy white and the plates do not exceed 30cm in length.
Range. Worldwide in temperate and polar waters. In the eastern Atlantic it is
found in all European waters from the Mediterranean to the Arctic, including
the North Sea and the Baltic. It occurs especially over the continental shelf
rather than in the deep ocean and is the rorqual most frequently stranded on
shore. It is hunted around Iceland and off Norway, the quota set by the
International Whaling Commission for the North Atlantic for 1981 being 2554.
Habits. Minke whales are more solitary than the large whales and usually travel
alone or in small family groups. They feed mainly on small fish such as capelin,
Mallotus villosus, but also on krill and small quid. Mating takes place in winter
or spring and a single young is born during the following winter.

HUMPBACK WHALE *Megaptera novaeangliae* **Plate 36**
Identification. Humpbacks are amongst the easiest of the large whales to
identify. As they dive the broad back emerges further from the water than in the
rorquals, the back fin shows clearly and the entire tail usually emerges from the
water. They are less streamlined than the rorquals and have enormously long
flippers which are predominantly white and with a corrugated front margin.
The overall pattern of black and white is extremely variable. The head carries
wart-like protuberances. The baleen is black and up to 80cm in length.
Range. Worldwide, migrating between subtropical and polar waters. Humpback whales used to occur all along the European Atlantic coasts but were
hunted almost to extinction earlier than the rorquals and are now very rare in
the eastern Atlantic although they still occur around Iceland and the Azores.
The International Whaling Commission has not approved quotas for this
species since 1955.
Habits. The Humpback is a slow swimmer compared with the rorquals and
occurs mainly in the shallower waters of the continental shelf or mid-oceanic
ridge. They sometimes 'breach', leaping completely clear of the water. They
make a great variety of remarkable singing sounds which can be detected
underwater at distances up to 100 kilometres.

RIGHT WHALES: family Balaenidae

Right whales are plump, slow-swimming baleen whales found especially in
coastal waters. The head is very large in relation to the body and the upper jaws
are arched to accommodate extremely long baleen plates, up to three metres in
length. There are no grooves on the throat, no back fin and the paired flippers
are broad and rounded. The blow is erect and double.

BLACK RIGHT WHALE *Balaena glacialis* **Plate 36**
Identification. A large whale, up to 18m, black all over, with irregular pale
excrescences on the head, especially on top of the snout. The head is about one
quarter of the total length and the baleen plates are black and up to 2.5m long.
Range. Worldwide in temperate waters. Formerly on the European coasts,
migrating between Spitzbergen and Iberian waters but almost exterminated
through whaling by the early 19th century. It is now almost extinct in the
eastern Atlantic but it survives in small numbers on the western side and
vagrants can be expected to occur in European waters.
Habits. Black right whales are sociable, slow-moving whales. They feed on
plankton, especially on even smaller crustaceans than do the rorquals.

BOWHEAD WHALE *Balaena mysticetus* **Plate 36**
Identification. The Bowhead or Greenland right whale has an even larger head
than the Black right whale, about one third of its total length, with baleen plates
up to 3m long. There is a variable amount of white, especially under the head.
Range. An Arctic whale, staying close to the margin of the sea-ice. The Atlantic
population was nearly exterminated by the 19th century. On the European side
it is only likely to occur around Spitzbergen but sightings this century have been
very rare. It survives in small numbers around Baffin Island and Alaska.
Habits. As for the Black right whale.

TOOTHED CETACEANS: suborder Odontoceti

This group comprises the majority of cetaceans, mostly dolphin-sized but with one 'big whale', the Sperm. They all lack baleen and have some true teeth, although these vary from continuous rows of numerous pointed teeth in both jaws, as in most dolphins, to a single tusk-like tooth in the lower jaw only, sometimes scarcely visible in females, as in the beaked whales. Of the European species all but the Sperm whale, the White whale and the Narwhal have a fin on the back.

SPERM WHALES: family Physeteridae

Sperm whales have numerous teeth in the lower jaw only, which is slender and overhung by the bulbous head.

SPERM WHALE   *Physeter catodon*   Plate 36
Identification. Male sperm whales reach 18m in length and are therefore comparable in size with the majority of baleen whales. The shape is unique, with an enormous rectangular head and a slender lower jaw, much shorter than the head. There is no clear back fin but there is a series of low irregular humps on the posterior half of the back. The tail usually leaves the water as the whale dives. Females are much smaller, up to 10m, but are otherwise similar to the males. The blowhole is unusual in being situated at the front angle of the head, on one side, and the blow is directed obliquely forwards.
Range. The Sperm whale is found throughout the world, mainly in tropical and warm temperate seas. Adult males migrate to the temperate and polar seas in summer and are usually the only animals found in northern European waters, extending north to Spitzbergen. This is the commonest large whale in the Mediterranean.
Habits. In the tropics sperm whales occur in matriarchal groups of females and young while the males are more solitary. They are slow swimmers but deep divers, reaching depths of a thousand metres and remaining below for up to an hour. When they surface after a deep dive they breathe repeatedly for a period of five to ten minutes before diving again. Sperm whales feed mainly on large squid. They become sexually mature at about ten and have a life-span of about 60 years. The Sperm whale is extensively hunted in warmer waters, for example around the Azores, the most valuable product being the waxy 'spermaceti' in the head. The quota for the North Atlantic for 1981 set by the International Whaling Commission was 130, males only.

PYGMY SPERM WHALE   *Kogia breviceps*   Plate 39
Identification. This is a dolphin-sized relative of the Sperm whale, up to 3.5m in length. The lower jaw is short, giving the head a shark-like appearance, and there are 12–16 pointed teeth in the lower jaw only. There is a prominent fin in the middle of the back as in many dolphin species.
Range. A worldwide but rare species, mainly in warm waters and known in

European waters only from a small number of stranded animals on the coasts of Portugal, France, Ireland and the Netherlands.

Habits. Little known. Pygmy sperm whales feed on squid and cuttlefish.

BEAKED WHALES: family Ziphiidae

Beaked whales are medium-sized whales that live in the open ocean. Most are very poorly known. The body is rather flattened from side to side, the flippers are small, the back fin is far behind the centre of the back and the hind margin of the tail fluke has no central notch. There is no baleen but teeth are generally limited to one pair of tusks in the lower jaws. These are well developed only in males but in females they generally remain in the jaw without fully erupting. The body is frequently marked with pale scratches, probably caused by the tusks during fighting. There are two to four grooves on the throat. Beaked whales are fast swimmers, diving deeply and feeding mainly on squid and cuttlefish. Apart from the Bottle-nosed whale, and perhaps occasionally Cuvier's whale, beaked whales cannot be identified with any certainty at sea. Stranded animals can best be identified by the position and shape of the tusks.

BOTTLE-NOSED WHALE *Hyperoodon ampullatus*   **Plate 37**

Identification. This is the largest, commonest and most sociable of the beaked whales, usually found in small groups. The forehead is bulbous, especially in adult males, a feature unique amongst beaked whales but which could lead to confusion with the Pilot whale (p. 213). The latter has a shorter beak and larger back fin, placed further forward. The tusks of the Bottle-nosed whale (in males) are at the tip of the lower jaws.

Range. Confined to the North Atlantic, migrating north to the edge of the ice in summer and south as far as West Africa in winter. It is the commonest of the beaked whales in European waters, especially off Iceland and Norway. In British and Irish waters they are seen mainly in August and September during the southward migration. It has been extensively hunted but is now protected by member countries of the International Whaling Commission.

Habits. This is a sociable species, seen in schools of up to 50 but more often in smaller groups. It is a deep diver and feeds mainly on squid and cuttlefish.

CUVIER'S WHALE *Ziphius cavirostris*   **Plate 37**

Identification. This is a typical beaked whale, lacking the bulbous forehead of the Bottle-nosed whale. The colour and pattern are very variable, including a distinctive form with the head and front part of the back white, but other individuals are a uniform grey as in several other species of beaked whale. The tusks are at the extreme front of the lower jaw and are bluntly conical, not flattened.

Range. Worldwide. Stranded animals have occurred on European coasts from the Mediterranean to the Baltic. British and Irish records have been mainly on the west coasts.

Habits. Unknown.

SOWERBY'S WHALE *Mesoplodon bidens*   **Plate 37**

Identification. This is a small beaked whale, up to 5m in length, black above and paler to a variable degree below. The tusks are situated near the centre of the lower jaws.

Range. North Atlantic. Amongst the species of *Mesoplodon* this is the one most frequently stranded on European coasts, mainly around southern Scandinavia and the North Sea but south to the Bay of Biscay.

Habits. This species is frequently stranded in pairs, male and female.

TRUE'S BEAKED WHALE *Mesoplodon mirus*   Plate 37

Identification. A small beaked whale, up to 5.2m long. It is dark above, grey on the flanks and white below, and is usually spotted to some extent. The tusks are at the extreme front of the lower jaws and are flattened sideways (compare Cuvier's whale).

Range. North Atlantic, known from only a small number of stranded animals, those on the European coast having been in France, Ireland and Scotland.

Habits. Unknown.

GRAY'S WHALE *Mesoplodon grayi*   Plate 37

Identification. A typical beaked whale, smaller and lighter than Sowerby's whale. The tusks are flattened and situated about one quarter the length of the jaw behind the tip.

Range. Southern Hemisphere, but one stranding has occurred on the Netherlands coast.

Habits. Unknown.

GERVAIS' WHALE *Mesoplodon europaeus*   Plate 37

Identification. A large beaked whale, up to 6m, dark slaty-grey above and only slightly lighter below. The tusks are flattened and situated about one sixth of the length of the jaw behind the tip.

Range. North Atlantic, but only one record of a stranding in Europe, in northern France.

Habits. Unknown.

BLAINVILLE'S WHALE *Mesoplodon densirostris*   Not illustrated

Identification. A typical beaked whale, black above and grey below, up to 5.2m in length. In adult males the posterior half of the lower jaw, bearing a single tusk, is swollen and bulges upwards outside the upper jaw. This gives the line of the closed mouth a sinuous shape, also seen in a less extreme form in females and young males.

Range. Tropical and warm temperate seas, north in the Atlantic at least as far as Madeira but not yet recorded on the European coast.

Habits. Unknown.

WHITE WHALES: family Monodontidae

The White whale and the Narwhal are the only members of this family. They are arctic species, related to the dolphins but differing particularly in the absence of a back fin.

WHITE WHALE *Delphinapterus leucas* **Plate 38**
Identification. This is a very distinctive cetacean, up to 5m long, and entirely white when adult. Young animals are pale grey. The forehead is bulbous and the flippers are rather short and blunt. There are eight to ten teeth in each upper and lower jaw.
Range. Confined to the Arctic, around the edge of the ice and especially in coastal waters. There is a population in the White Sea and individuals occasionally wander south with rare occurrences south to the English Channel and more frequently in the Baltic. They sometimes ascend rivers.
Habits. White whales are sociable animals, males and females forming separate schools outside the breeding season which takes place in spring and early summer when the calves are also born. In winter white whales sometimes remain within the ice zone, keeping small areas of water open by crashing the ice with their backs. They feed mainly on fish. White whales make a variety of sounds under water including a loud trilling whistle.

NARWHAL *Monodon monoceros* **Plate 38**
Identification. Narwhals are small whales, up to 5.5m, resembling white whales in lacking a back fin and in having the forehead swollen. The back is more or less covered in small dark flecks on a pale ground and the males are unmistakable in having a unique, spirally grooved tusk protruding forwards from the mouth for about half the total length of the body. The tusk represents a left upper incisor tooth. The only other tooth is the corresponding one on the right which remains small and concealed. In females both teeth remain concealed in the jaw. Very rarely in males both teeth develop as tusks.
Range. Confined to the Arctic, usually keeping close to the ice. They occur around Spitzbergen but are rare on the north coast of Norway even in winter. Occasional vagrants occur as far south as the southern North Sea.
Habits. Narwhals are gregarious and both sexes may occur in the same group, which now rarely number more than ten. The function of the tusk is not clear although it is likely to be concerned with competition amongst the males during the breeding season. Narwhals feed mainly on squid.

Narwhal tusks have been recorded up to 3m in length. They were objects of great wonder at the courts of medieval Europe and were one of the chief sources of stories of the mythical unicorn.

DOLPHINS: family Delphinidae

Most members of this family are small, fast swimming, fish-eating dolphins with numerous sharply pointed teeth in both jaws, a narrow beak, a prominent back fin and a notch in the centre of the hind margin of the tail fluke. Some species however are as long as 9m and these large ones are generally referred to as whales rather than dolphins.

LONG-FINNED PILOT WHALE *Globicephala melaena* **Plate 38**
Identification. This is a large sociable species that could be mistaken for the Bottle-nosed whale (p. 211) because of the bulbous forehead, but the beak is very short, the back fin is large, recurved and placed rather far forward on the

back, the flippers are long and slender and the underside is boldly patterned in black and white.

Range. The Atlantic and Southern Oceans. In the eastern North Atlantic this species occurs from the far north to the Mediterranean, frequently close inshore, and is especially numerous around Iceland, the Faroes and Shetland. It makes regular north-south migrations.

Habits. Long-finned pilot whales generally occur in schools which may contain more than a hundred animals, although about twenty or thirty is more usual. Such schools are conspicuous at the surface and this is one of the species of cetacean most easily and frequently seen from ships. It is also one of the most frequently stranded, sometimes whole schools becoming marooned on flat sandy beaches. The gregarious habit is exploited in the Faroes where schools are surrounded by small boats and driven into shallow bays where they can be easily killed. Pilot whales feed mainly upon cuttlefish and squid. They have a longer gestation period than the large whales, about 16 months, and three or four years elapse between successive births. The life-span is probably about 50 years.

KILLER WHALE   *Orcinus orca*   Plate 38

Identification. Fully adult male killer whales are easily distinguishable from all other whales and dolphins by the possession of a very large triangular fin in the centre of the back, but this can lead to confusion with some sharks, for example the basking sharks which tend to cruise at the surface. If the back fin of a shark breaks the surface it is usually followed by the similar tail fin which is vertical, not horizontal as in whales. Females and young male killer whales have the fin smaller and recurved. Killer whales also have a bold pattern of white markings on black and very large, broad, rounded flippers which, like the back fin, are disproportionately large in fully adult males. Females are distinctly smaller than males. There are 10–13 teeth in each row, about 25–30mm in diameter and oval in cross-section.

Range. Worldwide. In European seas killer whales occur throughout, from Spitzbergen and Iceland to Iberia and also in the Baltic and Mediterranean, frequently close inshore if the water is deep.

Habits. Killer whales usually occur in small groups. They are unique amongst the cetaceans in preying regularly upon seals and other cetaceans as well as large fish. They often congregate in large numbers around breeding colonies of seals – one killer has been recorded with 14 seals in its stomach. Killer whales attack the young of large whales and occasionally even make communal attacks on adults, going especially for the throat and tongue. They also eat carrion. Killers are frequently kept in dolphinaria where they become very docile and are easily tamed.

BOTTLE-NOSED DOLPHIN   *Tursiops truncatus*   Plate 39

Identification. This is the most familiar dolphin, being the one most frequently kept in dolphinaria. It is a large, grey dolphin, up to 4m in length without any prominent pattern. The beak is short and the lower jaw projects a little beyond the upper. In the water the combination of rather pale colour and large, pointed, recurved back fin is distinctive. There are 22–25 teeth in each row, all about 12mm in diameter.

Range. The Bottle-nosed dolphin is the most abundant dolphin in most European coastal waters from the Black Sea and Mediterranean north to the North Sea, and extending in summer to southern Norway and occasionally into the Baltic.

Habits. This is a sociable species, sometimes forming schools of over 100 but more often smaller groups of about 10 or 20. They are playful animals, sometimes leaping clear of the water and occasionally associating fearlessly with bathers or small boats. They feed mainly on fish. Breeding takes place in summer, with a 12-month gestation between mating and the birth of a single young one. They do not become sexually mature until an age of about 12 and the life-span is at least 30 years.

RISSO'S DOLPHIN   *Grampus griseus*   Plate 39

Identification. Risso's dolphin is a large dolphin, up to 3.5m in length, with no distinctive pattern but with a large pointed back fin, a bulbous forehead and no beak. The upperside is grey, frequently with pale scars, and there is a variable amount of white on the underside. There are three to seven teeth in each lower jaw but none, or occasionally one or two, in the upper jaws.

Range. A worldwide species, found in European waters from the Mediterranean to Scandinavia but rare in the far north.

Habits. Risso's dolphins usually occur in small groups of up to ten animals, but occasionally large schools of more than 100 are recorded. They feed on squid and cuttlefish and frequently follow ships.

ROUGH-TOOTHED DOLPHIN   *Steno bredanensis*   Plate 39

Identification. This is a small dolphin, up to 2.5m in length, with a pronounced beak which runs smoothly into the forehead without an intervening groove. It is dark slaty grey above and white below with large irregular pale spots which are sometimes pinkish. There is another dolphin with a spotted pattern, the Spotted dolphin *Stenella frontalis*, which has not been recorded in European waters but could occur in the south – it is dark with numerous very small white spots when adult, and the beak is sharply demarcated from the forehead. The Rough-toothed dolphin has 20–27 teeth in each jaw and they are very distinctive, with a matt surface caused by a network of very fine reticulate ridges and grooves, visible with a hand-lens.

Range. A species of the tropical Atlantic, north to the Mediterranean but only a rare vagrant further north, with strandings reported on the coasts of France and the Netherlands.

Habits. Little known. It is a gregarious species, found in groups of up to 50. They sometimes play on the bow waves of ships.

FALSE KILLER WHALE   *Pseudorca crassidens*   Plate 39

Identification. A large, slender dolphin, up to 5.5m in length and therefore comparable in length with small killer and pilot whales. It is black all over with the typical large central back fin of a dolphin. The snout is smoothly rounded with no beak. There are 9–11 teeth in each row, above and below, each tooth about 25mm in diameter.

Range. Worldwide in the open oceans. It is rarely recorded but occasional strandings occur, usually of large numbers, and these have been recorded from the Mediterranean to southern Scandinavia.

Habits. Little known. It is a fast swimmer, up to 30 knots. It has occasionally been seen in groups, and about 150 were stranded in northeastern Scotland in 1927.

COMMON DOLPHIN   *Delphinus delphis*   Plate 40

Identification. The Common dolphin is a small dolphin, usually about 2m, with a long slender beak, black above and white below and with a complex pattern on the flanks. The pattern is variable in detail and there is a variable amount of brown or yellowish colour on the fore half of the flank, but a constant feature is an elongated hour-glass or figure-of-eight pattern on the flank, with the constriction, or crossing over of lines, immediately below the back fin. There are 40 to 50 teeth in each row, each about 3mm in diameter.

Range. This is the commonest dolphin in the Black Sea and Mediterranean and north to the English Channel. It is scarcer further north but has been recorded as far as Iceland and Norway and occasionally in the Baltic.

Habits. Common dolphins travel in schools, often breaking the surface and diving rythmically and in unison, and sometimes leaping clear of the water. They frequently swim alongside ships or ride on the bow waves. They feed mainly on fish. Mating takes place in autumn and the young are born the following summer after a gestation of about ten months.

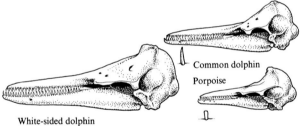

Common dolphin

Porpoise

White-sided dolphin

Porpoise is unique in having flattened teeth

Skulls and teeth of dolphins and porpoise

STRIPED DOLPHIN   *Stenella coeruleoalbus*   Plate 40

Identification. The Striped dolphin is similar in proportions to the Common dolphin, with a long slender beak, but the pattern is distinctive. There is a complex pattern of slender black lines extending backwards from the eyes. In other respects the pattern is variable but there is never a 'cross-over' point below the back fin as in the Common dolphin and there is no yellow nor brown pigment. There are 43–50 teeth in each jaw, each about 3mm in diameter.

Range. Worldwide in warm waters. It is rare in European waters but has been recorded from the Mediterranean to the English Channel.

Habits. Striped dolphins are gregarious and sometimes associate with common dolphins. They feed on fish.

WHITE-SIDED DOLPHINS   *Lagenorhynchus acutus*   **Plate 40**
Identification. This is a moderately large dolphin, with a short, ill-defined beak.
The hind part of the body is narrow and deep with a keel on the upper surface
between the large back fin and the tail flukes. The head, including the beak, is
entirely black and there is a distinctive pale band on each flank. There are 30–40
teeth in each row, all about 5mm in diameter.
Range. A common species of the northern North Atlantic, most abundant off
the Norwegian coast but extending from Spitzbergen south to the North Sea
and the Baltic.
Habits. White-sided dolphins are very gregarious and schools of over 1,000
have been observed, especially in the north. They migrate between polar and
temperate waters, breaking up into smaller groups during the winter and spring
breeding season in the south. They feed almost entirely upon fish, including
herring and cod.

WHITE-BEAKED DOLPHIN   *Lagenorhynchus albirostris*   **Plate 40**
Identification. This species is similar in size to the White-sided dolphin but it
differs in pattern and the hind part of the body is not so compressed. The back
fin is very large. The short beak is white and there is a pale band on the flank,
extending further forward than in the White-sided dolphin. There are 22–25
teeth in each row, each about 6mm in diameter.
Range. A North Atlantic species. It is the commonest dolphin in the North Sea
but it also extends north to the Baltic and to the Barents Sea and occasionally
south as far as Portugal.
Habits. As for the White-sided dolphin.

PORPOISES: family Phocoenidae

Porpoises are like small, dumpy dolphins without beaks, with a small back fin
or none at all and flattened spade-like teeth.

PORPOISE   *Phocoena phocoena*   **Plate 40**
Identification. The Porpoise is the smallest cetacean, up to about 1.8m in length
and rather dumpy in proportion. There is no beak and the back fin is much
smaller, broader and less recurved than in most dolphins. The body is black
above and white below with the black flippers clearly separated by white from
the black of the back and head. There are 22–27 teeth in each row and each
tooth is flattened and spade-like, quite different from those of any dolphin
species.
Range. Coastal waters from the White Sea in the far north and the Baltic along
all the Atlantic coasts to the Mediterranean (where it is scarce) and the Black
Sea (where it is common). Porpoises are very vulnerable to pollution and have
seriously declined in the Baltic and parts of the North Sea.
Habits. Porpoises are usually seen in small groups of less than ten and are
especially found in estuaries and even in large rivers. They are slow swimmers
and do not leap clear of the water as dolphins often do. They feed on fish,
crustaceans and cuttlefish. The young are born in late summer.

Checklist

This list includes the names of all the species that are given separate entries in the main text. In addition to the recommended scientific and English names, there are given, in parentheses, some of the more frequently and recently used alternatives. The scientific names of mammals occasionally have to be changed as information on the relationships of species accumulates, demonstrating for example that two forms previously believed to belong to the same species are really separate species or vice versa. The first part of the name, indicating the genus, is rather more vulnerable to change according to whether large or small genera are preferred. In this respect I have tried to follow a middle course, avoiding extremes of 'splitting' or 'lumping'.

The English names of mammals are not well standardized, especially in the case of those species that do not occur in Britain. As far as practicable I have tried to choose the names that are in most frequent use in recent publications provided they are unambiguous and not misleading. The names used are unambiguous in a European context (or North Atlantic context in the case of cetaceans) but not necessarily worldwide. A part of an English name that is in parentheses in the list, for example (Western) hedgehog, should be used in a European context but is superfluous in a British or Irish context.

The following symbols and letters have been used to indicate the status of each species in Britain, Ireland and continental Europe.

- ●   Regular, indigenous population
- ○   Regular but rare (cetaceans)
- ■   Introduced (deliberately or accidentally)
- V   Vagrant (irregular visitor)
- E   Extinct within the last 2000 years
- F   Feral (wild-living populations of domesticated stock, recognizably different from ancestral wild species)
- D   Primitive domestic form, not completely free-living
- 1,2 etc.   See footnotes.

		Britain	Ireland	Continent
Order Marsupialia	**Marsupials**			
Family Macropodidae	**Wallabies and kangaroos**			
Macropus rufogriseus	Red-necked wallaby	■		
Order Insectivora	**Insectivores**			
Family Erinaceidae	**Hedgehogs**			
Erinaceus europaeus	(Western) hedgehog	●	●	●
Erinaceus concolor	Eastern hedgehog			●
Erinaceus algirus	Algerian hedgehog			■
Family Talpidae	**Moles and desmans**			
Talpa europaea	(Northern) mole	●		●
Talpa caeca	Blind mole			●
Talpa romana	Roman mole			●
Galemys pyrenaicus	Pyrenean desman			●
Family Soricidae	**Shrews**			
Sorex araneus	Common shrew	●		●
Sorex coronatus	Millet's shrew	1		●
Sorex granarius	Spanish shrew			●
Sorex samniticus	Appennine shrew			●
Sorex minutus	Pygmy shrew	●	●	●
Sorex caecutiens	Laxmann's shrew			●
Sorex minutissimus	Least shrew			●
Sorex sinalis (*S. isodon*)	Dusky shrew			●
Sorex alpinus	Alpine shrew			●
Neomys fodiens	Water shrew	●		●
Neomys anomalus	Miller's water shrew			●
Suncus etruscus	Pygmy white-toothed shrew			●
Crocidura russula	Greater white-toothed shrew	2		●
Crocidura suaveolens	Lesser white-toothed shrew	3		●
Crocidura leucodon	Bicoloured white-toothed shrew			●
Order Chiroptera	**Bats**			
Family Rhinolophidae	**Horseshoe bats**			
Rhinolophus hipposideros	Lesser horseshoe bat	●	●	●
Rhinolophus ferrumequinum	Greater horseshoe bat	●		●

1. Jersey only.　　2. Channel Isles only.　　3. Scilly and Channel Isles only.

	Britain	Ireland	Continent
Rhinolophus euryale — Mediterranean horseshoe bat			●
Rhinolophus blasii — Blasius's horseshoe bat			●
Rhinolophus mehelyi — Mehely's horseshoe bat			●

Family Vespertilionidae — **Vespertilionid bats**

	Britain	Ireland	Continent
Myotis daubentoni (*Leuconoe daubentoni*) — Daubenton's bat	●	●	●
Myotis nathalinae — Nathalina bat			●
Myotis capaccinii (*Leuconoe capaccinii*) — Long-fingered bat			●
Myotis dasycneme (*Leuconoe dasycneme*) — Pond bat			●
Myotis brandti — Brandt's bat	●		●
Myotis mystacinus (*Selysius mystacinus*) — Whiskered bat	●	●	●
Myotis emarginatus (*Selysius emarginatus*) — Geoffroy's bat			●
Myotis nattereri (*Selysius nattereri*) — Natterer's bat	●	●	●
Myotis bechsteini (*Selysius bechsteini*) — Bechstein's bat	●		●
Myotis myotis — (Greater) mouse-eared bat	●		●
Myotis blythi (*M. oxygnathus*) — Lesser mouse-eared bat			●
Nyctalus noctula — Noctule	●		●
Nyctalus leisleri — Leisler's bat	●	●	●
Nyctalus lasiopterus — Greater noctule			●
Eptesicus serotinus (*Vespertilio serotinus*) — Serotine	●		●
Eptesicus nilssoni (*Vespertilio nilssoni*) — Northern bat			●
Vespertilio murinus — Parti-coloured bat	V		●
Pipistrellus pipistrellus — (Common) pipistrelle	●	●	●
Pipistrellus nathusii — Nathusius's pipistrelle	V		●
Pipistrellus kuhli — Kuhl's pipistrelle			●
Pipistrellus savii — Savi's pipistrelle			●
Lasiurus cinereus — Hoary bat	V		
Plecotus auritus — Common long-eared bat	●	●	●
Plecotus austriacus — Grey long-eared bat	●		●
Barbastella barbastellus — Barbastelle	●		●
Miniopterus schreibersi — Schreiber's bat			●

		Britain	Ireland	Continent
Family Molossidae	**Free-tailed bats**			
Tadarida teniotis	European free-tailed bat			●
Family Nycteridae	**Slit-faced bats**			
Nycteris thebaica	Egyptian slit-faced bat			4

Order Lagomorpha   Lagomorphs

		Britain	Ireland	Continent
Family Leporidae	**Rabbits and hares**			
Oryctolagus cuniculus	Rabbit	■	■	●
Lepus capensis (*L. europaeus*)	Brown hare	●	■	●
Lepus timidus	Mountain hare (Arctic hare)	●	●	●

Order Rodentia   Rodents

		Britain	Ireland	Continent
Family Sciuridae	**Squirrels**			
Sciurus vulgaris	Red squirrel	●	●	●
Sciurus carolinensis	Grey squirrel	■	■	
Pteromys volans	Flying squirrel			●
Spermophilus citellus (*Citellus citellus*)	European souslik			●
Spermophilus suslicus (*Citellus suslicus*)	Spotted souslik			●
Marmota marmota	Alpine marmot			●
Tamias sibiricus	Siberian chipmunk			■
Family Castoridae	**Beavers**			
Castor fiber	European beaver		E	●
Castor canadensis	Canadian beaver			■
Family Hystricidae	**Old-world porcupines**			
Hystrix cristata	Porcupine			●
Family Capromyidae	**Hutias etc.**			
Myocastor coypus	Coypu	■		■

4. One record on Corfu.

	Britain	Ireland	Continent

Family Gliridae — **Dormice**

Eliomys quercinus — Garden dormouse			●
Dryomys nitedula — Forest dormouse			●
Glis glis — Fat dormouse	■		●
Muscardinus avellanarius — Hazel dormouse	●		●
Myomimus roachi — Mouse-tailed dormouse			●
(*M. personatus*)			

Family Muridae — **Hamsters, voles, mice, rats etc.**

Subfamily Cricetinae — Hamsters

Cricetus cricetus — Common hamster			●
Mesocricetus newtoni — Rumanian hamster			●
Cricetulus migratorius — Grey hamster			●

Subfamily Microtinae — Lemmings and voles

Lemmus lemmus — Norway lemming			●
Myopus schisticolor — Wood lemming			●
Clethrionomys glareolus — Bank vole	●	■	●
Clethrionomys rutilus — Northern red-backed vole			●
Clethrionomys rufocanus — Grey-sided vole			●
Dinaromys bogdanovi — Balkan snow vole			●
(*Dolomys milleri*)			
Microtus agrestis — Field vole	●		●
(Short-tailed field mouse)			
Microtus arvalis — Common vole	5		●
(Orkney vole)			
Microtus epiroticus — Sibling vole			●
(*M. subarvalis*)			
Microtus oeconomus — Root vole			●
Microtus nivalis — Snow vole			●
(*Chionomys nivalis*)			
Microtus guentheri — Günther's vole			●
(*M. socialis*)			
Microtus cabrerae — Cabrera's vole			●
Pitymys subterraneus — Common pine vole			●
Pitymys multiplex — Alpine pine vole			●
Pitymys bavaricus — Bavarian pine vole			●
Pitymys tatricus — Tatra pine vole			●
Pitymys liechtensteini — Liechtenstein's pine vole			●
Pitymys duodecimcostatus — Mediterranean pine vole			●
Pitymys lusitanicus — Lusitanian pine vole			●
Pitymys thomasi — Thomas's pine vole			●

5. Orkney and Guernsey only.

	Britain	Ireland	Continent
Pitymys savii — Savi's pine vole			●
Arvicola terrestris (*A. amphibius*) — (Northern) water vole	●		●
Arvicola sapidus — Southwestern water vole			●
Ondatra zibethicus — Muskrat			■
Subfamily Spalacinae — Mole-rats			
Spalax microphthalmus — Greater mole-rat			●
Spalax leucodon — Lesser mole-rat			●
Subfamily Murinae — Mice and rats			
Rattus norvegicus — Common rat (Brown rat)	■	■	■
Rattus rattus — Ship rat (Black rat)	■	■	■
Apodemus sylvaticus (*Sylvaemus sylvaticus*) — Wood mouse (Long-tailed field mouse)	●	●	●
Apodemus flavicollis (*Sylvaemus flavicollis*) — Yellow-necked mouse	●		●
Apodemus microps — Pygmy field mouse			●
Apodemus mystacinus (*Sylvaemus mystacinus*) — Rock mouse			●
Apodemus agrarius — Striped field mouse			●
Micromys minutus — Harvest mouse	●		●
Mus musculus — House mouse	■	■	■
Mus spretus — Algerian mouse			●
Mus hortulanus — Steppe mouse			●
Acomys minous (*A. cahirinus*) — Cretan spiny mouse			6
Family Zapodidae — Birch mice			
Sicista betulina — Northern birch mouse			●
Sicista subtilis — Southern birch mouse			●

Order Primates   Primates

Family Cercopithecidae — **Old-world monkeys**

	Britain	Ireland	Continent
Macaca sylvanus — Barbary ape			■

6. Crete only.

	Britain	Ireland	Continent
Order Carnivora **Carnivores**			
Family Ursidae **Bears**			
Thalarctos maritimus Polar bear			●
(*Ursus maritimus*)			
Ursus arctos Brown bear	E	E	●
Family Canidae **Wolves and foxes**			
Canis lupus Wolf	E	E	●
Canis aureus Jackal			●
Vulpes vulpes (Red) fox	●	●	●
Alopex lagopus Arctic fox			●
Nyctereutes procyonoides Raccoon-dog			■
Family Mustelidae **Weasels etc.**			
Mustela erminea Stoat	●	●	●
Mustela nivalis Weasel	●		●
Mustela lutreola European mink			●
(*Lutreola lutreola*)			
Mustela vison (American) mink	■	■	■
(*Lutreola vison*)			
Mustela putorius (Western) polecat	●		●
(*Putorius putorius*)			
Mustela eversmanni Steppe polecat			●
(*Putorius eversmanni*)			
Mustela furo Domestic ferret	F		F
Vormela peregusna Marbled polecat			●
Martes martes Pine marten	●	●	●
Martes foina Beech marten			●
Gulo gulo Wolverine (Glutton)			●
Lutra lutra Otter	●	●	●
Meles meles Badger	●	●	●
Family Viverridae **Mongooses, genets, etc.**			
Herpestes ichneumon Egyptian Mongoose			?■
Herpestes edwardsi Indian grey mongoose			■
Genetta genetta Genet			?■
Family Procyonidae **Raccoons etc.**			
Procyon lotor Raccoon			■

	Britain	Ireland	Continent
Family Felidae — Cats			
Felis lynx (*F. pardina, Lynx lynx*) — Lynx			●
Felis silvestris — Wild cat	●		●
Felis catus — Domestic cat	F	F	F

Order Pinnipedia — Pinnipedes

	Britain	Ireland	Continent
Family Phocidae — Seals			
Phoca vitulina — Common seal	●	●	●
Phoca hispida (*Pusa hispida*) — Ringed seal	V		●
Halichoerus grypus — Grey seal	●	●	●
Monachus monachus — Monk seal			●
Pagophilus groenlandicus — Harp seal	V		●
Erignathus barbatus — Bearded seal	V		●
Cystophora cristata — Hooded seal	V	V	●
Family Odobenidae — Walrus			
Odobenus rosmarus — Walrus	V		●

Order Perissodactyla — Odd-toed ungulates

	Britain	Ireland	Continent
Family Equidae — Horses			
Equus caballus — Domestic horse	D	D	D
Equus asinus — Domestic donkey	D	D	D

Order Artiodactyla — Even-toed ungulates

	Britain	Ireland	Continent
Family Suidae — Pigs			
Sus scrofa — Wild boar	E		●
Family Bovidae — Cattle etc.			
Bison bonasus — Bison			●
Bos taurus — Domestic cattle	D	D	D
Bubalus bubalis — Domestic water buffalo			D
Ovibos moschatus — Musk ox			■

	Britain	*Ireland*	*Continent*
Ovis musimon (*Ovis ammon*)	Mouflon			■
Ovis aries	Domestic sheep	D/F	D	D
Capra ibex	Alpine ibex			●
Capra pyrenaica	Spanish ibex			●
Capra aegagrus	Wild goat			7
Capra hircus	Domestic goat	F	F	F
Rupicapra rupicapra	Chamois			●

Family Cervidae — **Deer**

	Britain	*Ireland*	*Continent*
Cervus elaphus	Red deer	●	●	●
Cervus nippon	Sika deer	■	■	■
Cervus dama (*Dama dama*)	Fallow deer	■	■	●
Cervus axis (*Axis axis*)	Spotted deer			■
Alces alces	Elk			●
Rangifer rangifer	Reindeer	D		●/D
Odocoileus virginianus	White-tailed deer			■
Capreolus capreolus	Roe deer	●		●
Muntiacus reevesi	Muntjac	■		■
Hydropotes inermis	Chinese water deer	■		■

Order Cetacea — Whales, dolphins, porpoises

	N. Europe	*British/Irish waters*	*S. Europe*
Suborder Mysticeti	Baleen whales			
Family Balaenopteridae	**Rorquals and Humpback whale**			
Balaenoptera physalis	Fin whale (Common rorqual)	●	●	●
Balaenoptera musculus	Blue whale	○	○	○
Balaenoptera borealis	Sei whale	●	○	○
Balaenoptera acutorostrata	Minke whale (Lesser rorqual)	●	●	●
Megaptera novaeangliae	Humpback whale	○	○	○

7. Some Mediterranean islands only.

	N. Europe	British/Irish waters	S. Europe
Family Balaenidae — **Right whales**			
Balaena glacialis (*Eubalaena glacialis*) — Black right whale	V	V	V
Balaena mysticetus — Bowhead whale (Greenland right whale)	V		
Suborder Odontoceti — Toothed whales			
Family Physeteridae — **Sperm whales**			
Physeter catodon (*P. macrocephalus*) — Sperm whale	●	●	●
Kogia breviceps — Pygmy sperm whale		V	V
Family Ziphiidae — **Beaked whales**			
Hyperoodon ampullatus — Bottle-nosed whale	●	●	●
Ziphius cavirostris — Cuvier's whale	O	●	●
Mesoplodon bidens — Sowerby's whale	O	●	●
Mesoplodon mirus — True's beaked whale		V	V
Mesoplodon grayi — Gray's whale			8
Mesoplodon europaeus — Gervais' whale			V
Mesoplodon densirostris — Blainville's whale			?V
Family Monodontidae — **White whales**			
Delphinapterus leucas — White whale (Beluga)	●	V	
Monodon monoceros — Narwhal	●	V	
Family Delphinidae — **Dolphins**			
Globicephala melaena — Long-finned pilot whale	●	●	●
Orcinus orca — Killer whale	●	●	●
Tursiops truncatus — Bottle-nosed dolphin	O	●	●
Grampus griseus — Risso's dolphin	O	●	●
Steno bredanensis — Rough-toothed dolphin			●
Pseudorca crassidens — False killer whale	●	●	●
Delphinus delphis — Common dolphin	O	●	●
Stenella coeruleoalba (*S. styx*) — Striped dolphin (Euphrosyne dolphin)		V	●
Lagenorhynchus acutus — White-sided dolphin	●	●	
Lagenorhynchus albirostris — White-beaked dolphin	●	●	V
Family Phocoenidae — **Porpoises**			
Phocoena phocoena — Porpoise	●	●	●

8. One record, Netherlands.

Mammals in Britain and Ireland

The diversity of mammal species in Britain is distinctly less than on the adjacent part of the continent of Europe, and Ireland has an even smaller range of species. Nevertheless, all the main groups are represented and, in any one district, there are many more species than are apparent to the casual observer. In mainland Britain (if well-established introductions are included) there are 5 insectivores, 15 bats, 3 lagomorphs, 14 rodents, 9 carnivores and 7 ungulates – 53 species in all. In Ireland the corresponding total is 29.

Some of the more common British mammals are not only widespread and abundant but very versatile in their choice of habitat. Wood mice, for example, are equally at home in woods, hedgerows and gardens and even on moorland and sand dunes wherever there are a few bushes. Foxes are equally enterprising, as familiar to some owners of suburban gardens in the south as they are to Scottish hill farmers. However, many other species are more restricted in their distribution. Amongst the bats and rodents the number of species diminishes as we travel north whereas the larger mammals are least common in the populous southeast of Britain where they have been more heavily persecuted.

Well-wooded country in the southeastern part of England, especially where it is interspersed with open country, probably contains the greatest variety of species. Many of these are ubiquitous throughout Britain, amongst them the Badger, Fox, Stoat, Weasel, Hedgehog, Mole, Common and Pygmy shrews, Pipistrelle, Bank and Field voles, Wood mouse, Grey squirrel and Rabbit. In addition there are more restricted southern species, although they tend to be less abundant and more difficult to locate. The Hazel dormouse is one of these, an elusive species found in woodland with a dense shrub layer. Others are the Yellow-necked mouse, which lives alongside the very similar Wood mouse especially in mature woodland, and the Harvest mouse, found on the edges of woods where there is tall grass. There are also several bats that are confined to the south or southeast: they include the Serotine, the Noctule and the Barbastelle. The presence of a river or pond will add several more species to the above list of widespread species, for example the Water vole, Water shrew and Mink.

Much of lowland Britain is farmland. Although the variety of species is less, many mammals have nevertheless adapted themselves to the unnatural conditions imposed by fields, especially where remnants of a woodland environment have survived in the form of hedgerows and copses. The Brown hare is probably the mammal best adapted to living in arable land and because it ranges widely over open fields it is less of a problem to the farmer than its relative the Rabbit, which concentrates its attentions on the edges of fields within reach of cover suitable for burrowing. Wood mice will occupy growing crops extensively during the growing season but are forced to retreat to the hedgerows and woods after harvest. Provided that they are not overtidied, hedgerows that contain a variety of shrub species are an ideal habitat for all the common small woodland mammals, and for some of the scarcer ones too, especially the Harvest mouse. They also frequently hold house mice and, especially if there is a wet ditch adjacent, common rats whose runs and holes are generally conspicuous in the sides of the ditch. Heavily grazed pasture provides little cover for animals like these but it is a rich habitat for earthworms which are in turn exploited underground by moles and on the surface by hedgehogs, badgers and foxes during their nocturnal forays from their homes in adjacent woods and hedges.

Towns and their suburbs are even more remote from the natural conditions to which most mammals are adapted but a few species thrive even there. Hedgehogs find playing fields and lawns good hunting grounds and are small enough to need little in the way of shrubbery or waste ground for their daytime nest. Foxes use their proverbial cunning and resourcefulness to survive right into city centres, hunting rats and mice and using railway embankments, factory sites and neglected gardens as refuges and highways. Badgers are less versatile but nevertheless find the outer suburban zone of cities such as London to their liking, using larger gardens and railway embankments for their sets. After the expected house mice and common rats, the ubiquitous Wood mouse is the next most common urban rodent, frequently found nesting in the warmth of the compost heap in the smallest of gardens.

Wales is marginal territory for most of the more restricted species mentioned above, but it has one mammal that is very much its own, namely the Polecat. Polecats were at one time found throughout Britain. By the 1920s persecution had reduced them to a small remnant in central Wales but they have now expanded to recolonize the whole of Wales and some of the adjacent parts of England. A small remnant population of Pine marten survives in North Wales but to find this elusive species in numbers we must go to the north of Scotland, especially north of the Great Glen where they have expanded from a small remnant, helped by afforestation. The Wild cat is another carnivore that has benefited from afforestation and is now widespread in the Scottish Highlands.

The plantations of exotic conifers that are replacing much of our natural woodland provide suitable habitats, at appropriate stages in their development, for many species of mammal. When open ground is first planted with trees it is generally fenced to protect the young trees from rabbits and deer (which can however thrive without doing much damage in mature plantations). The resulting lush growth of grass and other herbaceous plants provides ideal food and cover for field voles in particular whose runways are usually shared by both common and pygmy shrews. As soon as shrubby growth has developed, bank voles and wood mice move in along with their predators the stoats and weasels. The larger predators – Fox, Badger, Marten and Wild cat – also thrive in these conditions. As the trees mature, only wood mice and a few shrews survive in the deepest shade but all the other species survive in rides and clearings, and red squirrels occupy the canopy, especially when crops of seed-bearing cones begin to appear.

Throughout most of England and parts of lowland Scotland the Red squirrel has been replaced by the introduced American grey squirrel, but the greater isolation of the new Scottish forests gives the Red squirrel a better chance of surviving there. Another species that has survived better in Scotland than in England is the Otter, now very scarce on lowland rivers because of a combination of disturbance and pollution but still present on highland rivers and lochs and especially on the rocky west coast of Scotland where it is as much at home in the sea as in fresh water. Finally the Scottish hills hold Britain's only 'arctic-alpine' mammal, the Mountain hare, especially abundant on the lower heather-clad slopes of the eastern Highlands, but extending right to the highest summits of the Cairngorms.

Deer have a somewhat erratic distribution in Britain because of extinctions and introductions. Throughout Scotland the Red deer is the characteristic species of the open high ground, sometimes in herds of a hundred or more, while roe are abundant in woodland but much more solitary than the red deer. In England roe also occur in the north and the southwest, but introduced Fallow and Sika are the dominant deer in many places. The little Muntjac is much more elusive than the other deer but is now widespread in much of southern England.

Seals can be seen on most British coasts although they are rare in the Thames Estuary and the eastern half of the English Channel. The larger Grey seal is the dominant species on the more exposed coasts from Cornwall to Shetland and south along the east coast as far as Yorkshire. Breeding colonies may be large but are limited to a small number of sites, although they disperse much more widely outside the autumn breeding season and can be seen in the water and hauled out on rocks on most undisturbed parts of the coast. The smaller Common seal can be seen in many of the same areas but on the whole it favours more sheltered waters and is the commoner species in the east-coast estuaries such as the Tay and the Wash, where they adopt a very characteristic 'banana' posture, with head and tail clear of the ground, as they bask on sandbanks.

Seals are equally abundant in Ireland but, when it comes to terrestrial mammals, Ireland not only lacks most of the more restricted species found in Britain but several abundant and widespread ones as well, including the Mole, Common shrew, Field vole, Water vole and Weasel. Perhaps the most distinctive of Irish mammals is the Irish hare, a race of the Mountain hare that does not turn white in winter and is found on low and high ground alike. Besides more natural habitats, golf courses and airports are especially favoured by Irish hares and sometimes attract exceptional concentrations.

Distribution of mammals in Britain and Ireland

The maps that follow show the distribution of all those species that are to be found wild in the British Isles. The figures following the species name indicate the page on which the relevant main text appears and (in bold) the plate on which the species is illustrated in colour. Distribution is indicated as follows:

 area within which a species has been recorded

 area in which scattered sightings have been recorded

Wallaby (139, **10**)

Hedgehog (120, **1**)

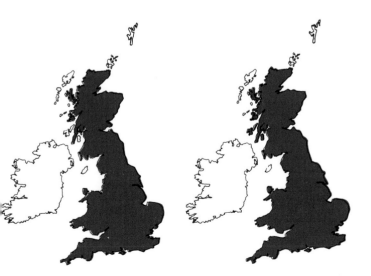

Mole (121, **1**)   **Common shrew** (124, **2**)

Pygmy shrew (125, **2**)

Water shrew (126, **3**)

**Lesser horseshoe
bat** (130, **4**)

**Greater horseshoe
bat** (131, **4**)

Daubenton's bat (132, **5**)

Brandt's bat (133, **5**)

Whiskered bat (134, **5**)

Natterer's bat (134, **6**)

Bechstein's bat (135, 6)

Greater mouse-eared bat (135, 6)

Noctule (136, 7)

Leisler's bat (136, 7)

Serotine (137, **7**)

Pipistrelle (138, **8**)

Common long-eared bat (140, **9**)

Grey long-eared bat (140, **9**)

Barbastelle (140, **9**)

Rabbit (143, **10**)

Brown hare (144, **10**)

Mountain hare (144, **10**)

Red squirrel (146, **11**)

Grey squirrel (147, **11**)

Coypu (151, **12**)

Fat dormouse (153, **13**)

Hazel dormouse (153, **13**)

Bank vole (157, **15**)

Field vole (159, **16**)

Water vole (164, **17**)

Common rat (167, **18**)

Ship rat (167, **18**)

Wood mouse (168, **19**)

Yellow-necked mouse (169, **19**)

Harvest mouse (170, **20**)

House mouse (171, **20**)

Fox (179, **22**)

Stoat (180, **23**)

Weasel (181, **23**)

Mink (181, **23**)

Polecat (182, **24**)

Pine marten (183, **24**)

Otter (184, **25**)

Badger (185, **25**)

Wild cat (188, **26**)

Common seal (189, **27**)

Grey seal (190, **27**)

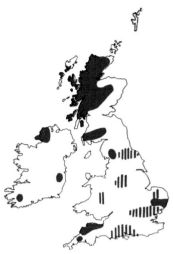

Red deer (201, **31**)

Sika deer (202, **32**)   **Fallow deer** (202, **32**)

Roe deer (204, **34**)

Muntjac (205, **34**)

**Chinese water
deer** (205, **34**)

Glossary

Baleen The flat horny plates on the upper jaw of the toothless whales, serving to filter food from the water.

Blow The visible cloud of vapour produced by whales when they exhale at the surface of the sea.

Blowhole The nostrils of cetaceans, situated on top of the head.

Calcar A cartilaginous or bony projection extending backwards from the ankle of a bat and supporting the edge of the tail membrane.

Canine The prominent conical tooth in carnivores, between the incisors and the cheek-teeth, and the equivalent tooth in other mammals irrespective of shape.

Carnassials The enlarged, shearing teeth found in most carnivores, one in each tooth-row.

Cartilage The rubbery tissue (gristle) that forms the skeleton of a young vertebrate animal, most of it replaced by bone as the animal matures.

Cetacean A member of the order Cetacea, i.e. a whale, dolphin or porpoise.

Cheek-teeth All the teeth behind the canine (or behind the gap in the toothrow in rodents and ungulates), comprising the premolars and molars.

Chromosomes The thread-like structures in the nucleus of every living cell, carrying the genetic material or genes.

Coppice Woodland in which the trees (e.g. hazel or chestnut) are cut periodically at the base and allowed to regenerate to produce a crop of poles from each stump.

Cusp A projection on the biting surface of a tooth.

Drey A squirrel's nest.

Echolocation The ability to assess the distance, direction and characteristics of objects in an animal's environment by the emission of sound (often ultrasonic) and the interpretation of the returning echoes.

Feral Living in a wild state, not dependent upon human help (used especially in the case of domestic forms of animals living thus).

Flippers The paired, paddle-like limbs of aquatic mammals (seals and cetaceans).

Fluke The flattened structure on the tail of a cetacean.

Forelock In a horse, the tuft of hair at the front of the mane that hangs forward on the forehead.

Guard hairs Long, stiff hairs that project beyond the main surface of the coat or pelage.

Hibernation A period of winter sleep accompanied by torpidity, i.e. a reduction of body temperature and of physiological activity.

Home-range The area usually used by an animal in its normal activity.

Incisors The front teeth in each jaw, in front of the canines, up to three on each side (more in some marsupials).

Indigenous Occurring naturally, not introduced.

Jizz The characteristic appearance of a particular species of animal that enables it to be recognized but that cannot easily be expressed in terms of particular features.

Krill Small shrimp-like crustaceans living in large shoals in the surface waters of the oceans and constituting the main element in the diet of many whales.

Lancet In horseshoe bats the uppermost, pointed projection of the noseleaf.

Molars The posterior cheek-teeth that are not preceded by milk-teeth.

Montane Found on mountains.

Pelage The hairy coat of a mammal (used in the same sense as plumage in birds).

Premolars The anterior cheek-teeth that are preceded by milk-teeth.

Rostrum The anterior part of a skull, in front of the orbits.

Rut The seasonal mating period in deer and other sociable ungulates.

Sella The central part of the noseleaf in horseshoe bats, above the horseshoe but below the lancet.

Set The system of underground passages excavated by badgers.

Sibling species Groups (usually pairs) of closely related species that cannot easily be told apart but which are believed not to interbreed in normal conditions.

Species An assemblage of animals whose members are capable of freely interbreeding and therefore show a high degree of similarity.

Territory An area actively defended by an animal against members of its own species.

Tragus A lobe growing upwards from the lower rim of the ear in bats, of a characteristic shape and size and useful in identification.

Tundra The dominant vegetation zone of the Arctic, consisting of open country with dwarf shrubs, sedge, lichen etc.

Tusk An enlarged tooth, usually confined to males and used in display or fighting to establish dominance. Usually a canine (e.g. in muntjac deer and in pigs) but an incisor in narwhals and the sole lower tooth in the beaked whales.

Ultrasonic Of sound, having a pitch too high to be audible to the human ear.

Unicuspid tooth In shrews one of the simple, conical teeth in the upper jaw, behind the prominent, two-pronged first tooth.

Velvet The soft, hairy skin covering the growing antlers of deer (when they are said to be 'in velvet'), rubbed off when the antlers are fully grown.

♂ Male

♀ Female

Further reading

General and regional works

Bang, P. & Dahlstrom, P. 1974. *Animal tracks and signs*. Collins, London.

Halstead, L. B. 1979. *The evolution of the mammals*, Peter Lowe, London.

Niethammer, J. & Krapp, F. 1978 —. *Handbuch der Säugetiere Europas*. Wiesbaden.

Corbet, G. B. 1966. *The terrestrial mammals of Western Europe*. Foulis, London.

Corbet, G. B. & Southern, H. N. (editors). 1977. *The handbook of British mammals*. Blackwells, Oxford.

Arnold, H. N. 1978. *Provisional atlas of the mammals of the British Isles*. NERC, Huntingdon.

Fairley, J. S. 1975. *An Irish beast book*. Blackstaff Press, Belfast.

Saint Girons, M.-C. 1973. *Les mammifères de France et du Benelux*. Doin, Paris.

Particular species or groups of mammals

Crowcroft, W. P. 1957. *The life of the shrew*. Max Reinhardt, London.

Mellanby, K. 1971. *The mole*. Collins, London.

Yalden, D. W. & Morris, P. A. 1975. *The lives of bats*. David & Charles, Newton Abbot.

Lockley, R. M. 1976. *The private life of the rabbit* (2nd edition). André Deutsch, London.

Crowcroft, W. P. 1966. *Mice all over*. Foulis, London (house mice).

Twigg, G. I. 1975. *The brown rat*. David & Charles, Newton Abbot.

Tittensor, A. M. 1975. *The red squirrel*. HMSO, London (Forest Record, no. 101).

Marsden, W. 1964. *The lemming year*. Chatto & Windus, London.

Burton, R. 1979. *Carnivores of Europe*. Batsford, London.

Neal, E. 1977. *Badgers*. Blandford, Poole.

Wayre, P. 1979. *The private life of the otter*. Batsford, London.

Hewer, H. R. 1974. *British seals*. Collins, London.

Page, F. J. T. 1971. *Field guide to British deer*, 2nd edition. Blackwells, Oxford.

Harris, R. A. & Duff, K. R. 1970. *Wild deer in Britain*. David & Charles, Newton Abbot.

Chapman, D. & N. 1978. *Fallow deer*. Terence Dalton.

Jewell, P. A., Milner, C. & Boyd, J. M. 1974. *Island survivors: the ecology of the Soay sheep of St Kilda*. Athlone Press, London.

Whitehead, G. K. 1972. *The wild goats of Great Britain and Ireland*. David & Charles, Newton Abbot.

Fraser, F. C. 1976. *British whales, dolphins and porpoises*. British Museum (Nat. Hist.), London.

Matthews, L. H. 1978. *The natural history of the whale*. Weidenfeld & Nicolson, London.

Index

References in bold are to the plate numbers of the coloured illustrations, others are to page numbers of the main entries in the text.

53891